THE
HISTORY OF
JAPAN

ADVISORY BOARD

THE HISTORY OF JAPAN

Second Edition

Louis G. Perez

The Greenwood Histories of the Modern Nations
Frank W. Thackeray and John E. Findling, Series Editors

Greenwood Press
Westport, Connecticut • London

Library of Congress Cataloging-in-Publication Data

Perez, Louis G.
   The history of Japan / Louis G. Perez. — 2nd ed.
      p. cm. — (Greenwood histories of the modern nations, ISSN 1096–2905)
   Includes bibliographical references and index.
   ISBN 978–0–313–36442–6 (alk. paper)
   1. Japan—History.   I. Title.
   DS835.P47   2009
   952—dc22   2008052242

British Library Cataloguing in Publication Data is available.

Library of Congress Catalog Card Number: 2008052242

ISBN: 978–0–313–36442–6

ISSN: 1096–2905

First published in 2009

Greenwood Press, 88 Post Road West, Westport, CT 06881
An imprint of Greenwood Publishing Group, Inc.
www.greenwood.com

Printed in the United States of America

The paper used in this book complies with the
Permanent Paper Standard issued by the National
Information Standards Organization (Z39.48-1984).

10 9 8 7 6 5 4 3 2

Contents

Series Foreword

The Greenwood Histories of the Modern Nations series is intended to provide students and interested laypeople with up-to-date, concise, and analytical histories of many of the nations of the contemporary world. Not since the 1960s has there been a systematic attempt to publish a series of national histories, and as series advisors, we believe that this series will prove to be a valuable contribution to our understanding of other countries in our increasingly interdependent world.

Some 40 years ago, at the end of the 1960s, the Cold War was an accepted reality of global politics. The process of decolonization was still in progress, the idea of a unified Europe with a single currency was unheard of, the United States was mired in a war in Vietnam, and the economic boom in Asia was still years in the future. Richard Nixon was president of the United States, Mao Tse-tung (not yet Mao Zedong) ruled China, Leonid Brezhnev guided the Soviet Union, and Harold Wilson was prime minister of the United Kingdom. Authoritarian dictators still controlled most of Latin America, the Middle East was reeling in the wake of the Six-Day War, and Shah Mohammad Reza Pahlavi was at the height of his power in Iran.

Since then, the Cold War has ended, the Soviet Union has vanished, leaving 16 independent republics in its wake, the advent of the computer age has radically transformed global communications, the rising demand for oil makes the Middle East still a dangerous flashpoint, and the rise of new economic powers like the People's Republic of China and India threatens to bring about a new world order. All of these developments have had a dramatic impact on the recent history of every nation of the world.

For this series, which was launched in 1998, we first selected nations whose political, economic, and socio-cultural affairs marked them as among the most important of our time. For each nation, we found an author who was recognized as a specialist in the history of that nation. These authors worked cooperatively with us and with Greenwood Press to produce volumes that reflected current research on their nations and that are interesting and informative to their readers. In the first decade of the series, more than 40 volumes were published, and as of 2008, some are moving into second editions.

The success of the series has encouraged us to broaden our scope to include additional nations, whose histories have had significant effects on their regions, if not on the entire world. In addition, geopolitical changes have elevated other nations into positions of greater importance in world affairs and, so, we have chosen to include them in this series as well. The importance of a series such as this cannot be underestimated. As a superpower whose influence is felt all over the world, the United States can claim a "special" relationship with almost every other nation. Yet many Americans know very little about the histories of nations with which the United States relates. How did they get to be the way they are? What kind of political systems have evolved there? What kind of influence do they have on their own regions? What are the dominant political, religious, and cultural forces that move their leaders? These and many other questions are answered in the volumes of this series.

The authors who contribute to this series write comprehensive histories of their nations, dating back, in some instances, to prehistoric times. Each of them, however, has devoted a significant portion of their book to events of the past 40 years because the modern era has contributed the most to contemporary issues that have an impact on U.S. policy. Authors make every effort to be as up-to-date as possible so that readers can benefit from discussion and analysis of recent events.

In addition to the historical narrative, each volume contains an introductory chapter giving an overview of that country's geography, political institutions, economic structure, and cultural attributes. This is meant to give readers a snapshot of the nation as it exists in the contemporary world. Each history also includes supplementary information following the narrative, which may include a timeline that represents a succinct chronology of the nation's historical evolution, biographical sketches of the nation's most important historical figures, and a glossary of important terms or concepts that are usually expressed in a foreign language. Finally, each author prepares a comprehensive bibliography for readers who wish to pursue the subject further.

Readers of these volumes will find them fascinating and well written. More importantly, they will come away with a better understanding of the contemporary world and the nations that comprise it. As series advisors, we hope that this series will contribute to a heightened sense of global understanding as we move through the early years of the twenty-first century.

Frank W. Thackeray and John E. Findling
Indiana University Southeast

Preface

I am amazed that an entire decade has passed since I wrote the original edition of this book. I am also amazed that some things I predicted then have actually come true. Alas, others have not. But then that should be expected. Japan is a wonderfully complex place. Its people are amazingly resilient, inventive, and adaptive. Wars, economic recessions, and natural catastrophes have come and gone and yet Japan prospers. I have heard it said that Japan perseveres in spite of its political leadership. That is a very good thing because its leaders have done and said some incredibly silly things. But, then Japan holds no patents or copyrights on incompetent political leadership.

I have tried to correct my own mistakes of 10 years ago in this revision. That being said, I am certain that I have committed even more in the editing. I am grateful for constructive criticism offered by my peers (especially the review written by Steve Erickson in the *Journal of Asian Studies*) and students.

I have maintained the original format with some revisions, notably chapter 9. I have revised the former last chapter into two (now chapters 9 and 10). The new chapter 9 now covers the Heisei Era (1989 to the present) with some new commentaries about what I have called the "Turbulent Years." Chapter 10 incorporates some revised material (from chapter 9) and is devoted to brief glimpses of Japanese society as one could find it today. I do so because many students have written to me asking about cultural matters in modern Japan.

I offer those observances as personal, idiosyncratic, and incomplete. What fascinates me about Japan may not be the things that interest you (and vice versa).

I am indebted to the long-suffering work of Greenwood's editors, among them Acquisitions Editor Kaitlin Ciarmiello. In particular, I wish to thank the Series Editors Frank W. Thackeray and John E. Findling. They campaigned tirelessly to have the series revised. My special thanks to Frank because he has had to persevere while suffering the slings and arrows of being a Pittsburgh Pirates fan. His loyalty and my own towards the fumbling Los Angeles Dodgers prove conclusively that intellect and sports loyalty are not interconnected.

As I did a decade ago in the first edition, I'd like to thank my wife, Karla, for her endless patience while I do this.

Timeline of Historical Events

1253	Nichiren sect founded
1274 and 1281	Attempted Mongol Invasions
1333	Founding of Ashikaga Bakufu
1336–92	Southern Imperial Court in Yoshino
1467–77	Sacking of Kyoto (Ōnin War)
1543	Portuguese arrive in Japan at Tanegashima
1582	Suicide of Oda Nobunaga
1587	Sword hunt and military unification by Toyotomi Hideyoshi
1587	Anti-Christian edict by Hideyoshi
1592–98	Korean Expedition
1597	Twenty-six Christians crucified at Nagasaki
1598	Death of Hideyoshi
1600	Battle of Sekigahara
1603	Tokugawa Ieyasu becomes shōgun; foundation of bakufu
1614	Battle of Ōsaka Castle; Toyotomi Hideyori dies
1637–38	Shimabara Rebellion; Sakoku instituted
1833–37	Tempo Famine
1837	Ōshio Heihachirō leads rebellion in Ōsaka
1853	Arrival of Commodore Perry
1854	Treaty of Kanagawa signed
1856–58	Beginnings of Unequal Treaties
1867–68	Meiji Restoration
1871–73	Haihan Chiken; universal male conscription; land reform
1871–73	Iwakura Mission
1873	Korean Affair, many resign from government

1874	Taiwan Expedition; Saga Rebellion; suicide of Etō Shimpei
1877	Satsuma Rebellion; suicide of Saigō Takamori
1878	Assassination of Ōkubo Toshimichi
1881	Ōkuma ousted from government; constitution promised
1889	Meiji Constitution
1890	First Diet Election; Imperial Rescript on Education
1894	Mutsu Munemitsu revises Unequal Treaties
1894–95	First Sino-Japanese War and Treaty of Shimonoseki
1895	Triple Intervention
1898	Civil Code enacted
1899	Unequal Treaties lapse
1900	Boxer Rebellion
1902	First Anglo-Japanese Alliance
1904–5	Russo-Japanese War and Treaty of Portsmouth
1906	San Francisco passes Anti-Japanese school laws
1908	United States announces foundation of Pearl Harbor
1909	Itō Hirobumi assassinated by Korean patriot
1910	Korea annexed by Japan; Great Treason Incident
1912	Meiji Emperor dies; Nogi and wife commit suicide
1914	Japan enters World War I, attacking German positions in China
1915	Twenty-One Demands on China
1918	Rice Riots; first Party Cabinet under Hara Takashi
1919	Treaty of Versailles and May Fourth Movement in China
1921–22	Washington Naval Conference; Four-Power Treaty
1921	Hara Takashi assassinated; Hirohito becomes regent

1923	Great Kantō Earthquake, thousands of Koreans killed
1925	Universal Manhood Suffrage; Peace Preservation Laws
1926	Taishō Emperor dies, Shōwa Emperor ascends
1928	Assassination of Zhang Zoulin by Kwantung Army
1930	London Naval Conference
1931	Mukden Incident
1932	Manchukuo established; Lytton Report; Inukai assassinated
1933	Japan walks out of League of Nations
1936	Anti-Comintern Pact
1937	Marco Polo Bridge Incident; start of World War II
1937	Rape of Nanjing; Panay Incident
1939	Anti-Comintern Pact with Germany and Italy signed
1940	Tri-Partite Pact (Japan, Germany, and Italy)
1941	Neutrality Pact with Russia
1941	Attack on Pearl Harbor
1942	Battle of Midway
1945	Battles of Saipan, Iwo Jima, and Okinawa
March 1945	Firebombing of Tokyo
August 6, 1945	Atomic bombing of Hiroshima
August 8, 1945	Russia declares war against Japan
August 9, 1945	Atomic bombing of Nagasaki
August 15, 1945	Japan surrenders to Allies
September 1, 1945	Allied Occupation of Japan begins
1946	"MacArthur Peace" Constitution was promulgated in 1946, but was not signed until 1947
1947	First postwar election
1951	San Francisco Peace Treaty signed
1951	U.S.-Japan Mutual Security Treaty signed

1952	Allied Occupation ends
1955	Foundation of Liberal-Democratic Party (LDP)
1956	Japan admitted to United Nations
1960	Mutual Security Treaty Demonstrations
1964	Tokyo hosts eighteenth Olympic Games
1970	Mutual Security Treaty revised
1972	Return of Okinawa; relations with China restored
1973	OPEC Middle East Oil Crisis
1989	Death of Shōwa Emperor, Heisei Emperor ascends
1995	Great Hanshin earthquake in Kobe region
1995	Aum Shinrikyō sect bombs Tokyo subway with poison gas
1998	Olympic Winter Games held in Nagano
1999	Nuclear accident at Tokaimura, Ibaraki Prefecture (two die)
2000	Empress Dowager Nagako (widow of Hirohito) died
2001	*U.S.S. Greeneville*, a U.S. nuclear submarine, collides with the *Ehime Maru* (nine killed)
2001	Russia agrees to return Shikotan and Hakomai of Kurile Islands to Japan
2001	Japan sends Self-Defense Force ships to help U.N. forces in invasion of Afghanistan
2002	With South Korea, Japan jointly hosts World Cup Soccer
2002	North Korea returns five kidnapped Japanese citizens
2004	Japan sends Self-Defense Forces to Iraq
2006	All Japanese Self-Defense Force troops returned from Afghanistan and Iraq
2006	Prince Akishino, and his wife have a baby boy, resolving succession crisis
2008	Japan recognizes Ainu as a separate race and culture

1

A Wonderful Place

Japan is a wonderfully unique place. It is a study of contrasts, anomalies, and anachronisms. It is many things to many people. On the one hand, it is Asia's first "modern" and industrialized nation and has been involved deeply in world trade for over four decades. Yet on the other hand, it is still a very traditionally conservative nation whose people as a whole are parochial and chauvinist in their world view.

One would think that the Japanese would be among the most cosmopolitan people in Asia, if not the world. They are so dependent on world markets that virtually anything that disturbs the flow of goods anywhere in the world has tremendous impact in Japan. Japan imports virtually all of its iron ore, bauxite, oil, copper, and nickel. It relies on foreign supplies for over 90 percent of its coal, natural gas, and lead. Over 85 percent of its total energy is imported from abroad. It is perhaps the greatest importer of agricultural goods; nearly 14 percent of its total food supply is imported. Japan is second only to the United States in terms of the total value of its industrial exports. It is the world's greatest exporter of automobiles; it has the greatest number of merchant ships in the world.

Yet the Japanese people are more intimately tied to their ancient ancestral roots than they are to events in the rest of the world. Third- and fourth-

Modern Japan. Courtesy of Jill Freund Thomas.

generation city dwellers, when asked where they are "from," still name the *furusato* "old home" of their ancestors. Their lives are tied more closely to the ancient rural agricultural rhythms than to the modern industrial cities where they reside. Despite the fact that with the possible exceptions of Asia's two city-states (Hong Kong and Singapore) Japan is Asia's most urbanized nation, the Japanese think of themselves as members of an ancient village. The nation's religious holidays still draw the city folk back into the countryside. Strong bonds of obligation link the Japanese to their roots.

Not surprisingly, the Japanese national ethic is more Asian, more traditional, and more conservative than the other large industrialized nations of the world. Thousand-year-old temples and shrines exist cheek-to-jowl with bustling industrial commercial centers. In a country where 98 percent of all families enjoy the most modern kitchen appliances (refrigerators, microwave ovens, electric rice cookers, and the like), most Japanese women shop daily for their foodstuffs at tiny neighborhood butcher, green grocer, and rice shops. Residents of Asia's most "modern" economy still buy their fuel, not at the most convenient or least expensive gasoline stations, but at the places where they have patronized for decades.

In politics, Japan can boast of Asia's most stable government, having peacefully changed governments without military coup or political putsch in over 50 years. The dominant Liberal-Democratic Party (LDP) continually ruled Japan from 1955 until the early 1990s. And yet Japan suffers from almost constant political turmoil, scandal, and financial improprieties. The largely urban population lags behind the rural sector in parliamentary representation.

In terms of gender equality, Japan has progressed far beyond the traditional social customs when women were little more than property. The constitution contains perhaps the most liberal and complete protections for the civil and political rights of women in the world. Yet although women no longer walk "two steps behind" their husbands as they did two generations ago, they are still discriminated against by custom within both public and private spheres. More than half of all marriages are still arranged by the parents of the couple. Women rarely are promoted beyond the middle level of management in private industry, and routinely are paid less than two-thirds that of their male counterparts. Only a very few women are elected to national offices, and they are scarcely visible in any social organizations other than those traditionally reserved for women only.

Yet women control much of the disposable family income. They make the sole decisions for the purchase of major consumer items and are the primary decision-makers in almost all aspects of their children's welfare including education and vocation. They wield tremendous power and influence in the consumer and environmental protection movements.

Although Japan is perhaps the most educated nation in the world, only about 20 percent of the population is admitted to a four-year college or university. Free compulsory education is available to every child, yet the entrance exams to colleges are so competitively difficult that only one in every three males and one in six females is admitted to college. The rest of secondary school graduates must settle for technical and professional training; young women are shunted off to junior colleges in what amounts to "finishing" or secretarial schools.

Virtually the entire population is considered literate (in perhaps the most complicated writing system on earth), and Japan publishes more reading material per capita than any other nation. The total combined readership of the some 30 newspapers in Tokyo amounts to 1.5 times the population! Among the best-selling books every year are books on Japanese linguistics, anthropology, and archeology. Novels are serialized in newspapers, and almost every newspaper has two or three professional historians on staff. And yet Japanese know very little about the rest of the world except fashion styles and the current statistics of their favorite expatriate baseball players now in the American Major Leagues.

Nearly every Japanese under the age of 40 has had at least five years of English language instruction and can readily parse even the most complex written sentences. Yet very few can speak more than a few words of English. Japanese have been known to walk across four lanes of traffic to avoid even the remote possibility of having to say anything to a foreigner.

Japanese schools are justly known for their excellent education, particularly in the sciences and mathematics. Japanese children score much higher in standardized tests when compared with Western children at the same age. Yet Japan can boast of very few Nobel Prize winners in any of the sciences.

The country justly prides itself for a very low violent crime rate. Armed assault, rape, and murder rates are tiny compared to virtually any other industrialized society. Women can and do walk alone at night throughout even large cities without fear. It is common for kindergarten children to ride public transportation alone without problem. Drunken men stagger home after payday with large sums of cash in their pockets without fear of robbery. Residents of even large cities do not lock their homes or cars at night. Yet perhaps 10 percent of all children suffer from some manner of physical bullying (*ijime*). Some cases were so serious that children have committed suicide rather than face their tormentors another day. It is estimated that 15 percent of all reported cases of physical violence in the nation are directed at school teachers by their pupils.

In a nation that prides itself in politeness, unspeakable acts of rudeness pass almost without notice every moment. The language is saturated with such extreme polite forms of expressions that no one thinks it strange to hear a sanitation worker say, "I humbly beg to remove your honorable garbage."

The art of bowing has taken on such importance that lessons are given and almost everyone can repeat the prescribed depth and angle of bow required for several different social situations. The parting scenes at train stations and welcoming scenes outside corporate board rooms are so comical in that they resemble aerobic exercise classes. Yet subway commuters push, shove, elbow, and knee strangers and friends alike in their haste to squeeze into railway cars. Baseball players and managers shove and even beat umpires.

Children shout obscenities at passersby, particularly foreigners. Able-bodied teenagers sit stolidly in subway cars, pretending to be asleep in seats reserved for the aged and handicapped, yet spring alive in time to make their stop. Old people occasionally soundly whack those youngsters across the shins when they refuse to move. It is rare for men to surrender their subway seats even to pregnant women. A standard joke on subways is that one can always spot a foreigner because they give up their seats even to a woman returning from her honeymoon. Mothers with infants, or even stooped old people, receive little better treatment on the subways.

The contrast in the rhythms of everyday life in Japan can boggle the mind. Millions of commuters dash to cram themselves into already overloaded trains in order to arrive at their jobs in time to leisurely drink a cup of tea for a half hour before work begins officially. At midday they wedge into tiny crammed restaurants, in order to wolf down scalding-hot bowls of noodles in a flurry of chopsticks and spoons, often standing while they eat, and then spend a leisurely hour reading or just watching the crowds. At the end of the day, they flee away from their jobs into bars in order to spend hours drinking with their coworkers, talking endlessly about the jobs they just fled. Or, they once again jam into the commuter trains, rushing to "make" this train lest they have to wait three minutes until the next one. They rush home to spend an hour soaking in a hot bath.

The same people who gulp down their midday meals in minutes can sit for nearly an hour while a cup of bitter green tea is ritually prepared, laboriously over charcoal heaters using bamboo utensils and poured into rough handmade ceramic bowls.

Japan is arguably the most beautiful rustic spot in the world. Soaring volcanic cones capped with snow rise out of deep verdant forests. Ruggedly picturesque coastlines are drenched with sparkling waters. Yet scarcely meters away from any of this pristine beauty are soda, cigarette, and even pornography vending machines. Ribbons of narrow streets are jammed with garish shops and ugly concrete apartment complexes. Prefabricated matchbox-sized houses jam against each other like rabbit hutches, but also against richly tiled ancestral homes that are two centuries old. Ancient postage stamp–sized Zen gardens are crowded about by McDonald's, Pizza Huts, and Mr. Donut shops.

Japan is a state of mind. This racially homogeneous culture hires private detectives to ensure that prospective marriage partners do not descend from a minority "caste" of people who are virtually identical to themselves genetically, religiously, and economically. Western visitors and residents are treated with civility, hospitality, and great tolerance, yet Asian aliens who have lived in Japan for generations are treated with vicious contempt and discrimination.

Japan has a national collective respect for its cultural traditions almost unrivaled in the entire world. (Please see chapter 9 for a full discussion.) Its theater, art, music, and historical architecture are heavily subsidized and protected by the government. Famous artists and crafts people are often designated as National Living Treasures and receive a hefty stipend to facilitate their arts. Museums and national institutes abound throughout the country and virtually no new building construction is allowed without prior archeological consultations to ensure that cultural artifacts will not be accidentally destroyed.

And yet, Japanese go to extraordinary lengths to copy and patronize Western culture at the expense of their own. Western styles of clothing, music, food, hair, and movies, to mention only the most obvious, are wildly more popular than their Japanese counterparts. Seemingly every month a new Western "boom" (the name given to new fads) arises and threatens to flood every minute of television time and every inch of newspaper and magazine column. Used American blue jeans sell for hundreds of dollars per pair. Oversized (at least to the Japanese foot), used American basketball sneakers cost 10 times what one would pay for new Japanese shoes that actually fit. The cost of French-made fashions bought in Tokyo make even the prices of trendy Beverly Hills boutiques pale in comparison.

Japanese traditional music remains popular with middle-aged people, but American rap, jazz, rock, and even country western music outsells the native music by a factor of 100 to 1. Millions of young girls spend long hours perfecting an ancient dance step or antiquated trill of the *shamisen,* and hundreds of Japanese teenagers congregate in Tokyo city parks every weekend to dance to 1950s-style American music. These young men spend hundreds of dollars to have their hair cut and slicked back in the style made popular by James Dean and Elvis Presley. They dress in leather jackets, tight blue jeans, and ankle boots, their girl friends in poodle skirts or pedal pushers, anklets, and Angora sweaters. Thousands of dollars are spent to import and maintain the "low-rider" American Chevrolets and Fords of the 1950s.

Traditional Japanese martial arts sports such as sumo, judo, jujitsu, kendo, and the like, are still quite popular among the young, but the most popular spectator sport in Japan is baseball. Basketball, soccer, and even American-style football are making serious inroads among the youth of Japan as well.

The richest (per capita of Gross Domestic Product, highest salaried workers, highest rate of personal savings, per capita foreign aid, and so on) nation in the world lives in the most cramped living quarters. Japan, which is the size of the state of California, is the eighth most populated nation in the world. Nearly 127 million people are jammed into a living area smaller than any *one* of 40 American states.

Because only 20 percent of Japan's total land is suitable for agriculture, residence, and industry, nearly 400 people live on each square kilometer of that space. Another way of thinking about it is that the total population of Japan lives in an area smaller than either tiny Portugal or Scotland. Japan's total living space could fit into Hokkaido, only one of its over 1,000 islands! The rest of Japan is too mountainous for many people to inhabit.

Consider the following: Japan has the least amount of per capita urban park land, the lowest ratio of sewerage, and the lowest crime rate of the greatest 25 industrialized nations of the world. It is an enigma.

Foreigners are startled to find that in 2006 out of a population of 127 million, nearly 92 million people considered themselves to be of the Shinto faith and another 80 million called themselves Buddhist. The sum of these two is 50 million more than the total population! In a world where monotheistic religions are mutually exclusive, the idea that the Japanese could profess two religions is unthinkable.

These are only a few of the contrasts and incongruities that make Japan an exotic and wonderful place. We now try to discover the roots of this fascinating culture.

GEOGRAPHY AND EARLY CULTURE

As much as any other culture (the river cultures of the Nile, Ganges, Yangzi, Tigris-Euphrates, and the seashore cultures of Holland and Great Britain, for example), Japanese society has been molded and shaped by its physical environment. Japan is at once a stunningly beautiful as well as a remarkably dangerous place to live. It is a cluster of over a thousand rocky volcanic islands some 250 miles off the coast of China and only half that distance from Korea. Nearly 75 percent of the California-sized land mass is mountainous forest. Its craggy coastline is washed by swirling swift ocean currents.

The tremendous strain on the underground layers of rock caused by a seven-mile drop in elevation from Mt. Fuji, its highest mountain (over 12,000 feet), to the five-mile deep offshore underwater trenches is worsened by the uplift pressures of nearly 500 active volcanoes. Averaging over four earthquakes per day (1,500 yearly), 20 of which through recorded history have killed over 1,000 people, Japan's land is very unstable. In addition to the continual shifting of the unstable ground, the volcanoes periodically erupt, spewing lava and volcanic ash for miles. Tsunami tidal waves, caused by the earthquakes and volcanic eruptions, crash against Japan's rocky coastline (in places along the western coastline, the difference between high and low tides is 40 feet) and are joined by seasonal torrential typhoons, monsoon rains, riptides, and whirlpools. In short, Japan is a very dangerous place.

Yet, the marriage of majestically high mountains and swirling seas has produced a rugged beauty rarely matched in the rest of the world. Its snow-capped volcanic cones are lushly covered by brilliant green forests. Its craggy black volcanic shoreline is sprayed by the pounding white foam of its deep blue ocean waves. In the fall, its deep river valleys are a riot of autumnal leafy colors; in the spring, its deep, dark mountain pools are embraced by thousands of colorful wildflowers. Summers are a shimmering checkerboard of sparkling green rice paddies, which turn to gold with the ripening grain; winters are a glistening hush in a deep blanket of pristine snow along its northwest coast.

But the spectacular beauty hides a harsh reality. Three-quarters of the land is too steep to farm; most of its short, often violent rivers are too shallow and too swift to navigate; much of its jagged coastline is too dangerous to fish except in deep-water ships; its ribbon of flat coastal land lies unprotected from typhoons and tsunami; its deep valleys are isolated from each other by steep jagged mountains and unfordable rapid rivers. All of which make life in Japan very difficult and very perilous. Added to these geographical problems, Japan has very little in the way of mineral resources. Its iron and coal deposits are sparse and of very poor quality; there are insufficient quantities of lead, copper, sulfur, zinc, and magnesium; and its petroleum is practically nonexistent. Gold and silver are in short supply and are very difficult to mine.

Yet the island archipelago has a long, rich history of human habitation. Its deep, lush forests and rich ocean currents have fed people for thousands of years. The abundant rain during the long hot summers makes the sparse but very rich river delta flatlands ideally suited for agriculture. Surprisingly, dangerous as it is, insular Japan, which is smaller than France (yet larger than Italy, Germany, or Great Britain) and has less farming, residential, and industrial land than the American state of Illinois, is perhaps the most densely populated country in the world. Its population (126 million in 1997, making it the eighth most populated nation in the world) was almost half that of the United States, with less than four percent of America's land mass.

The combination of geographic peril and insular isolation have molded a society of tough, hardy fatalists. A ruggedly self-sufficient people, creatively adaptive to their environment, the Japanese seem to thrive in the face of adversity. Isolated by treacherous seas from their Asian relatives, the Japanese have created a unique culture that responds to its rugged environment. The physical isolation from its Asian neighbors has kept it safe from the marauding armies that conquered India, China, Korea, and Continental Southeast Asia. In fact, it was not until 1945 that Japan was successfully invaded and occupied by a military enemy. This isolation has allowed Japan the "leisure" time to creatively adapt new foreign ideas to the Japanese reality.

Japan's relative isolation from the rest of the world has also created a remarkably racially and culturally homogeneous society. Virtually everyone in Japan shares the same genetic heritage. Almost everyone speaks, reads, and writes the same language, shares the same religious and cultural history, and has participated in the same educational system. In short, Japan is a strikingly unified and unique culture. It is certainly a culture worth studying.

2

Early Japan

JAPAN IN PREHISTORY

Archeological evidence of human life in Japan extends back perhaps 250,000 years. Evidence of a vibrantly active hunting and gathering culture dates back over 11,000 years. This society known as Jōmon (after its distinctive rope-decorated coiled-clay pottery) flourished in south central Honshu and northern Kyushu. The culture lived in circular earthen-pit huts; it used flaked-stone and bone tools and subsisted on forest fruits, nuts, berries, roots, and seeds. The Jōmon people supplemented their mostly vegetarian diets with the occasional small animal killed in the forest. Before long they began to harvest the rich variety of fish and shellfish from the surrounding rivers and oceans. They left huge shellfish mounds that are rich in broken pottery, worn tools, and discarded clay fertility fetishes, a treasure trove of information for archeologists who have reconstructed Jōmon life from its refuse piles.

The Jōmon were related to their neighbors in the Asian northeast: Korea and Manchuria; also to their even more distant neighbors in insular Southeast Asia and surprisingly also to the Central Asian Turks as well. Their religious artifacts resemble the fertility fetishes of those areas. Their genetic qualities link them most closely to the ethnic groups along Asia's northern frontier.

Evidence suggests that the Jōmon people were basically peaceful in their normal lives. They roamed as nomads along the ribbon of coastal river-delta flatlands following the seasonal food supply. Their religious cults (there were apparently a number of them) worshiped fertility in nature, bearing remarkable similarities to the religions of animist cultures in Africa and Southeast Asia, as well as North and South America.

The Jōmon culture was gradually replaced by that of the Yayoi (named after the section in Tokyo where their archeological remains were unearthed) who came to the islands from insular Southeast Asia and by the Southeast Chinese people who perhaps fled by ship or overland down through Korea, away from the invading Han Chinese armies on the mainland. There is no evidence of a military invasion, but rather a gradual mingling of two cultures; the Jōmon were supplanted by the technological superior Yayoi 2,200 years ago. The Yayoi brought metal tools, mirrors, bells, Chinese and Korean coins, wheel-thrown pottery, weaving technology, and wet-rice cultivation. They created an intricate and sophisticated system of crop irrigation that remained fundamentally unchanged for over 2,200 years (one can still see the outlines of the system from the Shinkansen "Bullet Train" in the area around Nagoya).

Like the Jōmon, these people worshiped the fertile powers of nature around them, but increasingly their gods became more sedentary in nature, reflecting the importance of the newly introduced agricultural patterns. That is to say, the Jōmon seemed to carry their portable gods with them as they roamed the countryside following the food supply. The Yayoi gods, however, "put down roots" quite literally in the soil where the people planted their crops. Most of the Yayoi holy sites seem to have been located along the forest and mountain line that girded their crops. Ancient Yayoi sites of worship correspond to locations where Shinto believers built their own shrines centuries later.

Linked in many cultural ways to Chinese agriculturalists, the Yayoi were themselves replaced by a technologically superior people five centuries later. These Kofun, or "Tomb" people, named after the distinctive keyhole-shaped massive tombs that they built, brought a military-dominated culture from their mainland Asia homeland. Whether the Asian mainland Kofun conquered from horseback as suggested by some anthropologists or peacefully intermingled with the Yayoi until their technology overawed the now-native people is uncertain; but by a.d. 250 the culture was decidedly more like that of Korea and China than that of the Yayoi. They lived in aboveground thatched houses similar in design to those of Southeast Asia. They carried single-edged iron long swords, spears, and arrows tipped with iron; they wore iron helmets and body armor made of thin slabs of iron sewn together with leather or silk. Their stirrups and reins resemble those of Korean horsemen. The swords, mirrors, and comma-shaped polished stones that they carried became the Three Treasures of the Japanese Imperial Regalia.

Their tombs were studded with rings of small clay figurines (*haniwa*) that tell us much about the diverse and sophisticated culture that flourished for hundreds of years. The haniwa are what archeologists call "burial furniture." They represent a shadow of the former life for the deceased and also to serve them in the next life as well. The figurines represented the human form: singers, shamans, priests, magicians, horsemen, artisans, farmers, cooks, fishers, soldiers, and servants. But they also represent human occupational environment as well. We can see houses, stables, workshops (particularly sword making), pottery kilns, and metal foundries. Remnants of mainland textiles, pottery, coins, mirrors, and religious objects found in the tombs attest to the fact that the Kofun culture maintained contact and trade with their relatives in the rest of Asia. Clearly this was a diverse, prosperous, and sophisticated culture. By the time of the Roman Empire in Europe and the Han Dynasty in China, the Kofun people probably numbered over a half million inhabitants.

The Jōmon, Yayoi, and Kofun cultures all struggled with another people, culturally distinct from them all—the Caucasian-like Ainu. This latter group of stouter and hairier lighter-skinned people did not intermingle very much with either the Jōmon or Yayoi, and by the time of the Kofun the Ainu had been pushed increasingly northward until they crossed over to the northern island of Hokkaido. When, why, and how they came to Japan is unknown, but they remained separate and distinctive from the people who would become the Japanese of today. For centuries they fought running battles and skirmishes with the Japanese, raiding their settlements for cattle, food, tools, and captives. They continue to live in very small numbers in Hokkaido today in nationally protected separate areas much like the Indian Reservations of the North American Southwest, with their distinctive language, religion (worshiping the bear like their Siberian distant relatives), and social customs.

EARLY HISTORICAL JAPAN

The first written historical accounts that we have of the Japanese are found in the Chinese records of the third century. The Chinese *History of the Wei* of a.d. 297 records that the Japanese had sent tributary and trading embassies to China as early as a.d. 57. They describe the Wa (or "dwarfs") as being a nearly nude, barely civilized people (but still managed the sea journey in their own ships) who tattooed their skins and worshiped many gods.

We are told that in the early third century, the country erupted into a long civil war. One ruler, however, managed to finally pacify the people—not militarily, but through diplomacy. Pimiku (Himiko or "Sun Princess," which was probably not a name but rather a title) was a shaman priestess who ruled "through magic and sorcery, bewitching the people." She surrounded herself with a retinue of "a thousand" young virgin girls but communicated to her people through the lone man in her government (her brother). The heads of the lineage groups or clans (*uji*) each worshiped their own kindred ancestral spirits (*kami*), but bowed to the supremacy of the Himiko's ancestor, the Sun Goddess *Amaterasu Omi-Kami*. Her kinship uji, the Yamato, unified the country through a system of alliances with other uji.

Himiko was clearly a spirit medium, interpreting what the spirits wished to say to the people of Japan. Whether she actually ruled or whether she "advised" the true ruler (perhaps her brother) as some historians suggest, it is clear that the Chinese recognized *her* as the legitimate Queen of Japan. After all, the embassy to China was sent in her name. The Chinese indicated their acceptance of her rule by sending imperial seals and ceremonial mirrors and bells. When Himiko (perhaps leading her armies in battle) died, she was buried in a huge keyhole-shaped tomb, indicating that the people still honored her memory. And when a man attempted to succeed her by force of arms, the various uji leaders resisted and fought against him. The succession dispute was settled when Iyo, a 13-year-old girl, was installed on the throne as the legitimate successor (and probable former disciple) of Himiko.

This evidence of the Himiko-Iyo peaceful succession (and hence the idea that it was "natural" and legitimate in the eyes of the people), when added to the information provided by the Chinese that males commonly went to live with the families of their wives, that inheritance came only through the female line, that both sexes practiced polygamy, and that the most important and powerful kami worshiped were female, all suggests that Japan was a matriarchy. Though history does not relate when and why Japan moved toward patriarchy, we can make some educated guesses.

First, the social, religious, and political philosophies that would influence Japan most heavily for the next thousand years were misogynist (hatred of women). The Chinese Confucianism (and Buddhism as well) that dominated East Asia during this time taught that women were not only physically inferior to men but emotionally, intellectually, and even spiritually inferior as well.

Second, the entire region was wracked by civil wars in the three centuries between the Han and Tang dynasties in China. The wars that raged on the Asian continent spilled down the Korean Peninsula towards Japan. Japan was constantly threatened by this unrest and probably found more comfort and security in male-dominated military governments than in the peaceful religious rule that characterized Himiko and Iyo.

Nevertheless, several Japanese emperors after Himiko and Iyo were women. Even after the male-dominated Confucianism was instituted in the seventh century, Japan continued to treat women with deference, perhaps due to their respect for female shamans.

THE HEIAN ERA (794–1185)

Beginning in the fifth century, Japan began to adapt creatively to a changing Asian political environment. The nearly four centuries of almost constant civil wars that raged on the Chinese mainland between the fall of the Han (a.d. 220) and the rise of the Tang (a.d. 618) dynasties seriously threatened Japan's political stability and independence. Hundreds, perhaps thousands of Chinese and Korean intellectuals fled for their lives to the islands and intermingled with the Japanese ruling aristocracy. The military leaders of Japan also became involved in various political adventures in Korea. The king of Paekche, one of three competing governments on the Korean Peninsula, in 552 sent the Japanese emperor a Buddhist missionary in gratitude for Japanese military help. The king recommended Buddhism for its magical and medicinal powers. When Buddhism came to Japan, however, it still had to contend with the indigenous religion, Shinto.

SHINTO

Shinto of early Japan has been called a formative religion because it lacked the basic elements of most world religions. It is rooted in the magical creation story of the "first family" of creative kami *Izanagi* and *Izanami,* descending through Amaterasu and her grandson Ninigi, the first human. Shinto, however, lacks divinely inspired holy scriptures. It lacks holy law and therefore also the sense of sin and ethics. To be sure, Shinto differentiated between what was considered holy and what was profane, but the difference was based on what was appropriate and that which was not. Ritual defilement or impurity could be washed away, sometimes literally with water, but also washed symbolically with paper or straw wands. Prayers were more like words to soothe the angry kami than requests to be granted by powerful spirits. Funerals had more to do with avoiding and symbolically negating the pollution and filth of death than to comfort the bereaved relatives and loved ones. This formative religion (or perhaps groups of cults) resembled the animist religions of surrounding cultures in Northeast and Southeast Asia at the time.

In this early period Shinto had neither an organized priesthood nor a system for personal salvation. Indeed, it had no real explanation of what the "other world," that is, the afterlife or the spirit world, was like or of how one got there (or avoided it for that matter). In fact, Shinto probably did not even have a proper name. When Buddhism came to Japan, it was called "Butsu-Do," the "way" or "path" of the Buddha. To designate the native religion, the name Shinto was developed (the Chinese ideograph used to write kami can also be pronounced "shin," and therefore it became "the Way of the gods").

Most significantly, whereas Buddhism was the religion of nearly all of East Asia, Shinto existed only in Japan. The ancestors of each uji were worshiped as kami, but then so were supernaturally shaped rocks and trees, as well as mountains, rivers, planets, the moon, and other inanimate objects in nature. One might say that Shinto in this period was localized and very personal. Some religious historians, in fact, have suggested that Shinto was never really a unified and distinct religion until the mid-nineteenth century when a new government created a national ethos out of many regional cults in order to legitimize a newly restored imperial court. Instead, there were several indigenous cults; each local uji worshiped their own kami in their own regional holy sites and deferred to the "national" kami of the Yamato because of political practicality. After all, it hurt no one to honor Amaterasu, the Sun Goddess of the imperial Yamato, as long as they continued to worship their local and personal kami as well.

EARLY BUDDHISM

Whatever the nature of early Shinto, it could not compete with the sophisticated social and religious philosophy called Buddhism. An exhaustive examination of the history and nature of Buddhism is far too complex to consider here. It should be enough to say that this new religion was technologically and philosophically much superior to Shinto. It came to Japan a thousand years after its founding in northern India.

Originally, the Buddha taught the following:

1 Life is illusion.
2 Life is painful, caused by desire.
3 Life continues through endless cycles of rebirth. Each incarnation is determined by the sum total of one's actions (karma) in the previous life.
4 Freedom from pain, realization of life's illusion, and release from the cycle of painful reincarnation could be attained by obliterating desire and thereby obtaining release (nirvana) from the world.
5 People should rid themselves of pain, desire, and illusion through proper conduct, meditation, and complete withdrawal from society.

In other words, Buddhism was a "religion without God." Salvation was to be found within oneself and could be accomplished independently without the need of teachers, priests, or any other religious agency. It was a quiet, gentle, contemplative, tolerant, monastic religion that required that one remove oneself from society.

When it came to Japan, however, it had been radically changed. It had taken on familial, social, and bureaucratic trappings during its five centuries in China and Korea. The *Mahayana* or "Greater Vehicle" school of thought that came to dominate China, Korea, and Japan taught that salvation was too difficult for humans to accomplish by their own good works. It was necessary for holy men (*boddisatva*) to intercede on behalf of humans. The boddisatva were thought to be men who had earned salvation but refused to leave the world until they could help other humans attain nirvana. In China they came to be worshiped like gods and were even mistaken by the common people as the Buddha himself.

So when Buddhism came to Japan, it did so in the form of several very complex schools of thought based on the Mahayana ideas. In the early period, the imperial and aristocratic houses competed with each other to patronize the various schools by funding the building of temples. In part this was to do spiritual good work, to effect positively their own karma. It was also seen as a civilizing element because the Chinese and Korean priests were educated urbane men. Buddhist priests also brought new technologies with them, not the least of which was the healing arts of Chinese medicine.

When the Japanese constructed their first permanent capital at Nara, they did so using the Chinese capital as their model. The massive temple complexes of Todaiji, Horyuji, and Toshodaiji surrounding the imperial palace became not only centers of religious instruction but also centers of learning, repositories of Buddhist art, and libraries of holy scriptures as well.

When Buddhist priests became involved in the business of government, however, the imperial house moved the capital northward to Heian-kyō (Kyoto) in 794, and the Buddhist establishment was required to remain in Nara. Two new schools of thought, however, gained power in the new capital. The *Tendai* school taught that all paths to enlightenment were equally efficient, but that salvation required many good works and much education at the feet of holy men in monastic retreat. The imperial family funded a growing temple complex on Mt. Hiei high above Heian where it protected the government from the surrounding forces of evil.

The *Shingon* sect taught that Buddhist truth was impossible to understand and therefore emphasized the powers of secret ritual practiced by holy men. Their monastery complex was situated on Mt. Koya to the south of the capital. The two schools were really for the imperial house and the rich nobles because farmers had little time or treasure to invest in Buddhist education or ritual. Because both schools received substantial support from the Yamato and other uji leaders, they became powerful and influential in later politics.

Significantly, both Shinto and Buddhism survived and prospered precisely because they reached a mutual accommodation. Tendai especially, with its highly developed sense of religious tolerance, preached that the Shinto kami were local Japanese manifestations of the boddisatva. Shinto shrines were encouraged to locate on Buddhist temple properties to act as native "protecting spirits." For its part, Shinto recognized that it could not hope to compete with the pomp and circumstance of Buddhist art, architecture, and music. It therefore accommodated itself to Buddhism, and attempts were made to combine the two faiths.

In the countryside, charismatic men and women went among the people as Buddhist missionaries. These unofficial priests and shamans, many of whom were probably Korean and Chinese refugees and immigrants, practiced their faith among the common folk, using their superior knowledge of magic and medicine. These *ubasoku* often intermarried within the regional nobility and formed a new layer of religious authority in the countryside. Many ubasoku went deep into the mountains where they lived as religious hermits, practicing a magical faith tied closely with native Shinto. These *yamabushi*, or "mountain priests," also served as guides for other Buddhists who wished to meditate and practice their faith in the mountains. This shamanist Buddhism interacted with all the other schools of Buddhism as well as with Shintoism.

CONFUCIANISM

An even greater influence on Japan in this early period, however, was the Chinese Confucian political ideology. After a series of imperial succession disputes, the Japanese under Shōtoku Taishi decided to follow the more sophisticated Chinese model, which consolidated and centralized power and authority under an emperor. Reasoning that the Confucian idea of rule by benevolent, wise, and moral bureaucrats was superior to constant military struggles, he managed to convince the warriors that they and their sons would prosper under a Confucian political system if they could enter it at the top. Of course it helped that their sons would become the educated elite. This gave the old aristocracy the social and political security that they could never obtain through military action alone.

Tired of constant warfare, the military leaders agreed to a truce wherein the emperor, being theoretically the most moral among them, could referee and arbitrate between them peacefully. Within a century, the Chinese-style government would be "permanently" installed under the so-called "Great Law" (*Taihō*) of 702. The system of national laws included a penal code as well as institutions for more efficient justice.

Confucianism is based on the idea that societies are best governed using the natural social models of basic human relationships. "Filial piety," the unquestioned love and loyalty that governed the relationship between father and son, became the model for all other relationships. Therefore, the emperor was to be honored and obeyed as the "father" of society, and the people were to behave as brothers to each other. Because in this model of natural hierarchies, wisdom comes with age and experience, moral education becomes the basis of governance.

Using the Chinese model, the imperial government instituted the Equal Fields System that reapportioned agricultural land every six years according to a national census. A national tax was imposed, as were systems for communal public works and a conscript army to keep the peace between themselves but also to fight the Ainu. A new capital city, Nara—modeled on China's great imperial city—was built on a checkerboard system of streets. The new government was based on a system of inherited noble ranks filled by the former uji military leaders. The final reform was the institution of a national religion: Buddhism. Despite lasting as the capital for less than a century, Nara became the center of social and political activity; indeed, the world's oldest (and largest wooden buildings) Buddhist temples are preserved there.

By 794 when the new capital Heian-kyō (later renamed Kyoto) was built, Japanese society was a unique synthesis wherein Confucian ideas were melded into Japanese political realities. For instance, only the sons of Japan's old uji military aristocracy could qualify to take the Civil Service Examination; in China, all literate males regardless of family occupation and social background were eligible. The all-powerful semidivine emperor of the Chinese became merely a puppet controlled by important families in Japan. The Fujiwara, themselves an offshoot of the imperial house, intermarried their daughters back into the imperial line and, before long, controlled child emperors (their grandsons) through the institution of regency.

Ironically, Confucian philosophy, which taught that women were incapable of being educated and were therefore unqualified for governing, was subverted by the Japanese. By the early Heian era, the imperial line descended through both the male and female lines.

The Fujiwara family system of government came to be superimposed over the imperial system but did not replace it, probably because it was easier to control it in that way. The Fujiwara family government ruled behind the throne like a theatrical "black curtain" (*kuromaku*), hiding the puppet masters who pulled the strings of government. Ironically, the Fujiwara kuromaku became the model for the future feudal puppet governments that would control the Fujiwara and the imperial house as well.

THE WRITTEN LANGUAGE

The Chinese written language itself underwent a similar creative adaptation. To be sure, the written language (like Latin in Europe) became the purview of educated aristocratic men. The official eighth-century histories *Kojiki* (Record of Ancient Matters) and *Nihongi* (Chronicles of Japan) and the early imperial poetry anthologies were written in classical Chinese. All of the business of government was conducted in Chinese; Chinese was the language of *sutras*, the sacred writings of Buddhism.

Because the Chinese and Japanese spoken languages are so different, it became necessary to adapt the written language to Japanese language structure. Spoken Chinese is tonal and mostly monosyllabic (one syllable per word). Japanese, however, is highly inflected (changing in tense) and polysyllabic. Word order is much more important in Chinese than in Japanese; Chinese contains almost no articles, whereas Japanese is full of them. How does one convey the rich nuances and meanings by inference of spoken Japanese in written form? It is done by creative adaptation, of course.

The ideograms of China were not only used for the transmission of distinct ideas but were modified into something like a phonetic symbolic alphabet (actually *two* syllabaries with each symbol representing the sound of a syllable) to transmit the sounds of native Japanese words. The syllabaries collectively called *kana* became the vehicle with which to sound out Japanese words. Later when Europeans introduced the phonetic alphabet, it too came to be used in Japanese writing. The combination of Chinese ideograms called *kanji* or "Chinese characters" with kana and *romaji* or "Roman characters" has been described by former American Ambassador to Japan Edwin Reischauer as "the most difficult writing system in common use anywhere in the world."

Women, according to Confucianism, were thought to be incapable of real intelligence and therefore were not educated in Chinese. They quickly mastered the simple kana system, however, and made the period the high point of Japanese literature. Poems, diaries, and romantic stories became the property of educated court women to the point that one male author disguised his gender, writing his celebrated *Tosa Diary* under a female pseudonym. But without doubt the greatest writers of the day were women. A court noblewoman wrote *Pillow Book,* an evocative and erotic account of eleventh-century court life. The greatest work of the era, the *Tale of Genji*—written by an eleventh-century court lady, Murasaki Shikibu—became the world's first novel. Full of rich poetic allusion, the novel depicts a dark, brooding, and fatalistic royal court where men and women alike engaged in complex conventions of courtly seduction. She described a court society wherein poetry, music, and other aesthetic pleasures became more important than anything else at all, including the business of governing.

The novel set the tone for a thousand years of Japanese artistic and aesthetic taste for the ruling class. Both genders used cosmetics, textiles, perfumes, textures, colors, and nature imagery to express their emotions. Letters of seduction incorporated the pleasures of all the senses. The rich poetic allusions to nature, to other poetry, and to Chinese and Japanese stories were written artfully in stylish calligraphy on lushly textured paper appropriate to the season.

Complex perfumes were wafted over the paper and colorful sprigs and flowers tied carefully to the message with richly textured, delicately dyed silk ribbons. Both men and women were expected to have mastered these conventions. Those in the court who did not were ridiculed and shunned, even if they happened to be otherwise physically attractive people.

Courtly costumes also defined aesthetic tastes. Layers of richly colored silk robes were arranged artfully by men and women alike. Costly brocades and painted patterns on silk conveyed artistic sensibility and good breeding. Often, because modesty demanded that unmarried women lurk behind richly textured screens, a suitor might never actually behold his lover's face or body until the seduction was physically consummated; and even then, it might be only a glimpse in the dimly lit corridors of the palace. A strategically draped hem beneath a screen or dangling artfully from a carriage, or a delicately penned note, might have to suffice in this game of seduction.

THE ARTS IN EARLY JAPAN

The period gave rise to other increasingly distinctly Japanese forms of art. The Chinese architecture that graces the ancient temple complexes blended with the native surroundings, particularly in Shinto religious buildings. Buddhist iconography sculpture also changed from the Chinese models to a more Japanese style. This came with the attempt to give human character to boddisatva and kami. Music evolved over the period as well. The chanting of sutras in Buddhist ceremonies served as models for chanting of stories and poems with secular themes. Painting went from the sophisticated pastel shadings and flowing lines of Buddhist art as seen in the temples of Nara to the flat, primary colors of *Yamato-e* ("Japanese paintings") in the sutra scrolls.

The Japanese developed their own distinctive forms of poetry based on Chinese models. Because Japanese contains far too many similar-sounding words to make a rhyming scheme interesting and challenging, the poets instead counted syllables and employed complex systems of puns and allusions for their poetry. The most popular form called *tanka* or "short poem" alternated lines of five and seven syllable lines that centuries later was shortened from 31 syllables to the 17 syllables of *haiku*.

Some would argue that the subtle nuances of the Japanese sense of beauty and representation were set in this period. Two hundred years later, another woman writer noted in the thirteenth-century court diary *Confessions of Lady Nijō* that the tastes and manners of Genji continued to rule the sense and sensibilities of the feudal age.

But perhaps therein lies the downfall of that society. While the aristocracy played, the military men began to take power into their own hands. The rustic military men would superimpose their rougher, masculine, and uneducated manners and tastes over those of the sophisticated, more feminine, aesthetic sensibilities of the Fujiwara Heian courtiers. But, like the Shinto religion that survived its encounter with Buddhism, like the system of uji leadership that survived the institution of Confucian imperial government, and like the imperial government that lingered after the imposition of the Fujiwara kuromaku, the imperial institutions and the aesthetic sensibilities of the Heian era would not be replaced completely by the rough tastes of the feudal warrior society that replaced them.

3

Feudal Japan

By the time of *Tale of Genji*, the Confucian and Buddhist civilian control of the country had been seriously undermined. Aristocratic civilian control by laws over society in general and over the military in particular had been gradually eroded away by economic changes in the society itself.

The imperial court had originally granted exemptions from the six-year Equal Fields distribution; temporary (for one generation only) tax exemptions to encourage costly, privately funded activities such as land reclamation (draining swamps, clearing forest land, irrigating arid land, terracing hillsides, and the like) and military campaigns against the Ainu; and exemptions to the Buddhist temples for their spiritual protection of the country. The great smallpox epidemic of 735–737, however, began to change that custom. Because perhaps one-third of the population perished in those two years, the country experienced a severe labor shortage.

In 745 the government made the tax exemption hereditary and permanent for land that had been reclaimed only. Before long, however, the privilege was extended to other land as well. Land reclamation and the maintenance of standing militias were very expensive enterprises that only large and powerful families could afford to do. Therefore only the very largest houses benefited from the exemption. Also, part of the problem was that the imperial government was granting these exemptions to members of its own family.

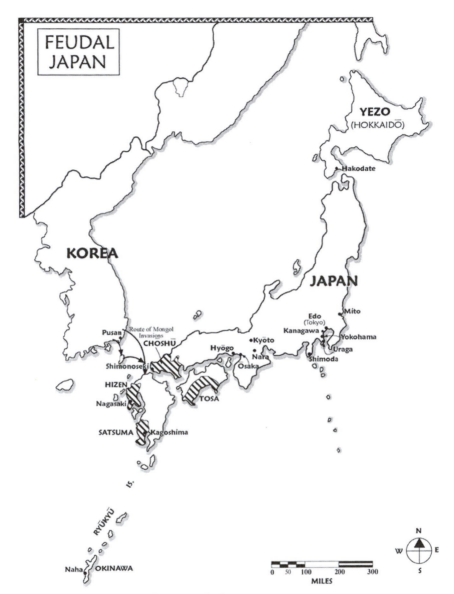

Feudal Japan. Courtesy of Jill Freund Thomas.

Often, sons who would never become emperor or inherit the leadership of the various branch families would be placed into positions within the leadership of the army or in the Buddhist establishments. To guarantee these young men a livelihood, the imperial government granted them tax exemptions. Unfortunately, it could not continue this practice for very long without endangering the economic, and therefore political, future of the government itself.

These semi-independent land holdings, called *shōen,* became so numerous that by the eleventh century more land was under the control of religious and military leaders than was taxed and controlled by the imperial government. With the tax exemptions came also the rights to exclude government inspection, census, and judicial jurisdiction. Therefore the shōen became, in effect, almost totally private estates.

Because the government could no longer raise enough revenue to pay for an imperial national army, the shōen owners began to raise and maintain their own militias made up primarily of former farmers, now called *samurai* (literally "men who serve") or *bushi* ("warriors"). Because the national government provided almost no other services for the shōen, the shōen owners were forced to create systems of administration. It then made sense to consolidate these small shōen into more efficient larger units. This was accomplished by ceding the land to powerful military and religious leaders. The former shōen owners became managers and stewards on their former lands and retained their rights to collect taxes (all this in exchange for the protection of their new patrons). Before long, the consolidated shōen evolved into semi-independent states. The small militias were similarly consolidated into armies, each with their own local commanders (usually the former owners) but now controlled by even more powerful military leaders.

Jealous military men began to vie with each other for the control of land and labor. Not surprisingly, the most important of these families were offshoots of the imperial house itself. In the same manner that the Fujiwara had wrested control of the imperial house in the early Heian period, other related houses began to use their influence to do the same. Rival political factions within the capital set dangerous precedents by using bands of samurai to enforce their claims at court.

By the 1150s, two Yamato-related families, the Taira and the Minamoto used the pretext of an imperial succession dispute (another dangerous precedent) to fight openly for power. The apparent winner of the decadelong struggle was the haughty patriarch of the Taira, Kiyomori who ruled Kyoto for over a decade. He absorbed hundreds of shōen and took for himself the right to grant even more shōen to his followers and to appoint them to positions as imperial governors and ministers. He used his armies to attack the holdings of the Nara-based Buddhist temples and absorbed their lands as well. Like the Fujiwara to whom he was distantly related, he married his daughters to emperors, forced the emperors to abdicate, and then installed a grandson who resulted from one of those marriages as emperor. Like the Fujiwara, Kiyomori became a kuromaku regent for the infant. In fact, so complete was his control in the capital that the motto of the day was "If one is not a Taira, then one is not even considered human."

Ironically, despite the fact that Kiyomori had hunted down and viciously killed virtually the entire Minamoto family, his "mercy" would be his undoing.

He arrogantly spared the young sons of his rival to demonstrate his power. That mercy was not to be repeated or appreciated. Yoritomo, the oldest of those boys was made hostage to the Hōjō family, who were Kiyomori's relatives living in the small fishing village of Kamakura 300 miles to the east of Kyoto. In 1180, Yoritomo took advantage of another attempt to restore power to the emperor. He raised an army of dissatisfied military men, including Hōjō Tokimasa, his jailer who became his father-in-law. After five years of bloody fighting, Yoritomo's coalition defeated the Taira and then he founded a military government on the basis of his newly won title as the emperor's military deputy or *shōgun* (the full title *Sei-itai Shōgun* meant "Barbarian subduing Commander" and usually had been filled by a Fujiwara prince). Instead of moving to Kyoto as the Taira had done, the Minamoto, and their allies the Hōjō, remained in their Kamakura stronghold and forced the rest of the country to come to them. In fact the eastern military capital gives its name to the first "feudal" period of Japan's history.

Yoritomo did not make the mistake of showing mercy to his defeated rivals. Virtually the entire Taira family was hunted down and murdered. Even babies were put to the sword, drowned, and even buried alive. Yoritomo's blood lust knew almost no bounds, however, as he eventually had rivals within his own family killed as well. His cousin Yoshinaka, who had been his staunchest and most loyal ally during the war, was assassinated. Yoritomo's greatest general was his younger brother Yoshitsune. Fearing his growing popularity, however, Yoritomo had him hunted down before Yoshitsune was "allowed" to commit suicide. When Yoshitsune's widow gave birth to a posthumous son, Yoritomo had him killed. Within two years Yoritomo had another half-brother and one of his sons-in-law murdered as well.

THE KAMAKURA BAKUFU: 1192–1333

By 1192, Yoritomo seemed to be in complete control of the country. He transformed his private military government into something resembling a national government. Similar in some ways to European feudalism, the political system that evolved was based on the personal, contractual, and military relationships between the shōgun and his regional subordinates, the *gokenin* or "house men" (implying a kinship). These men, who were sometimes the descendants of former shōen owners, often were former peasants and samurai who had risen through the ranks of Yoritomo's armies. They provided the shōgun with the military power of their own personal, contractual military bands of samurai. They collected local taxes and administered lands in their capacities as imperial stewards and constables. The shōgun usurped the emperor's right to appoint or dismiss these men, and thereby the gokenin were tied to him personally. Unlike feudalism in Europe, however, the gokenin did not own this land or the farmers who tilled the soil. In Japan, the farmers were independent peasants who owned their own land.

Also, unlike the semiautonomous knights who lived on their own personal feudal manors in Europe, the samurai often lived in the castles of their feudal lords, the gokenin, and were paid a salary when they were called to fight. Finally, unlike Europe, the imperial government continued to exist in Kyoto, but the shōgun, the emperor's military deputy, controlled the country from Kamakura, 300 miles to the east. Some tax land remained in the hands of the emperor and of the noble aristocracy in Kyoto and therefore out of the direct control of Kamakura.

The Kamakura government, often called shōgunate (or *bakufu*—"tent government"), was a mixture of military and civil administration. The Minamoto and their Hōjō regents (discussed later) controlled the lives and properties of their own direct feudal subordinates by virtue of the power to appoint and dismiss them. But the bakufu left the administration of the outlying regions to their gokenin warlords in their capacities as civil governors, stewards, and constables. And because the imperial house continued to appoint stewards and constables to imperial land, the political map was considerably clouded by this mixture of powers.

Model laws were passed by the shōgunate, and the gokenin were encouraged to copy them, but as long as the gokenin kept the peace in their areas, the bakufu left them alone. The shōgunate maintained a liaison office in Kyoto to watch over the almost powerless court, mostly to keep the emperors from trying to restore power to themselves, because that was how Yoritomo came to power. Mostly, the bakufu left the effete nobility alone to play their inconsequential games as before. In reality, there was no "national" government in Kamakura. Yoritomo and the shōguns who succeeded him controlled the ability to appoint men to some imperial positions, but once those men began to consolidate power in their districts, they became increasingly more independent. The gokenin commended their lands to the shōgun and became his vassals, but they retained considerable regional autonomy as long as they did not challenge the bakufu's national authority. After a while very few gokenin were deprived of their offices. Their sons could expect to inherit not only their father's titles and offices but indeed also the control of these increasingly autonomous lands.

By the late thirteenth century the government had become something more like a coalition of semi-independent, gokenin-led states who swore loyalty to the office of the shōgun. There were, similarly, no national systems for taxes, justice, or even common defense. Gokenin could be called upon by the shōgun to spend their revenues on projects for the common benefit of the Japanese people as a whole, but each such request was personal and had to be negotiated individually. The Minamoto and Hōjō houses controlled extensive tracts of land (at one time almost 25 percent of all the agricultural land except for the island of Hokkaido) and therefore could garner huge amounts of taxes and raise large armies with that revenue, but these were not national, they were private.

The fiction remained that a national government continued to function in Kyoto; that the Minamoto-Hōjō were only the emperor's military deputies. When they spoke to the people of Japan, they did so in the name and under the authority and legitimacy of the emperor. Yoritomo, like the Fujiwara and Taira families before him, had been very careful to get imperial sanction for every appointment, law, and military order that he made.

The Minamoto and Hōjō played a complex and intricate game of marriage politics in order to extend their control all over the country. Favored gokenin were "adopted" or married off to relatives. Ironically, when the shōgunal line fell fallow in 1252, a Fujiwara-Yamato prince was "adopted" into the Minamoto-Hōjō house and the four families were briefly united.

At the foundation of the bakufu in the 1190s, Yoritomo instituted a rough sort of family government in Kamakura that increasingly evolved into something of a model for future feudal governments. A Samurai Board was set up to administer to the needs of the soldiers; a Board of Inquiry functioned as a judicial office; and an Administration Board took care of everything else. These boards were staffed by Yoritomo's most trusted gokenin. Curiously, the rule of order demanded a unanimous vote to keep any one of them from controlling the others. Some historians, notably Mikiso Hane, have argued that this is perhaps the beginnings of the Japanese love of rule by collectivity and consensus. Many of the gokenin modeled their own regional governments on that of the Kamakura, and often regional disputes were settled by the bakufu as sort of a national referee.

The Kamakura government fell into the hands of the Hōjō family soon after the death of Yoritomo in 1199 (ironically two of his sons and a grandson were themselves assassinated by a third son) to be controlled by his strong-willed widow Hōjō Masako. Masako, who was only 32 when Yoritomo died, retired to a Buddhist convent. Yet she wielded so much power, in fact, that she was called the "nun-shōgun." This remarkable woman (perhaps in the manner of her distant ancestor Himiko) installed and removed emperors, shōguns, and regents for both emperors and shōguns (including her own father whom she sent into exile) and had to be consulted whenever any successor to Yoritomo's original gokenin was confirmed. She presided over a substantial increase in the fortunes of the bakufu when thousands of shōen were confiscated from the imperial house after an attempted imperial restoration by an ex-emperor in 1221. The Hōjō family continued to hold sway over the coalition of gokenin for more than a century after her death in 1225 despite the greatest external threat to the country until World War II.

In 1274 and again in 1281 the continental Mongol forces, who had already conquered most of China and all of Korea, attempted to invade Japan. Led by the courageous young regent Hōjō Tokimune, the Japanese put up a fierce defense. The Mongol forces were technologically superior, however, employing complex coordinated troop movements of large infantry and cavalry units, whereas the Japanese were more accustomed to fighting as individual samurai. The Mongols also used powerful crossbows and catapults that fired exploding fireballs. The Japanese still used swords, spears, and longbows. The Mongols were also a numerically superior force. In the 1274 attempted invasion they brought nearly 30,000 Mongol and Korean warriors, in 1281 a huge armada with a combined Chinese, Mongol, and Korean force of nearly 140,000 men. The Japanese put up a determined fight, but ultimately the Mongols were driven away by typhoons both times (which the Japanese called *kamikaze* or "Wind of the Gods") off the northwestern coast of Kyushu.

Because all gokenin warlords collected their own taxes and paid their own expenses, the shōgun had no national treasury with which to reward those who had defended the country. The Kyushu defenders naturally were angry because they had borne the brunt of the fighting and now were not rewarded with any spoils of war because they could not confiscate the lands of their enemies. And because no one knew if the Mongols would try yet another invasion, the warlords in Kyushu had to remain alert as well to maintain the huge defensive seawall built along the coast. The superstitious Hōjō, however, hastened to reward the Shinto and Buddhist priests whose prayers had brought the kamikaze twice.

Resentments continued to stew for several years until a series of attempts to restore actual power to the Emperor Go-Daigo gave many gokenin an opportunity to form a new coalition to replace the Kamakura shōgunate. Interestingly, Yoritomo had used a previous imperial restoration attempt to wrest power from Taira Kiyomori; his widow Masako had used a similar attempt to extend feudal control in 1221. A restoration attempt five centuries later (1867) would spell the end of another feudal regime.

Ashikaga Takauji, a former subordinate and ally of the shōgun, changed allegiances in the middle of the campaign and rallied other warlords around the emperor until the shōgun's forces were defeated. Takauji attacked his own allies, arrested the emperor, and then installed himself as the new shōgun. He returned the capital to Muromachi, a district of Kyoto that lends its name to the era. The imperial house was briefly split between rival claimants to the throne when Go-Daigo fled Kyoto in 1336 and set up his own rival Southern Court at Yoshino, which lasted until 1392.

RELIGIOUS DEVELOPMENTS

This period was also one of religious ferment as several contesting schools of Buddhist thought struggled to explain the war and bloodshed that ran through the society. As early as the eleventh century, new interpretations of

Buddhism vied with the established sects of Tendai and Shingon, the latter two having received most of the imperial patronage. Many of the new religious reform movements were led by priests who fled the turmoil of feudal warfare in search of enlightenment in China.

The Buddhist religious teaching of *mappō* had a great deal to do with the search for alternate paths to salvation. The Buddha had taught that sometime in the future, a time would come when the ways of men would become so perverse and wicked that not even the power of the Buddhist Law could prevail. Many religious leaders looked around them during the height of the wars between the Taira and Minamoto and thought that the time of mappō had surely arrived. Despite the Buddhist laws against the taking of any life, the killing of one's warrior enemies in combat had become commonplace and even seemed to make some sort of perverse logic: Kill or be killed. But the idea of Yoritomo slaughtering innocent babies, not only of his Taira enemies, but his own nephew as well, must have convinced many that humanity had reached the ultimate depths of depravity.

One priest, Hōnen, lived through the wars and began to preach that people could never attain salvation on the basis of their own religious work because of the evil in the world. Therefore they must depend on the power of the Buddha Amida to intervene on their behalf. The faith in Amida would rescue them after death, and they would be reincarnated in the Amida's Western Paradise where they could live serenely, work out their karma of past lives, and ultimately attain salvation. This Pureland (*Jōdo*) sect, as it came to be known, with its simplistic and direct message of salvation, gathered much support from the peasantry. Honen's disciple Shinran expanded the Pureland idea even further. He argued that to live one's life in a self-conscious and smug attempt to attain salvation through good works was even worse than living an evil life. "If a good person can be saved, cannot an evil person be saved as well?" he asked. Better to put complete faith in Amida than to waste one's life doing good works just to attain salvation. A single sincere call for Amida's merciful intercession (called *nembutsu,* or "Hail to the Buddha") could guarantee salvation. In fact, in order to demonstrate his contempt for what he considered to be hypocritical religious laws, he put aside his saffron-colored Buddhist robes and wore normal clothing; he broke his celibacy vow, married, and had several children; he ate the meat forbidden by Buddhist law and generally changed the face of the Buddhist priesthood.

His True Pureland (*Jōdo Shinshū*) sect gained thousands of believers. Because these reformist ideas were simple and easy to comprehend, the peasantry flocked to them. Because the schools taught that anyone, even women, could attain salvation through the nembutsu, the leadership of some religious communities was assumed by peasant men, and occasionally charismatic women. Before long, Jōdo and Jōdo Shinshū had more followers than the rest of the Buddhist sects combined (they continue to enjoy great success in Japan today).

Another reform sect founded by the priest Nichiren argued that one could call on the power of one particular holy scripture, the Lotus Sutra, for salvation. There was no need to study or understand the meaning of the scripture, he argued; the power of the sutra was sufficient to save. Nichiren argued that all the other Buddhist sects were completely wrong, and he tried to destroy them by force. He formed his own militant nationalist sect that preached that only Japanese could attain salvation. "If we were to find the Buddha among the Mongols, we should kill him," he maintained. Nichiren-shū, as the sect itself came to be known, enjoyed widespread popularity (it would become the focus of many ultranationalist groups in the 1930s and has enjoyed a renewed popularity in the post–World War II era within the "Value Creating Society," *Soka Gakkai*).

The period also witnessed more attempts to synthesize and combine Buddhism and Shinto, including a school called *Ryōbu-Shinto* ("Two-Way Shinto") that preached that Shinto was merely a Japanese manifestation of Buddhist truth. Again, charismatic shamans (called ubasoku), and "mountain priests" (yamabushi) combined the religious messages of several schools, creating even more distinct religious sects and cults. Some religious historians have argued that the almost constant warfare of feudal Japan created the numerous cults to fit nearly every need, to soothe every fear, to answer every religious question.

The adherents of another Buddhist sect, *Zen,* argued that because everything is illusion, one must concentrate the mind on this "nothingness" to allow one's inner truth to break through unimpeded. In other words, salvation was to be found internally through personal enlightenment. All attempts to "obtain" salvation were themselves part of the desires that clouded the mind. "The clutching hand cannot grab itself" was the argument.

The founder of one Zen school, Eisai, traveled to China for enlightenment (he is regarded as the man who brought the tea ceremony to Japan). He argued that it was necessary to "shock" the mind out of its habit of thinking logically (and therefore creating more illusion) with impossible riddles called *koan* ("What would you look like if your parents had never met?"). Dōgen, the founder of another Zen school, returned from a pilgrimage to China convinced that a physical discipline of prolonged quiet meditation (*zazen*) would settle the mind and allow one to attain enlightenment.

Both schools appealed to the rough and uneducated samurai. The warriors had neither the education nor the leisure time to spend their lives in the pursuit of knowledge as required by Tendai and Shingon. The basic anti-intellectualism of Zen as well as the physical discipline and training required in zazen appealed to them. Some Zen monks argued that truth could only be passed on secretly from one enlightened monk to his discipline disciples. This, of course, was not very different than feudal lords passing on the secrets of combat to one's samurai disciples. Also, Zen's emphasis on concentrating mind and body for a single purpose was similar to the discipline required in the martial arts. The feudal warlords also found Zen to be an excellent form of discipline for their troops and therefore patronized Zen monks and established monasteries for them. The Kamakura Bakufu founded and patronized five Zen centers in its capital.

Samurai flocked to them to gain release from the horrors and guilt of warfare, and to prepare themselves to face the enemy and death. They found zazen to be a cleansing exercise for the mind. Because all of life was illusion, death and killing were no worse than ordinary human acts such as breathing, eating, or sleeping. They chose the *sakura* cherry blossom as their symbol because their lives bloomed and died much like the short-lived blossom.

All of these religious sects, as well as the older ones that continued to keep some believers, struggled with the horrors of war. The samurai developed their own twisted philosophy based on honor among warriors. This amalgam called *Bushidō* (although it would not be so named until a century later), the "Way of the Warrior," combines Chinese Taoism, Shinto, and elements of the various sects of Buddhism. Bushidō suggests that the only worthy truth is the honor of being the true warrior. Everything, even one's own life, must be sacrificed to that honor. The warrior was expected to be honest, sincere, strong, manly, fearless, frugal, stoic, and selflessly devoted to one's comrades and feudal lord. Family and loved ones were less important than honor and trust between samurai; honor must be preserved even to death. The greatest expression of this honor was to seek death in service to one's lord instead of trying to avoid it. *Hara kiri*, or "belly slitting" suicide, demonstrated one's sincerity and preserved one's honor. It could also convey one's contempt for the material world, demonstrate one's sincere regret for one's bad behavior, or even shame and force one's lord to obey the rules of bushidō.

Of course not all samurai lived up to this ideal. Consider the bestial behavior of warriors like Yoritomo, who killed his own family; the treacherous Ashikaga Takauji, who switched sides in the middle of a battle; or later samurai who turned against their lords, their fathers, their sons, or anyone else, depending on personal needs, jealousies, or paranoias. It is clear that power was more important than honor to these men.

Even the emotional love of women was inferior to the "pure" love between warriors. Previously, samurai women could and did inherit not only wealth and land but also their father's, husband's, or son's samurai status. Women occasionally led troops into battle. Among the list of Yoritomo's many gokenin can be found the names of some women. By the end of the period, however, the necessity of concentrating one's land in the hands of a single warrior successor made inheritance by women impossible. There is little wonder, then, if Japan's treatment of women had degenerated to the point that primogeniture, the total inheritance by one son, was the order of the day, and that women became, as one samurai put it, "little more than rented wombs."

If the Kamakura era was one of brutality and misogyny, the Muromachi era that followed it was even worse. And the Sengoku Era that followed the Muromachi was characterized by even more horrible acts of savagery and perversion. Japanese society would have to sink to horribly perverse and evil depths before it could rise again to the humanity and culture of the Heian Era.

THE MUROMACHI ERA: 1333–1467

The end of the Kamakura Bakufu ushered in a brief period of actual imperial rule. The emperor Go-Daigo managed to "restore" real political and military power to his own house for slightly more than two years. The warlords who had flocked to his side now watched warily as he began to set up a government very different from any that they had experienced. He laid claims to Hōjō lands and began to appoint his own loyalists as stewards and constables. The warlords were angry and suspicious when Go-Daigo did not reward them, his "loyalists," with offices or confiscated land. But when he began to try to wrest land and power away from his allies, they quickly sprang into action. Of course any real attempt to restore actual power to the emperor had to be at the expense of the feudal warlords. At the forefront of this reaction was one of the men who had helped Go-Daigo seize power, Ashikaga Takauji.

Takauji was related to the Hōjō regents whom he had helped defeat. He had joined the rebellion when ordered by the bakufu to put it down. None of the "loyalist" generals managed to defeat their enemies completely. Often, the armies of the bakufu gokenin simply switched sides as Takauji did. Allies today were the future enemies of tomorrow. Takauji in 1335 took the field at the head of his considerable personal army and quickly gained allies among the dissatisfied warlords around him and moved against the imperial house. Perhaps the last straw for him had been when Go-Daigo had appointed his own son as shōgun, a post that Takauji coveted.

Warfare raged on intermittently for nearly two decades as both sides won and lost skirmishes, but by 1336 Takauji managed to win the war of coalitions. Warlords changed sides from time to time, and Takauji was almost constantly in the field, but by that date, he had managed to win the loyalties of the majority of the most powerful warlords. Takauji was forced to turn over the task of actual government to a younger brother while he stayed in the field. The loyalist forces continued to rally around Go-Daigo, who had escaped from Kyoto to set up a rival throne in Yoshino. In 1338 Takauji felt secure enough to assume the title of shōgun, and shortly thereafter he passed the position on to his son, thus forming the basis of the Ashikaga Bakufu.

Skirmishes continued for two decades more with the forces of Go-Daigo raiding Kyoto at least three times. Takauji had to take the field against his younger brother and his nephew as the political situation remained unstable until the third shōgun managed to consolidate the new bakufu.

The Ashikaga (or Muromachi, named after the district of Kyoto where the shōguns resided) Bakufu was never really very much like the Kamakura Bakufu that preceded it. The Kamakura had based its power and legitimacy on its right to appoint and remove imperial governors, land stewards, and constables. The military changes in the country, however, forced the Ashikaga to mutate into something closer to European-style feudalism.

The first three Ashikaga shōguns had set up a government in the Muromachi northern suburbs of Kyoto. They had maintained a liaison office in Kamakura and had established the rudiments of a national government, but it never approached the power and influence of the Kamakura Bakufu. The shōguns tried to extend their power over the warlords, which forced the latter to build up their own power to keep from being swallowed up by the shōgun. The bakufu seized the lands of the Hōjō, as well as those of all the gokenin who had fought on the losing imperial side. Together with their own land, the Ashikaga now directly controlled nearly one-quarter of the country. Building on that large holding, they attempted to bring in the lands of the men who had fought for the emperor. But when their own allies saw the Ashikaga keeping the land for themselves, they began to fear for their own futures.

This inadvertently gave rise to a new type of feudal warlord. Although the term would not gain full currency for another 50 years or so, the designation *daimyō* (literally "great names") came to be used increasingly for this new class of military men. Many came from old gokenin, steward, governor, constable, and even Yamato, Fujiwara, and Minamoto cadet houses, but the majority were "men on the make." They were the former subordinates of other feudal lords who had lost their positions in war, through theft and subversion, or who had been overwhelmed by their own former samurai. The era has been characterized as the "Age of *Gekokujo*" (Rule of the Mighty by the Lowly) as one proud family after another was supplanted by their former subordinates. It rang as true for the imperial house that was controlled by the Ashikaga, as it did ironically later for the Ashikaga themselves. Scarcely a handful of the proud gokenin houses survived the era. The rest lost out to their former political and military inferiors.

These daimyō, who had only recently won their wealth and power by wresting them away from their feudal superiors, were not about to let anyone, even the shōgun, take them away. When the Ashikaga tried to rein them in, they resisted. When the bakufu tried to limit their landholdings, their armies, or the extent of their power, they entrenched their defensive positions within castles. They consolidated their lands and men, their samurai were now required to reside within the castle all the time, and no one was thereafter granted land as a reward for service.

Inheritance was no longer divided among all the children. Now, because warfare and politics required strong central leadership, a primogeniture of sorts became the order of the day. Only one male heir inherited the entire domain, all siblings became feudal vassals to the leader. Very often, the heir was not even a son. Daimyō often adopted a charismatic subordinate as a "son-in-law" and heir. Needless to say, this practice disinherited all women and made them dependent on their male relatives. It also caused tremendous jealousies among brothers. The practice of a daimyō being killed by brothers, cousins, sons, or other relatives "on the make" became very common. Occasionally a daimyō would be killed by his wife, concubine, sister, or even mother attempting to install their favorite as the new daimyō.

The daimyō knew from personal experience that land was power; so they never allowed their samurai the right to actually live on the land. Many of the new daimyō had parlayed small tracts of land into larger holdings, often at the expense of their own direct feudal lords. Some had been adopted into powerful houses, others had killed their lords, still others had ridden to the top behind their loyal peasant-samurai. They did not wish that their samurai would do the same to them.

The samurai now "lived as in an inn." Everything was provided for them by the daimyō within the castle—meaning that they had no personal loyal retainers, and therefore no loyal band of followers with whom to plot against their lords. Samurai were often shifted about so that they could not build up personal cliques. They had become professional soldiers.

The daimyō were so independent that they no longer even bothered to seek the official imperial offices that had meant power in the Kamakura era. Control of the land, the taxes, and the samurai was all that counted now. Even the bakufu had become unimportant in the lives of the daimyō. By the middle of the fifteenth century, the only people who cared about the bakufu offices were those who actually held them.

The nature of warfare changed as well. Japanese had learned something from the Mongol forces at the end of the thirteenth century. They found that unmounted infantry armed with long iron-tipped pikes could be devastatingly effective, even on well-armed cavalry. A battalion of pike men standing behind stout earthen shields, backed by ranks of archers, could withstand the fiercest samurai cavalry attack.

The Japanese did not move toward Mongol crossbow and catapults, but they did begin to use large mobile phalanxes of archers to good effect. They also understood and appreciated the effectiveness of strong defensive walls and so began to experiment with positional castle warfare as well. All of these new military technologies involved the use of thousands of men. The hundred or so well-armed and well-armored mounted samurai that had been the scourge of the battlefield in the wars of the 1180s were rapidly being replaced by "light foot" (*ashigaru*) soldiers who were cheaper to arm and easier to train. One mounted samurai armed with a longbow, a good razor-sharp steel long sword, and protected (as was his horse) by lacquered armor and helmet cost more than 50 ashigaru armed with iron pikes and protected by thick twisted straw rope layered over leather armored vests. A samurai took years to train, an ashigaru, only days.

Of course the need for such large armies of men changed the nature of political and administrative control as well. Extensive training and drilling of troops was now necessary as tacticians experimented with complex strategies. Coordinated movements of large armies required better communications on the battlefield. Battle flags, smoke, drums, couriers, whistles, and gongs were employed, but all of these methods required a well-trained disciplined military. Gone were the days when samurai-farmers could leave their fields briefly and return home after the battle. In due course the samurai left the rice fields, and the peasants left the battlefields. The daimyō kept their samurai and ashigaru nearby and their farmers on the land producing food for his military. So the samurai became castle-dwellers, and the peasantry remained rural people.

The daimyō realized that their power depended on the productivity of the land and undertook public works projects to improve their holdings and to increase their revenue base. Flood and coastal water control projects as well as irrigation works vied with land reclamation, hillside terracing, crop rotation, road building, and experiments with better rice strains. The best domains gave the peasants material incentives to produce more by decreasing the tax levees on increased productivity. In most areas, the peasants were allowed a great deal of freedom to govern themselves as long as they kept the peace and paid their taxes on time.

Because the samurai had been removed from the land, however, the peasantry usually had to arm and defend themselves against bandits and brigands. Discontented peasants swelled the ranks of the ashigaru and even became samurai themselves as the social class lines were blurred at best. So it should not come as a surprise that occasionally the peasants used their weapons in other ways as well. From time to time they rose up in protest and even challenged their feudal lords. Usually, however, they sought temporary relief from taxation, particularly in times of famine or natural disasters. They demanded that the daimyō grant "acts of grace" (*tokusei*), that is, forgiving of debts. These were aimed, not at the daimyō-imposed taxes (though occasionally they wanted these too), but rather to cancel all debts owed to moneylenders and pawnbrokers. Not surprisingly, daimyō occasionally profited from the tokusei by imposing a fee of 10 percent on all debts canceled. It was not money owed to them anyway. As one would expect, the moneylenders and pawnbrokers also sought protection. They and wealthy merchants, sake and soy brewers, and even smaller temples paid license fees to other armies as bodyguards. All of this led to the need for even more armies, of course.

The daimyō began to develop free markets around the castles in order to attract artisans and wholesale merchants to feed and supply the samurai. Previously, markets were periodical in nature, appearing as if by magic, on regularly scheduled days of the month at crossroads, forks of the river, temples, shrines, or river fords. But now these castle-town merchants set up permanent dependable markets that specialized in one or two products: vegetables, meats, fish, rice, straw products (mats, sedge hats, sandals, etc.), leather goods, hemp, cotton, silk, tea, pottery, metal implements, and the like. These independent city-folk (*chōnin*) formed castle-town *za* (guilds) and monopolies in order to control prices, to maintain quality and quantity of goods, and to avoid taxation. Often, the daimyō would promise artisans and merchants a free hand in their own self-government in order to attract them to his castle. Rich local merchants began to form commercial and marriage alliances with merchants from other castle-towns, and before long the intercastle trade took on an inter-regional character as well.

The customary use of barter exchange gave way to the use of currencies. Japan had for centuries imported Chinese copper coins, called "cash," or had devised mediums of exchange such as lengths of silk, cotton, or linen. Often rice itself became the medium of exchange, with commodities priced at specified amounts of grain. Now daimyō, guild or individual merchants, and temples began to mint their own coins or even to print their own paper money. Pawnbrokers, wholesale merchants, sake and soy brewers, and moneylenders struck up a lively and sophisticated commerce.

The Ashikaga tried to rein in the increasingly independent merchants and daimyō but with little success. They had even less success with the rising power and wealth of the Buddhist establishment because they were organized on religious principles as well as on land and wealth considerations. Because the temples concentrated a great deal of land and agricultural wealth, they also became involved in moneylending and pawnbroking. As in the end of the Heian period, the Buddhist temples found it necessary to maintain their own armies to defend their land and wealth in the rising lawlessness of the period. Several established monasteries and one lay congregation association gave the bakufu the most trouble.

The Tendai mountain temple complex on Mt. Hiei above Kyoto had grown in size and wealth during the chaos of the early fourteenth century. It had acquired large tracts of land surrounding the capital. In order to protect the land against the greedy daimyō around them, as well as against the Ashikaga, temple leaders raised large militias. These militias were sometimes made up of the peasants who farmed the land, but more commonly of mercenary soldiers who flocked to whoever offered them pay. The warriors shaved their heads like monks (hence the name "warrior-monks"), but they were samurai nonetheless. They protected the mountain monasteries, but occasionally, this growing army of unruly men swarmed down into Kyoto to raid tax collectors, pawnbrokers, and the Ashikaga themselves. By the 1460s they participated in a wanton destruction of half of the city itself during the Ōnin War of 1467–1477.

Another mountain monastery was the Shingon complex atop Mt. Koya on the Kii Peninsula south of the capital. This group of warrior-monks also controlled a huge land estate in the surrounding area. Occasionally their militia engaged in military adventures in the area, often adding to their extensive land holdings by conquest rather than religious bequest.

The other troublesome monastery was the Kofukuji complex in Nara. This ancient temple had long been patronized by the Fujiwara family, and its army had been used in that family's struggles with other political factions in Kyoto. They too engaged in military campaigns and thereby contributed to the instability in the capital.

The lay Buddhist group was the *Ikkō* or "single-purpose" community of True Pureland believers in west-central Honshu. Their otherwise isolated communities of co-religious farmers banded together (hence the name of "single-purpose") for common defense. They established an extensive network of parish militias that ranged far and wide in coordinated military campaigns. They established a tithe-like religious tax controlled by a single religious patriarch at the Honganji complexes in Kyoto. For the most part they refused to pay taxes to anyone else, so large tracts of rich farmland were controlled by the religious leaders in Kyoto. Because their faith promised a release to the Western Paradise of Amida, they did not fear death. This of course made them an extremely dangerous enemy.

Eventually the Ikkō built a huge castle on the plains of Ōsaka controlling the surrounding area for miles. This was clearly a force to be reckoned with. Not even the bakufu could totally control them. Most surrounding daimyō steered clear of them or made military alliances of convenience with them.

The Ashikaga were more successful in dealing with what might be called "national" affairs. They forced the imperial family to bow to their wishes. The emperor lived his life basically under house arrest. Very few courtiers (and virtually no outside daimyō) were allowed access to him in order to avoid any attempts at restoring power to the imperial court. The bakufu provided the court with a stipend but seized all tax lands in order to control the imperial family. Finally in 1392 the shōgun tricked the descendants of the Emperor

Go-Daigo's Southern Court into reuniting with the court in Kyoto by promising that the two courts would alternate as emperor. The Ashikaga never kept this promise, but after the throne was reunited in Kyoto, they kept it tightly controlled.

The Ashikaga also took the lead in reestablishing foreign relations with China. Because of the Mongol raids, commercial and diplomatic relations between the two countries quite understandably had lapsed. Also, the chaos caused by the collapse of the Mongol dynasty in the mid-fourteenth century allowed the rise of piracy that preyed on trading ships between China and Japan. The Ashikaga dealt harshly with these brigands called *wako* (Japanese pirates) and managed to establish relations with the new Ming Dynasty in China. Official so-called Red Seal and Tally ships plied their way between the two new governments. Ashikaga ships were given Ming imperial red seals or jagged-edged tokens, which would then be tallied or matched up against the Ming half of the token in Chinese ports, designating them as sanctioned monopoly traders.

Trade goods from China and Korea were silk, brocades, cotton, tea, books, copper coins, and porcelain. Japanese wares were swords, folding fans, sulfur, copper, and silver. Japanese priests on religious pilgrimages often went along on these journeys as well. Chinese and Korean artists, potters, and priests also made the journey to Japan. The political chaos at the end of the Mongol and the beginning of the Ming Dynasties brought political refugees from China and Korea to Japan. The era, then, was one of shared cultural exchanges, and new Chinese philosophies such as Neo-Confucianism made their mark in Japan.

Japanese merchants ranged far afield in Southeast Asia as well. Whole communities of Japanese merchants set up shop in the Philippines, Siam, Taiwan, and the other islands. By the sixteenth century, Japanese trading ships were familiar in ports throughout the area.

Although the era was not a particularly important one in Japanese history, it was influential in terms of establishing new norms for social and political behavior. Historians have argued that the stoicism, perseverance, and austere bureaucratism that came to define Japanese personality had its origins in the Ashikaga period. The militarization of the society as a whole was born during this era. Peasants and chōnin alike began to emulate the taciturn brusque character of their samurai leaders. There is evidence that the Japanese were more open, gregarious, emotional, and free-spirited before this era. The ideal warrior ethic of Bushidō became the model for men of all social classes. Similarly, their long-suffering wives became the models for chōnin and peasant women too.

The origins of the lower-class *eta*, the ancestors of the modern-day *burakumin*, can be found in the era. These outcast folk were probably the descendants of captive slaves who performed disagreeable and dirty occupations like butchers, grave diggers, executioners, tanners, and surprisingly, straw workers (perhaps because they made sandals, associated with dirty feet). Thought to be ritually polluted and subhuman, they were made to live in the most dangerous places: the undefended outskirts of castle walls, under bridges, and temporarily dry river beds. They were not allowed to worship in temples or shrines (they often set up their own), and they were virtually separated from the rest of society for centuries. Denied entry into "normal" occupations, they formed a netherworld "shadow government" of self-help and self-defense. In many cities, they controlled the criminal element and were allowed to govern their own neighborhoods. The social stigma continues to effect some of their descendants today. In some regions, private detectives are hired to investigate family histories of prospective marriage partners to be certain that they are not the descendants of these unfortunate people, who are still considered by some to be polluted with "bad blood" and suffering from hereditary diseases and psychoses.

THE ARTS

Although the period was one of almost constant warfare and degradation, it was a time of artistic and aesthetic triumph as well. While the country at large suffered from warfare, treachery, and atrocity, the new urban aristocracy sought refuge and solace in the arts. Religious ferment during the Kamakura period had heavily influenced the arts of the country, and now aesthetic appreciation flourished.

Zen priests returning from pilgrimages to China brought new art forms and styles. The very best painters, like Sesshu (1420–1506) and Miyamoto Musashi (1584–1645) (also a famous swordsman), employed monochrome ink-wash (*sumi-e*) styles as well as ornate gold-leaf painting techniques. The latter style was employed by the masters Kanō Eitoku (1543–1590) and Hasegawa Tohaku (1539–1610) to decorate the interiors of daimyō castles. Sumptuously illustrated scrolls such as the *Tale of Genji* spread both literacy as well as art throughout the country. Woodblock printing, which would have its heyday two centuries later in the Tokugawa Era, would have its origins in this era as well.

Calligraphy became a true art form, given free expression in the development of vertical hanging scrolls where nature melted into writing. Indeed, the spare, unadorned, rustic aesthetic of Zen spread throughout the arts. The idea that truth can be encapsulated in an instant flash of enlightenment gave impetus to what has been called the "miniaturization" of art. The so-called Zen Arts of flower arrangement, rock and moss gardening, the tea ceremony, and plant sculpture (*bonsai*) all blossomed in this period. In the hands of a master gardener like Musō Kokushi or Sōami, the designer of the famous Ryōanji rock garden, the universe could be created in a small plot of gravel, rock, moss, and sand. When practiced by Zen masters such as Sen no Rikyū, the art of tea could exhilarate yet calm the mind. Under the influence of Zen architects who studied in China, new heavy-roofed temples rose as if in flight over the Zen complexes in Kamakura and Kyoto. The simple, weathered lines of the humbling tea huts merged with the ornate gold leaf of Sung Dynasty Chinese-style imperial palaces. The result was the splendidly tranquil shōgunal garden retreats of Kinkakuji (1397) and Ginkakuji (1483) in Kyoto.

Music and other aesthetic forms of art flourished among the aristocratic houses of Kyoto as well. Virtually every noble (and many merchant) house boasted a postage stamp–sized garden, and virtually every home incorporated the austere aesthetic architecture of the Zen teahouse. The lushly glazed ceramic tea bowls brought from Korea and China by Zen priests gave rise to a rich cottage industry in the hillsides of central Honshu. The nights were lit by the firefly-like glow of clay kilns surrounding Kyoto. By the end of the era, huge treasures were spent by tea aficionados for the rough, asymmetrical tea bowls developed by pottery masters. A similar trade sprang up in the crackled-glaze bowls used for flower arrangements that graced nearly every Japanese home.

A new form of literature bloomed in this military dominated era. A series of "warrior tales" began in the early Kamakura period and continued well into the Muromachi. The main focus was on the heroic and sometimes tragic exploits of famous warriors in the various wars. The most famous of these tales include *The Tale of the Heike, Tale of the Hogen,* and the *Tale of the Heiji*. Not surprisingly, a whole genre of tales, sagas, and romances sprang up around the romantic character Yoshitsune. The tragic life of the young handsome brother of Yoritomo was told over and over again with new, sometimes improbable embellishments. The birth of the Ashikaga Bakufu was recorded in the epic *Chronicle of the Grand Pacification,* which romanticized the exploits and tragic deaths of the loyalists who had fought against Ashikaga on the side of the emperor. Other more Buddhist-influenced secular writing included *Record of My Ten-Foot Square Hut* and *Jottings of a Fool*. New imperial poetry anthologies and histories flourished as well.

Clothing styles emulated the colorful painted silks and brocades described in the *Tale of Genji* and *Confessions of Lady Nijō*. Women's already elaborate hairstyles once again took flights of fancy. These feminine styles were embellished by the costumes worn by the actors in the various theatrical forms.

Several forms of theater competed for the attention and patronage of the aristocrats and the people, but the *Noh* theater eventually won out. Noh, a heavily Buddhist-influenced stylistic theater, flourished primarily within the warrior aristocracy. Its Zen symbolism of repressed longing and its studied fatalism appealed to the stoic samurai. It had its beginnings in the simple shrine dances (called *sarugaku* or "monkey music") of Shinto festivals but evolved into a complex ritualized theater that employed dance, mime, chorus chanting, masks, and elaborate costumes. The father-son theatrical masters Kan'ami Kiyotsugu and Seami Motokiyo helped to formalize both style and content through nearly a century of embellishment. The bakufu patronized Noh because of its strong emphasis on the warrior ethic, and nearly every religious complex had a Noh theater stage.

Other forms of theater developed within the chōnin merchant class, but would wait until the Tokugawa era before they matured into distinct genres with their own histories and traditions. The most popular forms began among the traveling balladeers. Troupes of wandering minstrels roamed from one village or castle town to another, entertaining the common folk reciting warrior tales often accompanied with lutelike *shamisen*, flutes, and drums. Very often these minstrels were blind, because this, along with the art of massage, was one of the few occupations open to the sightless. Other entertainment forms incorporated dance, music, and narration. More often than not, however, these amusements were merely methods to advertise the real occupation of the dancers: prostitution. Fortunately, while the country and society reached perhaps its lowest point in human depravity, the arts managed to soothe the minds of at least some of its people.

THE SENGOKU ERA: 1467–1598

Unfortunately, with the exception of the third shōgun, Ashikaga Takauji's heirs were not charismatic military leaders. Therefore the daimyō in the countryside once again looked for new political coalitions. As in the end of the Heian era three centuries before, the urban civilian administrators lost power to the rising class of military men in the countryside. While aristocrats in the city enjoyed the pleasures of the capital, they neglected to tend to the business of administration. This time, however, the country dissolved into civil war, and Kyoto itself was raided and burned several times beginning in the 1460s. A succession dispute within the Ashikaga house gave rise to a series of battles called the Ōnin War (1467–1477). This decade of fighting in turn gave birth to even wider civil war called *Sengoku* or "Warring States." Vicious warfare continued on for nearly a century even after the Ashikaga had settled their family dispute.

No single strong military leader was able to consolidate power, and Japan suffered the depravity of civil war. For nearly a century ambitious daimyō jealously guarded their feudal powers. Military coalitions rose and fell, often within the same week in which they had been "eternally" sealed. Every time that a charismatic and able daimyō would seem to be on the brink of reconsolidating the country through a coalition, jealous rivals (sometimes within his own family) would rush to form a counter coalition, which in turn would quickly fall apart from treachery and deceit. Women and children were used as hostages to "cement" these alliances, but ambitious men often sacrificed wives and children (they had plenty more of both) and even mothers, breaking these temporary alliances whenever a better opportunity presented itself. Sons turned against fathers, brothers against each other. No quarter was asked or given; retribution and revenge reached horrible proportions. Even the Buddhist armies of Mt. Hiei and Mt. Koya and the Ikko sects of True Pureland believers committed atrocities. The mutual distrust, the moral degradation, and the rough military equality of these warlords kept the country at war for over a century.

The change that broke this impasse came from abroad, brought by Portuguese merchants. These hardy seamen stumbled onto Japanese soil in 1543 bringing with them not only trade from abroad, primarily in Chinese silks, but also the two items that would help break the century-old deadlock: (1) a superior military technology in the form of guns and (2) Christianity. In combination, when used by ruthless, ambitious, and brilliant men, the country was reunited.

The last three decades of the sixteenth century saw the country descend into the most horrible warfare to date. The country was led by three horrifically cruel yet equally brilliant military men whose eventual goal was reunification and national peace. Fortunately, the country emerged from this national bloodbath in 1600 into an era of 268 years of relative peace.

ODA NOBUNAGA

The first of these military warlords was Oda Nobunaga, a minor daimyō from Owari in central Honshu. His father had overthrown his own feudal lord, and the son would be even more crafty, more vicious, and more ambitious. Nobunaga was cruel beyond belief; he was also a military genius. A daring tactician and charismatic warrior, Nobunaga fought a succession of battles between 1560 and 1570 that succeeded beyond all reasonable expectation. With a battle-hardened cadre of some two thousand ruthless warriors, he defeated armies 10 times that size. His strategies and tactics often risked everything for the one quick, decisive victory that almost always rewarded the sheer nerve and courage of his warriors. The retribution, rape, pillaging, and wanton destruction that followed these victories were too horrible to even imagine.

Nobunaga's cruel reputation had a more positive effect. Before long, other minor daimyō flocked to his side to avoid the fate of his former enemies. But he refused military coalitions. He would only accept complete and total

surrender to his power. The men who became his vassals were tested immediately, being placed in the vanguard between Nobunaga's forces and the
enemy. If they faltered, they were butchered; if they proved able and courageous, they were tested again and again. Nobunaga trusted virtually no one.
He assumed that everyone was as ambitious, as treacherous, and as dishonest
as he was. During this period he was more often right than wrong about his
enemies and allies.

Daimyō would be required to put their entire families in his trust as hostages. Warlords who displeased him would have their whole families slaughtered before their eyes, before the daimyo himself was tortured and butchered,
often by Nobunaga himself. Even Buddhist priests who refused to surrender
to his will were treated horribly. Perhaps two thousand "monks" on Mt. Hiei
were killed or burned alive with their women and children when their leaders refused Nobunaga's offer to "Join or Die" in 1571. The number of men,
women, and children of the Ikkō who were killed by his troops in 1580 may
never be known; estimates range as high as forty thousand. Little wonder
why he is known to history as the "Destroyer."

Of course he was much more, but his notoriety served him well. The terror
that he struck in the hearts of all daimyo kept most of them in line. They had
only to look around them to see the results of his displeasure. Entire regions
of the country were put to the sword and burned if for no other reason than a
daimyō had not obeyed as fast as Nobunaga liked.

Nobunaga immediately recognized the power and possibilities of the new
Portuguese weapons. The *arquebus* was an expensive imported weapon that
was clumsy, inaccurate, and very heavy. Many daimyō had experimented
with it, primarily as a siege weapon. Others used them in small numbers,
primarily to repulse cavalry charges. More powerful than the longbow, the
arquebus had several serious deficiencies.

First, because it had to be imported, it cost 100 times more than a longbow
and 10 times more than an ordinary sword. Second, it was a machine, and all
machines require expensive and specialized maintenance. After all, the working parts had to be imported from Portugal. Third, the tremendous power
came from gunpowder. That too, as well as the gunshot ballistics, had to be
imported or manufactured. Fourth, because the barrel bores were not perfectly
round (much less rifled), the arquebus was horribly inaccurate. A marksman
could dependably hit a man-sized target from about 30 yards, less than the
killing range of a longbow. Further than that, one might as well throw rocks.

Nobunaga solved these problems so that other daimyō could not match
his innovations. He rounded up iron makers and put them to work as gun-
smiths. He bought the ingredients for making iron barrels (iron ore and coal
or charcoal), gunpowder (niter and sulfur), and gunshot (lead and brass) and
was soon rewarded with hundreds of serviceable and even improved guns

since the Japanese had been making steel for swords for over two centuries. Next, he trained thousands of ashigaru foot soldiers to fire the guns. Finally, he invented new tactics for their use. He trained men to fire together in alternating ranks. In effect he invented a machine gun of arquebusers. Before his enemies could react, he used these ranks at oblique angles, in crossfire, in flanking ranks, behind mobile iron shields, and finally mounted on horses. He had developed a lightning-quick, light armored cavalry who could destroy or dishearten even the most heavily armored samurai-led army ranks. His use of cannoneers was similarly innovative.

Of course the lightweight but flexible armor that was almost impervious to arrows, pikes, and swords had to undergo a similar evolution. The "Saint's Breastplate," a single piece of tempered iron covering the torso, resulted, as did more sophisticated helmets. Naturally the temporary earthen defensive castles of old mutated into huge, elaborate complexes of high stone walls backed by rammed earth and intricate moats.

In addition, Nobunaga encouraged the European Jesuit priests to come to practice and preach their religion among his troops. He did this not only because this would guarantee the continued supply and monopoly of weapons, but also because he used Christianity against his Buddhist enemies. Because sixteenth-century Jesuit Christianity was organized on military principles of discipline and administration, Nobunaga knew that if he controlled the religious head, the body of troops would obey. Because Christianity, like the Pureland sects, promised an immediate spiritual salvation in one single lifetime for those who died in holy war, it could be used to develop a fearless army of soldiers.

Obedience and humility preached by the Jesuit fathers also appealed to Nobunaga as well. He used Christianity like the arquebus, as a tightly controlled killing tool. In 1570 a daimyō ceded the tiny fishing village of Nagasaki to the Jesuits in order to guarantee that the silk-bearing ships would dock there. Nagasaki within two decades was a thriving port city of over 300,000; about half of the population worshiped Jesus Christ in the seven cathedrals there. When Nobunaga gained control of the surrounding area, he continued to allow the Jesuits to govern the city but under his control.

As in his treatment of the Christians, Nobunaga showed himself to be more than just the brutal beast who struck fear in the hearts of his enemies. He was a very able administrator as well. He created uniform measurements to facilitate a land survey and a census, as well as a uniform system of taxation. He began to disarm the peasantry in the 1570s to control them better, as well as return them to the land and improve crop yields. He abolished unnecessary fees, and other barriers to interregional trade. He improved roads and dredged rivers and canals to facilitate delivery of supplies. A profitable Chinese silk monopoly through the Portuguese was set up that also facilitated trade with Korea and China. In short, his long-range plans looked far into a future when Japan could once again be united under a single powerful government, his own.

Nobunaga was a tactical genius who recognized brilliance in men. Most of his best generals "came up through the ranks." He was generous in his rewards; he was brutal in his punishments. His greatest general, Toyotomi Hideyoshi, was a peasant who had begun his illustrious career as Nobunaga's sandal bearer.

TOYOTOMI HIDEYOSHI

Hideyoshi's family was so poor that, like other poor peasants, they did not own even a family surname. Hideyoshi was reputed to be among the ugliest men in the country (Nobunaga cruelly called him "the bald monkey"), but Nobunaga recognized a brilliant mind within Hideyoshi's deformed head. Hideyoshi rose through his tactical and strategic brilliance until by 1576 he led an army of over 50,000 men. He was rewarded for his brilliant strategies and battle successes, being placed in the vanguard against Nobunaga's fiercest enemies. Time and again Hideyoshi repaid Nobunaga, defeating enemy after enemy. Again and again Hideyoshi was grandly rewarded and promoted by Nobunaga. By 1582 the Nobunaga onslaught had conquered two-thirds of the country, and Hideyoshi was hot on the heels of the powerful Mori family in the west when Nobunaga was assassinated.

Ironically, Nobunaga, who was the murderer of tens of thousands, was forced to commit suicide by one of his own generals. The man sought to avenge his mother who had been treacherously abandoned by Nobunaga in a hostage exchange. Nobunaga had ordered him to assist Hideyoshi against the Mori when he suddenly turned against Nobunaga and surrounded him. Nobunaga knew what manner of tortuous death awaited him at the hands of this man, so he took his own life. But his assassin did not live long enough to benefit from his treachery. Within days Hideyoshi made a hasty peace with the Mori and turned his army against the murderer who was soon captured, killed, and decapitated.

It was at this point that Hideyoshi showed his own mettle. He managed to convince Nobunaga's heirs that the benefit for all lay in completing the work of reunification rather than in fighting for succession. Within two years after this coalition of Nobunaga's sons and generals was made, Hideyoshi managed to eradicate everyone in the coalition except Tokugawa Ieyasu with whom he made an uneasy peace.

Ieyasu, a former hostage and later vassal general to Nobunaga, was rewarded for his loyalty to Hideyoshi with the huge *Kantō* plain in the east which was larger than Hideyoshi's own extensive fief. Ieyasu was married to Hideyoshi's sister (Ieyasu's former, now "inconvenient," wife was quickly divorced), and he was required to leave his entire family as hostage to Hideyoshi. By 1585

Hideyoshi was in command of all the country except for small pockets of resistance. By 1590 every daimyō in the country had sworn loyalty to him, and
he began to further consolidate power.

Like Nobunaga, Hideyoshi ruthlessly and cruelly destroyed those who
dared to resist him. Unlike his patron, however, Hideyoshi could afford to
compromise. He did not find it necessary to slaughter whole families of the
daimyō who fought against him. He allowed them to save their families by
committing suicide to atone for their mistakes. He kept hostages as Nobunaga
did, but he honored them and kept them safe, which Nobunaga did not always do. People feared Hideyoshi, to be sure, but they knew that they could
trust him. He came to be known as the "Conciliator" for his readiness to bar-
gain and to compromise.

Nevertheless he was a ruthless and brutal man when he needed to be. He
was also a great administrator. He followed in the footsteps of Nobunaga in
his pacification of a warring country. His "sword hunts" disarmed the peasantry; his land survey unraveled the complicated titles to land and taxation.

To keep his fellow peasantry from destabilizing the political settlement of
the day, he "froze" society into eternal social classes. Using the idealized social model of Sung China Neo-Confucianism, he declared that "heaven and
nature" decreed that all men should remain in their occupational, social, and
therefore, economic classes. He argued that the karma of previous lives (mixing Buddhism with Confucianism) had determined their present social station; their future incarnations depended on their actions in this one.

At the top of the social system were the warriors who kept the peace and
acted as administrators; below them were the "backbone" of society, the peasantry who fed everyone else. Below the peasants were crafts people: people
who made things with their hands. At the bottom were the parasitic merchants
who contributed nothing to society except the movement of food and goods.

He forbade movement and marriage between classes, thereby keeping
wealth and land out of the hands of the military and the weapons out of the
hands of peasants and merchants. He effectively drove a wedge of mutual
suspicion, resentment, and hatred between the classes in order to maintain his
own control over all of them. He was a master of "divide and conquer."

The daimyō were kept in mutual antagonism as well. Those men whom he
trusted (he was not stupid, he still kept their families as "guest" hostages) he
placed strategically between the daimyō whom he did not trust. Daimyō were
moved so that they resided cheek-to-jowl with their ancient rivals and enemies. They were moved around so that they could not depend on loyal peasants under them. Intermarriage or adoption between daimyō families was
forbidden. In short, he kept the daimyō in jealous opposition to each other.

He placed tighter controls on the Christians after he no longer was in need
of their services. Edicts against the Jesuit priests were passed in 1587, but he

did not really enforce them after he was satisfied that they were now in check. When threatened by a Spaniard, he rounded up 26 Franciscans (unfortunately several Jesuits were mistakenly taken in that group) and had them crucified on the hill overlooking the Christian city of Nagasaki in 1597 as a lesson to all. Additionally, he seized control of all the port cities in the country, including the Christian Nagasaki, which he administered directly. He did likewise with the silver, copper, and gold mines. He slowly tried to remove or nullify every possible enemy.

In 1585 Hideyoshi briefly toyed with the idea of having himself adopted by the last Ashikaga shōgun, who Nobunaga had deposed in 1573, but instead he had himself adopted by the Fujiwara and had himself designated regent for the emperor. The emperor was "restored" to something of his former splendor but none of his power. Hideyoshi rebuilt and refurbished the palace and held costly sumptuous celebrations in the emperor's honor. But he kept the emperor and his courtiers virtual prisoners in their palaces.

Although he did not tax the daimyō directly, he imposed upon them a number of costly public works to drain their treasuries. Daimyō were forced to pull down "excess" castles (each was allowed only one) and used the materials to build huge castles for Hideyoshi at Ōsaka and in Momoyama, south of Kyoto, all at their expense. The daimyō were also forced to contribute samurai to his army in proportion to their land holdings and annual revenue. These soldiers were designated with a specially colored red armor that separated them from other samurai. The expenses for their upkeep were paid by the daimyō, who could not control them.

Most importantly, Hideyoshi raised an army, larger even than the Mongol horde, from the contending daimyō, which he sent abroad to conquer Korea. Whether he was mad with ambition and really meant to conquer first Korea, then China, and perhaps India, or whether he merely wished to rid Japan of this excess of samurai is open to discussion. Perhaps he intended to do both. For several years beginning in 1592, however, this huge Japanese army spread war, famine, and devastation on the Korean Peninsula.

When the Japanese forces approached the Chinese-Korean border at the Yalu River, the Chinese entered the fray (a lesson lost on the American General Douglas MacArthur four centuries later). The war ground to a stalemate, but resumed with new vigor in 1597. The adventure ended a year later when Hideyoshi died. But not before tens, perhaps hundreds of thousands Koreans died horribly in the five years of war and famine.

One other thing that Hideyoshi failed to accomplish during his lifetime was to establish a dynastic succession. Had he been able to do so, perhaps the next three centuries would be known as the Toyotomi Era. It would be known as the Tokugawa Period instead.

When Hideyoshi died in 1598, he left a five-year-old son, Hideyori, hardly an able military successor to his feared father. Hideyoshi had scores of concubines, none of whom could provide him with a male heir until it was too late. Once the boy was born, Hideyoshi tried to ensure his succession. He forced his heir apparent nephew to commit suicide and then brutally butchered the man's children, wife, concubines, and all of their servants. On his deathbed Hideyoshi had his most "trusted" allies swear loyalty to the young boy, but within two years the collective regency had dissolved into warfare.

One of the five regents was his old rival Tokugawa Ieyasu. Ieyasu managed through patience and cunning to succeed where Nobunaga and Hideyoshi had not. The dream of a Japan unified under one government did not die with Nobunaga and Hideyoshi; Ieyasu lived to see it fulfilled. He saw his adult son appointed shōgun and the future of his family made secure. The Japanese adage says, "Nobunaga planted the rice; Hideyoshi harvested and cooked it; but Ieyasu ate it."

4

The Tokugawa Era, 1600–1868

TOKUGAWA IEYASU

Tokugawa Ieyasu was the son of a recently established minor daimyō house from the area around Nagoya, close to the home of Nobunaga. At one time Ieyasu had been a hostage for his father to Nobunaga. When he succeeded his father as daimyō, he then became one of Nobunaga's vassals and generals.

Ieyasu was a pragmatist. He was not a brilliant and charismatic military leader on the order of Nobunaga or Hideyoshi, but he was patient, observant, and quick witted. His every action was carefully considered, and he always sought advice from his subordinates. He actually encouraged constructive criticism from his men; they therefore were devoted to him. He rewarded his loyal followers well and was careful never to squander his warriors in battle needlessly. He was no more honest than he needed to be, having several times broken his solemn oath when he found it necessary to change alliances. Once when Ieyasu's wife and son were suspected of plotting against Nobunaga, the latter demanded that Ieyasu prove his loyalty by killing them both. Ieyasu hardly hesitated in his compliance. After all, Ieyasu married many women and had several concubines, producing many sons. He could ill afford to endanger his life and his career for the sake of only one wife and one son.

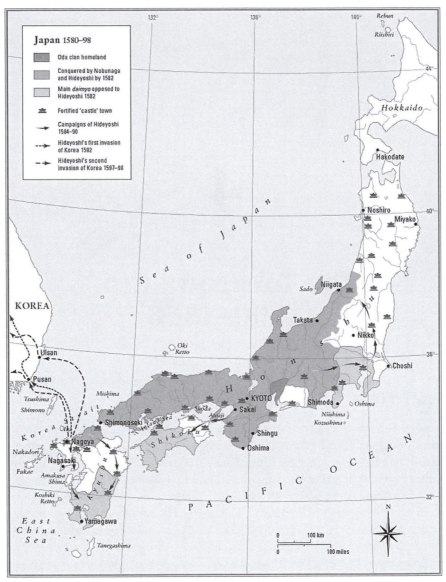

Japan during the Wars of Unification, 1580–1598.

After the suicide of Nobunaga in 1582, Ieyasu for a time was a rival to Hideyoshi as the successor to their dead feudal lord. Their armies struggled briefly without clear result before Ieyasu determined that he could not win against Hideyoshi. Ieyasu had "tested the wind" and survived that encounter when he swore loyalty and assisted Hideyoshi in extinguishing his enemies in eastern Japan. Ieyasu accepted the Kantō plain as his reward for that loyalty, giving up control over his former central Honshu homeland. His former homeland lay astride the main road between Kyoto and Kamakura and therefore was a threat to Hideyoshi. The Kantō Plain, which included the city of Kamakura as well as the small fishing village of *Edo* where Ieyasu built his castle, was 300 miles away and therefore remote from Hideyoshi's center of power.

Ieyasu was something more of an uneasy ally to Hideyoshi than an abject lackey. He was therefore able to stall when asked to lead Hideyoshi's Korean expedition, and ultimately he remained in the Kantō, building his new castle in Edo during the entire ill-fated adventure. When Hideyoshi died in 1598, Ieyasu swore loyalty to his young son Hideyori but quietly bided his time until the other regents made their moves to seize control. He consulted his vassals, sounded out potential allies, and engineered a carefully timed plot whereby a large portion of the enemy coalition suddenly turned against their allies at the Battle of Sekigahara in 1600. The battle turned into a rout in his favor, and within months Ieyasu was the champion of the land. Typically, Ieyasu did not risk his own army in the encounter, preferring others to do his work.

It is truly an indication of how seriously divided the country was in 1600 that Ieyasu was never able to completely centralize and consolidate control. He followed Nobunaga's and Hideyoshi's examples of political control by coalition and vassalage. He created an elaborate system of land division; of hostages; of social, political, and economic controls; and ultimately of national seclusion. The fact that he could do this is an indication of his power; the fact that he had to do this was indication of his weakness.

Ieyasu was neither an innovator nor a great thinker. But he understood power: He liked what he had, used it wisely, and wanted more. He was patient. He understood well the advice of the ancient Chinese military genius Sun Tzu, who said, "If I wait patiently at the banks of the river, the body of my enemy will eventually float by." Ieyasu correctly felt that if he froze the status quo, he would be no worse off than he was. If he ventured to change the system, then he might lose what he had. So he risked very little and refined much. He copied much from Nobunaga and Hideyoshi, adapting what seemed to work and discarding that which did not. Being a pragmatist, he did not care very much where the idea originated, as long as it worked.

He wisely adapted the Neo-Confucian social system to his needs. Understanding that if real peace came to Japan after a century of civil war, he would not need the nearly one million warriors to keep the peace. Therefore, following Hideyoshi's lead, he clearly defined the division between samurai and the rest of society. Each daimyō was allowed to keep a specific number of armed samurai, proportional to the productivity of their land. Estimates of the number of former warriors who were demoted into the peasant class run as high as 60 percent.

The ashigaru were coerced and coaxed into a netherworld of "village leadership." In effect, they became the local village hereditary headmen, constables, justices, and tax collectors. They were allowed to keep their surnames as well as their now largely ceremonial short swords (traditionally used for only two things: to take the heads of enemies and to commit suicide) as badges of authority, but they were otherwise disarmed and placed squarely back into the peasant class. They were at the top of that class, but they were henceforth peasantry to be sure.

Similarly, Ieyasu forbade anyone moving up or down in class. Harsh punishments, usually death, were meted out to anyone caught trying to change social class. Chōnin were not allowed to acquire farm land, and peasants were forbidden to migrate to the cities or move from one domain to another. Intermarriage between classes was forbidden as well.

Obviously Ieyasu wished to make time stand still. He would have preferred to have seized power from the daimyō and perhaps also to have trimmed the number of samurai to save expenses. But because he could not do so, he reduced as much as he could and forbade any substantive changes in the status quo. He hired Confucian political philosophers who could rationalize why a merchant should remain so, and why peasants should be content with their lowly rustic lives. But what was most important to him was that they do so because it ensured his family's future, and possibly that of Japan as well.

THE POLITICAL SETTLEMENT: A DELICATE BALANCE

Ieyasu was faced with a badly divided country when he became shōgun in 1603. The country had been at war for more than a century, and no one could remember how a centralized government actually operated. The daimyō had long survived by their wits and by their armies; they could not be counted on to automatically obey any commands that did not seem to be in their own immediate best interests. The mere swearing of feudal allegiance was not worth the time, effort, or paper. The long history of constantly shifting military coalitions made Ieyasu's task doubly difficult because he had excelled at the "double-cross" himself. He had to devise a method to keep the possible political powers at bay. It is to his credit that the complex and intricate system that he devised would continue virtually unchanged for over 260 years.

The most pressing danger of his time was the need to keep approximately 250 semiautonomous daimyō in check. Each, even his relatives and most trusted vassals, was a potential threat to the delicate balance of coalitions that resulted from the Battle of Sekigahara in 1600.

He stipulated that a daimyō was entitled to that title provided that he: (1) controlled a *han* ("domain") with an agricultural productivity of over fifty thousand bushels of rice (ten thousand *koku*) and (2) swore complete loyalty to the shōgun. He divided the daimyō into three groups. His own extensive family of over twenty directly related houses or *shimpan* ("collateral domain"), three of which (Kii, Mito, and Owari) were allowed to contribute heirs to the main house if it failed to produce an appropriate shōgunal successor. This group controlled about one-third of the total agricultural area of Japan.

The non-kinship group of over 200 daimyō were divided into two groups. His longtime allies called "house" (*fudai*) daimyō were men whom Ieyasu trusted and whom he had created as daimyō. Their han were usually modest in scale but were located in strategic areas. Collectively the fudai controlled a little less than 30 percent of the farm land.

His former, yet still powerful enemies, the *tozama* ("outsider") daimyō, controlled nearly 40 percent of the land. Most of the tozama controlled larger han. The fact that they were even allowed to remain powerful is the most significant indication that Ieyasu walked a political tightrope. Any attempt to destroy them piecemeal would cause the others to band together quickly despite their mutual hatred and suspicion of each other. And, there was no guarantee if war resulted that he could rely completely on the loyalty of his shimpan, let alone his fudai. Ieyasu knew that when the emperor Go-Daigo and later the Ashikaga had attempted to do this, all the daimyō had resisted. Better to maintain the uneasy status quo than to tip the balance to an uncertain future.

He and his heirs forced every daimyō, tozama, and fudai alike, to spend half their lives in his capital Edo, and the other half in their home province. This system of "alternate attendance" or *sankin kotai* served other purposes as well. This way the shōgun could keep an eye on all of the daimyō. Also, the tremendous costs involved in maintaining separate residences in their han, another in Edo, plus the onerous travel expenses, served as indirect and unofficial taxes. He kept their families hostages in Edo the entire time. Guardians at the gates into the city were always reminded to watch for weapons going in and women coming out, because either indicated a possible plot. Adoption, marriage, and political and economic alliances between daimyō were forbidden, and an extensive and pervasive network of spies to keep many eyes on the daimyō was employed.

Ieyasu used the age-old jealousies, hatreds, resentments, and suspicions between the daimyō to keep them from forming coalitions. He placed his shimpan daimyō astride the major roads to Edo and settled his fudai allies in between tozama. He moved many of them around during the first two decades of the period and often placed old blood enemies next to each other to keep each other in check. He retained the right, used rarely and judiciously after the first decade of the bakufu, to deprive daimyō of their land for reasons of gross insubordination, criminally poor administration of their han (used only when the peasants were in full-scale revolt), and for failure to produce a suitable male heir. Ieyasu also retained the right to approve and legitimize every political succession. But this, too, he used very carefully lest the other daimyō suspect that some kind of evil plot was at work.

Like the Muromachi shōguns before him, Ieyasu was forced to grant virtual administrative independence to his vassals. He interfered into their lives as much as he dared, but he had to be careful not to push mutual enemies into alliances. He had sophisticated law codes written as models for the daimyō to emulate, but he could not enforce compliance unless the daimyō showed themselves to be incompetent as administrators.

Ieyasu could not tax the daimyō directly, but he did require them to provide, at their own expense, for the defense of the country. These indirect taxes included the costs of maintaining public roads and horse-exchange stations for the use of bakufu couriers. They were called upon to maintain and defend the now ancient seawall defense in northwest Kyushu, in case another Mongol attack was in the offing. They dredged canals, harbors, and river ways; they forested hardwoods and bamboo; and occasionally they were forced to donate rice and other foodstuffs to relieve famines. In short, Ieyasu made the daimyō his public works administration and forced them to pay their own expenses. It is significant that both Nobunaga and Hideyoshi had experimented with these systems of political control, but it was Ieyasu who perfected them.

Despite these elaborate systems of control, Ieyasu still had three sources of power that worried him greatly: the imperial house, Toyotomi Hideyori, and Christianity. All three were potential time bombs that threatened the still uneasy political settlement, and all three had thousands of potential supporters. He had to tread very lightly until his position grew stronger and more secure.

He dealt with the imperial house immediately because he saw it as the greatest potential source of mischief. Ieyasu knew that at least three times in history an attempted imperial restoration had caused a change in government, so he was careful to control the emperor. In 1603 Ieyasu accepted the title of shōgun (after having proved his very doubtful Minamoto ancestry), which he turned over to his successor son two years later. Ieyasu established a liaison office in Kyoto staffed with his most loyal retainers and forbade any daimyō from even passing through the ancient capital without the express written permission of the shōgun himself. The emperor, he treated with great deference and respect. The court was endowed with a large tract of tax land, administered by the Tokugawa of course, and rebuilt the palace to high grandeur. But the fact remains that the emperor and the court were hostages of the Tokugawa. Every imperial action was closely monitored. No ceremony could take place without a Tokugawa "guest" present.

Hideyori's threat was more difficult initially. Ieyasu had lost direct control of Hideyoshi's son in 1598 and had to monitor his actions from afar. He had several trusted men lodged as spies within the boy's entourage, but the child was under the control of his strong-willed mother as well as several Tokugawa enemies in the Ōsaka region. The boy had been allowed to keep some three million bushels of his father's extensive tax land and therefore was potentially very powerful. Ieyasu ringed the boy in with loyal troops in every direction, and in fact when his son became shōgun in 1605, Ieyasu made his home in nearby Sumpu (modern-day Shizuoka) to watch over Hideyori. But the threat would remain for many anxious years until it exploded in 1614. Two years before his own death, Ieyasu personally directed the siege of the Ōsaka castle where almost 100,000 troops loyal to the boy were lured into revolt. Near the end of the standoff, he managed by trickery to break the siege, and the 30,000 remaining defenders were killed. Hideyori and his mother committed suicide, and the threat from the Toyotomi forces was over.

THE CHRISTIAN THREAT

The threat from Christianity took somewhat longer because the threat was within his own army. Ieyasu at first used the Christians as Nobunaga and Hideyoshi had done. But like Hideyoshi, who had outlawed (but never enforced the edict) Christianity in 1587, Ieyasu feared the foreign faith. Increasingly he started to use other Europeans against the Portuguese. The Spanish Franciscan, Augustinian, and Dominican priests were jealous of the Portuguese Jesuits. Ieyasu also used the English and the Dutch. The latter two he used because they were Protestants, and, unlike the Roman Catholic Portuguese and Spanish, they did not even try to proselytize their faith in Japan. He granted them trading rights and tried to break the Portuguese lock on the Chinese silk market with Chinese and Korean traders also.

The greatest threat was not from the foreign Christians, however, but rather from his own vassals who were in some cases now second- and third-generation Christians. He began to experiment in 1606 to see just how loyal they were to their God and to the Pope. He commanded a few of his vassals to renounce their faith or to leave the country. When the Christian daimyō chose exile rather than recant, he had his answer: Christians were loyal first and foremost to God. He could never trust them again.

In 1614, during the midst of the siege at Ōsaka Castle, he commanded that all foreign priests leave Tokugawa domains within a month. Two years later priests were banned from all of Japan. All Japanese Christians were ordered to renounce their faith and to become Buddhists virtually overnight. Those who refused faced death. Only about two-thirds of the some 150 priests left; the others were ferreted out, tortured, and eventually killed. Many Japanese Christians went into hiding, many more recanted, not a few died as martyrs to their faith. But the end was very near. In 1637–1638 a Christian-led rebellion against discriminatory taxation broke out in Shimabara, close to the Christian city of Nagasaki. The Tokugawa reacted predictably. They surrounded the area, forcing any Christian sympathizers into the ruined castle on that peninsula and slowly created a hell for them there. After starving the defenders for several months, the Tokugawa marched in and slaughtered the remaining 40,000 defenders.

By 1640 the Tokugawa had nearly eradicated every vestige of Christianity in Japan. The Roman Catholic Church recognizes only 3,125 martyrs during this period, but there were thousands more. Only a handful escaped two centuries of persecution by hiding in remote islands and mountains. For the next 200 years everyone in Japan had to annually prove that they were not Christians by registering with their neighborhood Buddhist temple and then performing the ritual of *fumi-e* or "treading pictures." This meant that every man, woman, and child had to walk on pictures or bronze replications of Christ or the Virgin Mary to symbolically prove their contempt for Christianity.

The Portuguese merchants were replaced by the Dutch who themselves were all but imprisoned on the tiny artificial island of *Deshima* in Nagasaki harbor. They, too, had to perform fumi-e to prove that they had no Roman Catholic sympathies. The Dutch had proved their animosity to Roman Catholicism by bombarding the Shimabara Christians from their ships off the peninsula. Chinese and Koreans were also allowed to conduct carefully monitored trade, but they were tested as well. The English and Spanish had left of their own accord. The next step was almost inevitable: The bakufu made laws to ensure a *sakoku* or "closed country." Japanese were forbidden to go abroad; those who did could never return on pain of death. Ships larger than those that could carry 500 koku of rice were made illegal. Only the small coastal ships were allowed to ply Japan's waters. Unauthorized ships were fired upon. Shipwrecked foreign sailors were to be "killed in the surf," before they could hit dry land. Foreign books were now illegal. Those brought by the Dutch for their own use were carefully searched for any references to Christianity. In short, Japan was now more isolated from the rest of the world than perhaps it ever had been in its history.

THE TOKUGAWA BAKUFU: CENTRALIZED FEUDALISM

The government of the Tokugawa lasted for 268 years and therefore must be considered a qualified success. Like the Kamakura and Muromachi Bakufu before it, the government was a mixture of military and civil administration. It was also a combination of private and public, regional and national administrations.

Ieyasu's most loyal personal retainers called "bannermen" (*hatamoto*) staffed his family council. They administered the sprawling Tokugawa lands and governed the tens of thousands of vassal samurai. They served as justices, quartermasters, armorers, inspectors, spies, and all the other occupations that made any army run efficiently. During Ieyasu's lifetime there was scarcely any waste and inefficiency because he was reputed to be the "stingiest miser in all of Japan." He appointed able and honest men to positions of power regardless of their family and social standing. His descendants were not so astute in promoting able men, but the system was so closely monitored and so administratively simple that it very nearly ran itself for over a century before it needed substantive reforms.

The "national" government was something of an oxymoron. It has been called "centralized feudalism" by Edwin Reischauer, which aptly characterizes the anomaly. It remained decentralized in its treatment of the semi-autonomous daimyō, but forced them to live in Edo half of their careers and thereby centralized the government in the capital. One council made up of senior fudai councilors debated policy and advised the shōgun before he made laws and issued edicts. Another council of "junior advisers" oversaw the hatamoto, the army commanders, and the administrators of the giant Edo castle complex. The "senior" and "junior" rankings designated not age but the size of the daimyō's holdings. "Senior" men were those with han larger than 25,000 koku in evaluation.

NEO-CONFUCIAN SOCIAL CONTROL

The sociopolitical philosophy developed by the twelfth-century Chinese Confucian reformer Chu Hsi was a godsend for the Tokugawa political settlement. Although more suited for the secular bureaucratic Sung Dynasty in China, it suited Ieyasu's needs very well. Brought to Japan by traveling Zen monks and Chinese and Korean refugees, it was popularized in the late sixteenth century by men like Fujiwara Seika and his chief disciple Hayashi Razan. Ieyasu, like Hideyoshi, also employed the separation of society into four occupational social classes, patronizing the Neo-Confucian masters within his government to good effect.

Like ancient Confucianism, the reformed version was based on the concept of benevolent moral rule modeled on the filial piety that governed family and other social relationships. But Neo-Confucianism suggested that nature itself demanded efficient rule by the "best and brightest": the educated, moral sages. It argued that the moral earthly order was best served when "men of talent" were allowed to rise in society and government regardless of their family and social standing. The four social classes based on functions helped to keep the society running efficiently. But that did not preclude men of talent from moving up in social class according to their demonstrated abilities. When used effectively, this philosophy avoided the inefficiency caused by nepotism and other favoritism.

Neo-Confucianism, with its preference for an educated civilian cultural elite instead of the aristocratic, powerful military, or landed wealthy leadership had to be adapted to Japanese reality, of course. But ancient Confucianism had undergone a similar creative adaptation nine centuries before in the Heian era as well. At that time, the "Mandate of Heaven" in China allowed the sages to replace inefficient and immoral emperors; in Japan it was interpreted to mean that corrupt ministers and governors of the emperor could be removed, but not the semidivine emperor himself.

Because the country was officially at peace, the rough uneducated samurai had to become administrators anyway, so it made a great deal of sense to educate them in Neo-Confucian principles of moral administration. To be sure, some samurai were never able to make the transition to bureaucratism, but those who wished to prosper under the new regime began to study seriously. For his part, Ieyasu appointed and promoted only the ablest administrators regardless of their family backgrounds. For over 200 years the samurai continued to pride themselves on their military prowess, but their careers very much depended on their mastery of Neo-Confucianism.

As with any other cultural adaptation, the creation of the warrior-bureaucrat required considerable compromise and invention. Men like Yamazaki Ansai and Kaibara Ekken helped the samurai incorporate the Neo-Confucian principles of benevolent and moral rule into their Bushidō code of ethics, retaining their martial virtues of loyalty, courage, honesty, selflessness, perseverance, and contempt for comfort and personal wealth. In short, they helped create the most frightening creature known to man: the military bureaucrat.

Ieyasu set up Confucian academies for his samurai in all of the shimpan domains, and the other daimyō rushed to do the same. Within a generation there was scarcely an illiterate samurai to be found throughout the country. The schools were staffed primarily by the samurai themselves, but also by learned Buddhist and Shinto priests who knew the Chu Hsi doctrine. The education consisted of learning to write the complex Sino-Japanese kanji characters and kana by rote. Their primers were the simplified writings of the Neo-Confucian masters. To be sure, each samurai boy learned the various martial arts of the sword, the bow, and later the unarmed arts of *judo* and *sumo;* his status and pride demanded that. But his career and future socioeconomic standing very much depended on his mastery of the literary arts.

At the heart of this new ethic was the idea that all people, regardless of status and social station, could fulfill their duties and obligations in an appropriate manner. This idea called "propriety of status" found honor in proper conduct according to one's lot in life. Everyone had a place in society, everyone's duty was to behave in a manner appropriate to that place. Peasants were not to behave like samurai, and merchants were not to behave like peasants. Each class was to defer to the others, and the language even reflected the minute levels of stratification between roles. Different verbs were to be used according to the status of the speaker and listener. The practice continues today in an abbreviated form called "honorifics." Younger people, women, and subordinates always use humble verbs; elders, males, and superiors use somewhat condescending ones.

Even women had a place—a low, demeaning one to be sure, but nevertheless, they were expected to fill that role. Kaibara Ekken wrote a treatise called *Onna Daigaku* or "Greater Learning for Women" in which he delineated what the Confucians called the "Three Obediences." The idea was that women could have three masters in their normal lifetimes: their fathers, their husbands, and later if widowed, their sons. Women were always to obey and defer to men in everything. In turn, men would protect them and treat them with respect and benevolence. In short, women were to be treated as eternal children. Girls might be sold into slavery and prostitution by their fathers and be expected to "honor" their fathers by persevering despite their miserable lives.

The Confucian-Bushidō ethic had its counterpart among the other classes as well. The chōnin (city folk) found their own philosophy in the honest completion of their filial duties to their merchant and artisan families. Although not very elaborate compared to Bushidō, the *Shingaku* ("Heart Learning") of Ishida Baigan demanded that the merchant sacrifice personal emotional needs for the good of society. Theatrical plays were rife with the emotional tension of *giri* (duty) versus *ninjō* (human emotion). The social obligations of giri won out at the end of each story.

The chōnin endowed and patronized neighborhood schools—called *terakoya* or "parish schools," not because they gave religious instruction but because they were conveniently housed in neighborhood temples. The basic curriculum was the rudiments of writing with an emphasis on the arithmetic necessary to run their merchant establishments. Very little of the poetry and ancient history was taught in these schools—no merchant really needed them to prosper in business.

Girls also were taught the rudiments of arithmetic, if only to help run the family business while the males were away. Often, in fact, women became highly educated almost by accident, perhaps when helping a dullard brother learn. Women entertainers called *geisha* learned to read well enough to become familiar with the poetry and warrior tales that helped entertain their customers.

Estimates of literacy are highly suspect, but Japan has a long history of high regard for the literary arts, so perhaps a quarter to a third of all the males (certainly every samurai, and they were 6 percent of the population) could read, and half that number of women probably could as well.

The elite landed peasants accepted the Neo-Confucian ideas, if only because it put them just below the samurai and high above the merchant class in social status. Most peasant families possessed a highly prized "house code" of ethics that mirrored those of the samurai and the rich merchant houses. These simple codes uniformly preached the virtues of honesty, frugality, hard work, and selfless devotion to the family. It would not be an exaggeration to suggest that the peasantry accepted their lowly niche in society because the philosophy tied them to the greater and grander whole of Japanese society in much the same way that peons and serfs took pride in their place in the "chain of being" in Medieval Christian Europe.

Suffice it to say that Neo-Confucianism worked very well as an instrument of social control. Everyone had a place determined by nature. Peaceful obedience and fulfillment of one's role in society contributed to the greater good. Buddhism, trying desperately to fit into this secular humanist philosophy, weighed in with a social message that agreed with Neo-Confucianism. One's place in society was determined by one's actions in previous lifetimes; one's future life could be improved by good karma in this life.

As a rule, the various Buddhist establishments in the country fared well under the Tokugawa and therefore fell into line philosophically. Whereas the Buddhist military power had been destroyed by Nobunaga, Hideyoshi, and Ieyasu, the Tokugawa persecution of Christianity had helped Buddhism tremendously. Because everyone in Japan was required to register with a neighborhood temple (and later with Shinto shrines as well) and perform the ritual of fumi-e annually, the temples used the opportunity to set up Buddhist festivals and ceremonies as well. The temple registers provide demographers with the first reliable census data available.

Zen continued to flourish because of its appeal to the samurai, but the several other sects also thrived in the two centuries of peace. Buddhist sects that catered to chōnin blossomed during this period. The various rural Pureland sects did well because the Tokugawa usually left the governing of villages to their inhabitants and the surviving Ikkō leaders naturally rose to prominent positions in the countryside.

THE CULTURAL ARTS

Although the period was dominated by the social and political philosophies of the samurai class, the cultural arts of the time would reflect the tastes of the chōnin class. The Tokugawa method of political control, sankin kotai at Edo, created a tremendous urbanization in the seventeenth century. The semi-annual forced migration of every daimyō family to Edo created not just one metropolis but many. Edo increased in population from about 30,000 in 1590 to nearly a million a century later (it was probably the largest city in the world at the time). Also, each daimyō had his own capital city established around the one castle each was allowed to keep. By 1650 there were over 40 cities of over 10,000 population where there had been scarcely a handful at the time of Sekigahara 50 years before. The ancient capital of Kyoto maintained a population of a quarter million for a century, and by 1750 had grown to perhaps twice that. Ōsaka would grow to match and surpass Kyoto's population, and several other cities like Nagoya and Kanazawa would reach 100,000.

This explosion of urbanization created perhaps the world's most urbanized country by 1700. Perhaps 10–12 percent of the population was urban, about half of that number was samurai. The other half could be called chōnin because the class distinction between merchant and artisan was blurred at best. Their tastes in entertainment and in decorative, literary, and theatrical arts were very different from their samurai masters. Where the samurai preferred the austere Zen Arts, the chōnin reveled in loud, joyous, profane, and colorful street entertainment.

Whereas the Noh theater continued to be supported by the bakufu and daimyō, the chōnin flocked to the *Jōruri* puppet shows put on by small informal theater troupes. Like Noh, Jōruri had its origins in the Shinto festival dances. During the Ashikaga period, Noh had been patronized by the bakufu, Jōruri had not. Wandering minstrels had often employed small puppets behind screens to "act-out" the warrior tales they recited. As cities and audiences grew larger, these troupes settled down into regular theaters and began to perfect their "craft." Before long, the puppets grew increasingly larger in size so that they could be better seen by larger audiences. Eventually the puppets grew to about two-thirds life size and required more than one puppeteer to manipulate.

Jōruri became the ancestor of the *Bunraku* puppet theater, which continues to thrive in Japan. The elegantly costumed puppets are marvelously constructed to mimic the most subtle human movement. Eyes roll, eyebrows arch, and lips move in artfully carved wooden heads that swivel and nod. Hands and feet dance in the hands of puppet masters. The entire ensemble of three persons per puppet create an altogether amazingly lifelike movement. Chanters and musicians accompany the puppet action off stage. Bunraku became so enormously popular that human actors began to mimic the puppets! The result was the equally popular *Kabuki* theater that also continues to prosper in Japan.

Kabuki, like Bunraku, had its primary support among the chōnin. Their main themes mirrored the concerns of the merchant class: the psychological conflicts between giri (duty to society and family) and ninjō (emotional love). They also included romanticized warrior tales that incorporated the giri-ninjō struggle as well as stylized acrobatic combat that appealed to almost every theatergoer.

Because puppets can always do and say things for which human actors would be imprisoned, Bunraku took on satire and social commentary as well as pure entertainment themes. The best writers for these chōnin theater genres often ventured to spoof and criticize their samurai "betters." Takemoto Gidayu mounted such productions in Ōsaka, and Chikamatsu Monzaemon did the same in Edo. Chikamatsu rivaled Shakespeare and Cervantes with his ribald, evocative, and richly emotional plays that gave real expression to the lives of the chōnin folk.

Writing for both the puppet and Kabuki theaters, Chikamatsu developed character, mood, and psychological tension for his actors. By the early eighteenth century the puppets and actors had become social lions, setting the style for fashion and behavior. Curiously, common folk emulated the actions of the Kabuki actors, who took their cue from the puppets, who of course mimicked the common folk!

Kabuki was rowdy, acrobatic, ribald, erotic, and great entertainment in its heroic tales. Because some theater troops often degenerated into prostitution, Kabuki, like Noh, after the seventeenth century was performed by men only. Predictably, many male actors who specialized in women's roles were also homosexual prostitutes. Ironically, the male actors also set the fashion in clothing, hairstyle, makeup, dance, and even behavior for women of the day. Tragically, women were in effect being told that only these men could define femininity.

Both Kabuki and Bunraku experimented with music, dance, sumptuously decorated costumes, and elaborate stage props and devices (revolving stages, trapdoors, and elaborate entryways) to curry the favor of the lower classes. The bakufu tired of trying to suppress the ribaldry, so they began to control and tax it instead. "Licensed Quarters" were set up in Ōsaka, Edo, and other cities where theaters could ply their trade. The "red-light" districts became home to brothels, bathhouses, restaurants, inns, and other nighttime establishments. The area was supposed to be restricted to chōnin, but traveling peasants and disguised samurai joined in the revelry as well. The bakufu turned a blind eye toward the areas as long as the chōnin proprietors kept the peace and paid their license fees.

The playbills and advertisements of these establishments came to create another art form. Monochrome woodblock printing had long been employed in China primarily for the printing of Buddhist sutra and Confucian writings. Korean artists had long used this method and had brought them to Japan four centuries before. Japanese printers had experimented with color print illustrations, mostly to attract common folk to the cheap pamphlets that they produced. Before long, however, more and more colors were used. Each application of color required a separately carved block to be matched precisely to the print of a previous woodblock. As the need for colorful action playbills increased, the printing took on a serious artistic style.

By the eighteenth century a group of artists had created a new art form: *ukiyo-e.* Ukiyo-e, meaning "pictures of the Floating World," referred to the riotous evenings spent in theaters, geisha houses, brothels, restaurants, and tea shops in the demimonde of Ōsaka and Edo. Masters such as Suzuki Harunobu and Kitagawa Utamaro applied scores of intricately laced colors to each print of actors and courtesans. Later artists like Katsushika Hokusai and Andō Hiroshige employed similar techniques to create picturesque travel scenes that sold as souvenirs for people on sankin kotai journeys and religious pilgrimages.

Other forms of painting flourished in the Tokugawa era, but none so vibrant as the ukiyo-e. Zen masters continued to paint in the sumi-e ink-wash style, and others created lushly colored folding and sliding screens employing gold leaf and other sophisticated techniques. But these later painters produced replicas rather than develop new forms and genres. The same may be said of calligraphers who continued to produce the distinctive hanging scrolls that graced nearly every samurai formal reception room.

Poetry changed somewhat. The old tanka syllable-counting style evolved into an even shorter version called haiku of 17 syllables (two five-syllable lines divided by one of seven syllables). Complex rules and conventions developed to guide this new poetic form, while other poets continued to master the tanka and *renga* "linked verse." The greatest haiku master was without doubt Matsuō Bashō, who, although born a samurai, traveled the country composing poems for the chōnin.

The period saw an explosion of other literary forms as well. Chikamatsu's plays were printed in large numbers, as were stories written by men like Ihara Saikaku who specialized in writing about the lives of the people who bought his stories: the chōnin. He published scores of ribald and erotic tales that were richly illustrated with woodblock prints, selling hundreds of thousands of copies. Indeed, some historians have argued that more books were published in eighteenth-century Japan than in the rest of the world. This is, of course, an unprovable exaggeration, but there is evidence of more than 50 printing houses in Edo alone, and many of Saikaku's novels and books had several publishing runs of 10,000 each. Other novels like Jippensha Ikku's *Adventures of Shank's Mare* were published serially in weekly installments and later published in collections. One collected issue had several publishing runs of over 10,000 as well.

More serious writing flourished as well, but not in the numbers of issues as the entertainment writing. Histories, collections of ancient poetry, commentaries on Neo-Confucianism, religious, and other serious writings were published. Intellectual activity of many kinds flourished throughout the era.

Perhaps because the country was at peace for nearly two centuries and certainly because the society was relatively isolated from the rest of the world, the Tokugawa era was one of conscious reexamination of Japanese culture. Without the constant influence of other cultures, the Japanese became introspective. They consciously developed what they considered to be the truly native arts, differentiating them from the foreign. So even though Japan was almost isolated from the rest of the world and thereby missed the benefits (as well as the human excesses, one might add) of the Industrial Revolution, it did not lag behind Europe and the Americas in terms of cultural and artistic development.

EARLY MODERN JAPAN: 1700–1850

Far too many historians have looked upon the second century of the Tokugawa era and have seen only the negative aspects of that society. To be sure there are many: Feudalism, misogyny, national seclusion, religious persecution, philosophical intolerance, and social bigotry are only the top of a long list of social, political, and economic ills perpetuated by a repressive military aristocracy.

But too often we have also criticized this era for what it was not. It was not "modern"; it was not democratic; it was not universal in its thinking; it was not Western; it was not Christian; in short, it was not like whatever ultimate social goal good people aspire to.

Unfortunately most of the criticism, well intentioned as it might be, held Tokugawa Japan up to impossible standards for the time. If it was not egalitarian, one must remember that it had no intention of being so. If it was not truly democratic, neither was any other society at the time. If it was not "modern" in its technology, its religious philosophy, or in its "world view," one must remember that every other society in the world was struggling with some or all of those problems as well.

Tokugawa Japan between 1700 and 1850 was more peaceful, more equitably fed, and more secure than any other society in the world. For the most part, its population was content with their lives. In the main, its people lived without fear of invasion, confident in their government to protect their livelihoods, and reasonably certain that they could enjoy justice in their lives. How many people on earth in 1750 could do the same? The Chinese to be sure, maybe the British; certainly not the French, the Russians, the Germans (or Prussians), the Poles, Koreans, Africans, Indians, Mexicans, or even the rebellious people who were just beginning to think of themselves as "Americans."

The century and a half beginning in 1700 was one of turmoil in the world. One has only to glance briefly at the litany of violence in the next hundred years to begin to appreciate how fortunate Tokugawa society was. In the next century or so, the world would shudder from several revolutions (American, French, German, Italian, Latin American); countless rebellions and insurrections (Irish, Taiping, Sepoy); and dozens of wars (Napoleonic, Crimean, 1812, Opium, French and Indian, American Civil, Mexican—to name but a few). Japan remained at relative peace for the entire period.

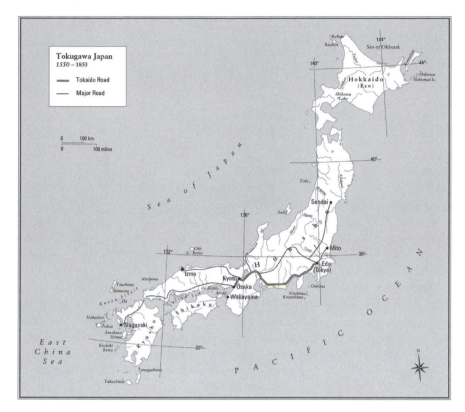

Tokugawa Japan, 1550–1853.

The political tranquility, which historian George Sansom called *Pax Tokugawa*, was marred occasionally by peasant uprisings, political assassinations, and interfamily vendettas to be sure. But the period was characterized by peace and by studious, serious attempts by the samurai aristocracy to govern fairly, benevolently, and morally.

Ironically, the Neo-Confucian ideology that was the sinew and muscle that held Tokugawa society together was also the source of many of its problems. Historians have claimed that it would be its ultimate "undoing" in 1867; that because it was socially rigid, economically shortsighted, and philosophically feudal, it prevented Japan from competing with a "modern" West. Perhaps they are correct. The difference between the Neo-Confucian strengths in 1600 and its weaknesses in 1850 is time. The system did not adjust to the needs of a different age. The Neo-Confucian philosophies that govern the Asian economic powerhouses of Japan, Taiwan, South Korea, and Singapore in the early twenty-first century have been adapted creatively to a new world reality. The philosophy in eighteenth-century Japan tried to adapt as well. But not very successfully, as we shall see.

The social ideas of Neo-Confucianism are based upon a twelfth-century Chinese rural, self-sufficient agriculturalist society. The social divisions of bureaucrats, peasants, artisans, and merchants were premised on the social and economic needs of such a society.

Japan in 1600, however, had already developed a complex and sophisticated interregional and international economy. Japanese wore Chinese silks and Korean cottons, smoked American tobacco, ate South American sweet potatoes, enjoyed Indonesian spices, drank Chinese teas, and read European books. They shipped swords, folding fans, copper, sulfur, silver, and dried sea products throughout the world. Thousands of Japanese merchants lived in port cities in China, Taiwan, Korea, Siam, Luzon, Malacca, and Java, and tens of thousands of sailors visited these places when Japanese ships plied Southeast Asian waters. Hundreds of foreigners lived in Japan for long periods, thousands more visited for a short time.

When the Tokugawa shōguns instituted the principles of Neo-Confucianism in the early part of the seventeenth century, they sought to "freeze" society not as it really was in 1600, but as they thought it should be. The maintenance of the delicate political balance status quo demanded that this be so. Artificial social barriers had to be erected between the occupational classes. At about 6 percent of the total population, there were too many samurai. Japan did not need any more people at the top. So, peasants could no longer become samurai much less military war lords like Hideyoshi had done. They could never become rich merchants, nor could merchants become samurai, nor samurai anything else.

Everything depended on Japan being re-created on the Neo-Confucian model of a social economy where peasants produced food, artisans created tools, merchants transferred food and goods where needed, and samurai governed and regulated all. Tensions created by this creative adaptation taxed the finest minds for ways to channel these energies into socially productive avenues. The proud, fearless, and determined aggression of warriors had to be channeled to create the patient, doggedly honest, moral bureaucrat. The grasping self-interest and ambition of the merchant had to be focused to allow the social pariah some pride and honor in what was always characterized as parasitic behavior. What pride and ambition could drive a peasant to produce food for society if peasant boys and girls could never aspire to be wealthy, powerful, or creative? It worked for 268 years because all segments of society really believed that what they did in their lives was honorable and valuable.

But a century after Sekigahara the system needed some serious adjustment. Most of the attempts at reform, unfortunately, were based on the same Neo-Confucian ideas that had caused them. The shōgunal ministers, as honest and well intentioned as they may have been, did not understand that the problems of inflation and social unrest created by the philosophical contempt for commerce could not be solved by more contempt. Several shōguns and almost all shōgunal ministers tried to solve the economic problems by retrenchment—that is, for the samurai to "tighten their belts" and spend less, to force the merchants to cancel debts and lower prices, and to force peasants to produce more. The fundamental idea was for everyone to stop acting selfishly (and therefore immorally) and collectively return to the ideal model. Better morality meant a better society. Confucius and Chu Hsi had said so; so it must be true.

High-ranking samurai administrators cut their own salaries, placed their wives on tighter budgets, and generally tried to show the way by increased frugality. They naturally required that their subordinates and the samurai beneath them do the same. Of course it did not occur to the top administrators that a 10 percent recision in their own comfortable salaries meant doing without a few luxuries; a proportional cut for most of the lower-ranking samurai meant not eating for a day each week.

They could not conceive that the answer might lie in an honest and fair taxation of commerce. That would fly in the face of the idea that the only "noble" tax was on agriculture. A tax on commerce would only raise prices as well as raise the social status of the merchants! To make money off "parasitic" activity was to lower the status of government to the level of money-grubbing merchants.

Of course the samurai were not spending extravagantly, so they could not "cut back." Instead they borrowed from moneylenders, pawnbrokers, and merchants. Or, they swallowed their considerable pride and took secret "side jobs" like acting as paid bodyguards for rich merchants or as collectors and "enforcers" for pawnbrokers and moneylenders; or they produced cottage industry piecework such as making folding fans, umbrellas, straw sandals, hats, raincoats, or toys. One can well imagine how happy they were to be doing this menial work and how happy artisans would be to have samurai moving into their occupations.

Merchants who had accumulated wealth were just as discontented to have to hide their assets lest they be confiscated or forcibly "loaned" (never to be repaid of course) to the bakufu or regional daimyō. Whenever a seemingly annual reform retrenchment program was announced, rich merchants would be rounded up to be humiliated and "squeezed" for their wealth. Great public sport would be made of displaying the costly clothes, the expensive furniture and jewelry, and the rich food that the merchants enjoyed. Obvious comparisons would be made by all to their own meager possessions. Clearly, here were the reasons why some people suffered: the greed of the merchants.

Stories are told of how rich merchants would hide their wealth with poor exteriors, of wealthy chōnin lining their drab cotton *kimono* robes with sumptuous silks. Some merchant families kept very little in their simple homes, preferring to eat rich foods in hidden restaurants and sleeping in richly decorated secret inns far away from the prying eyes of bakufu spies.

Often the bakufu would "forgive" and cancel all debts owed by samurai to merchants in feudal "acts of grace" (tokusei) similar to those of the Kamakura and Ashikaga shōgunates. It was after all a measure of their benevolence for their subordinates to ensure their well-being. This solved nothing, of course, because it drove up interest rates charged on subsequent loans. Often, merchant moneylenders, all members of the same guilds, refused to loan money to samurai until they had repaid the forgiven debts owed to other merchants. Or, the moneylenders simply stopped lending until the retrenchment reforms had ended.

The lot of the lower-ranking samurai actually worsened when this happened because inflation inevitably got worse—their income was a never-changing (unless it was actually reduced by thrifty feudal bureaucrats) salary or stipend. They could not increase their income by charging more for their services. That would be immoral. And since they made nothing but governance, they could not increase their production in order to cover rising prices.

A very few bakufu administrators such as Tanuma Okitsugu experimented with real economic reforms such as regular commercial taxes in exchange for commodity monopolies of selected licensed wholesalers or in new exports such as dried sea products to be sent to China. But these men were always ultimately branded as morally corrupt (and of course it did not help that Tanuma was himself financially corrupt) because Neo-Confucianism had great contempt for bureaucrats who "soiled their hands" with money. The good samurai, it was said, had such contempt for money that he "does not even know the price of rice." Most lower-ranking samurai knew the price, most could not afford it.

When the daimyō or the bakufu needed to increase their own incomes, they simply raised the agricultural taxes on the peasants. Because merchants usually actually handled the agricultural produce, tension increased between the merchants and peasantry. The peasantry resorted to arms (pitifully, with short swords, rakes, hoes, scythes, sticks, and cleavers) and revolts, usually not against the government but against moneylenders, pawnbrokers, and grain merchants.

Although the daimyō and bakufu harshly squashed these rebellions as quickly as possible, they had more sympathy with the peasantry than with the merchants. The government always blamed the merchants because they had caused the samurai to raise taxes to cover expenses. Usually only the peasant ringleaders were punished. It took a very courageous village leader to lead such an uprising, because death was always the reward. Often the government made no attempt to collect debts, recover land or goods, or otherwise recompense the merchants. Occasionally, in his benevolence, the daimyō actually lowered the taxes temporarily, because his own debts to the merchants had been obliterated too. This of course made the rebellions something of a success, if not for the executed leaders, at least for the peasantry at large. Songs were sung and stories told for generations honoring the courage and morality of these martyred peasant leaders. Japanese folk history is full of them.

In general the lot of the peasantry was a bleak one. George Sansom has noted tersely that the Tokugawa "cared much for agriculture; but little for the agriculturalists." Farmers were routinely charged half of their crop in taxes. And in the lean years very little adjustment was made to lessen their suffering. They were also required to do unpaid labor as part of their obligation to society. They repaired roads, dredged rivers and canals, maintained sea and river dikes, forested trees, and labored endlessly at other menial tasks. In times of extreme hardship, farmers often sold members of the family into temporary bondage. Historian Mikiso Hane, who has best documented the lives of the peasantry, notes that because the bondage continued until a debt was repaid, often the temporary conditions continued for life. Countless young girls were indentured to brothels, a life that usually meant humiliating slavery.

Of course the economy was not always so bleak for either the peasants, lower-ranking samurai, or the chōnin. The population of the country almost miraculously stabilized for over a century. Demographers like Kozo Yamamura and Susan Hanley have suggested that the entire society had collectively made sophisticated family-planning decisions based on economic reasons.

Some historians claim that the ever-dwindling plots of land inherited by large families convinced Japan to have fewer children. If the amount of land remained basically the same, but more people were being born to inherit it, the plots became increasingly smaller and smaller. Left to "nature," eventually the land would not be able to sustain the population. The Tokugawa tried to avoid this by making it illegal to subdivide a plot smaller than one *chō*, about 2.45 acres. Others have suggested that the Japanese controlled their population by infanticide, the killing of unwanted babies. Recent scholarship seems to indicate that the Japanese used other less drastic methods of birth control.

The fact remains that the Japanese consciously limited their population growth. With increased crop productivity through better strains of rice, better methods of land reclamation, irrigation, fertilization, crop rotation and diversification, as well as more efficient means of storage and transportation, the life of the average Japanese probably improved during the period. One former peasant, Ninomiya Sontoku, wrote extensively on agriculturalist topics, helping to spread technological innovations throughout the country. His pamphlets were printed by the thousands and circulated heavily.

Famine was not unknown during the period, but as long as it was regional and localized, the daimyō themselves managed to weather the storm by shifting supplies around. National famines like the three-year catastrophe of the early 1830s were ineptly handled by the bakufu simply because it was not really a national government. It had to depend on individual daimyō who would prefer to hoard their grain rather that feed strangers and ancient regional enemies.

Economic historians suggest that the real "crunch" to the economy came in the early nineteenth century from the increase in "cash crops." The daimyō, who spent half their lives in Edo and the other half in their castle-towns, were not around to experience the suffering of the peasants whom they had forced to grow mulberry for silk worms, tea or tobacco, flax for linen, cotton or jute. The peasants could not eat these crops when times were bad. But they still had to pay their taxes. At least the traditional peasants could eat their tax rice when times got bad, or rise in revolt to break down the granaries of rice merchants.

The urban economy grew in size and sophistication during the period. Because the samurai and chōnin had to be fed and clothed, a system of commercial transportation had to be developed. And because each daimyō had to spend both time and treasure in his sankin kotai in Edo, a system quickly developed to pay for these journeys. Every daimyō found it necessary to keep commercial agents, originally his vassals, but eventually merchants themselves, in places like Ōsaka, Sendai, and Edo to handle his finances. Rice and other crops were sold to wholesale merchants in exchange for coins, or more commonly, for paper credit to be redeemed in Edo, or along the way.

Many merchant houses grew rich in this national trade and developed powerful commercial and even political influence. Even the Tokugawa employed such agents and were constantly in debt to them. In fact there is considerable evidence that at the end of the era the rigid divisions between samurai and merchants were breaking down. Many cases are known where samurai adopted the daughters of merchants in exchange for the forgiveness of huge debts. These now-samurai girls would be married to samurai men making the grandchildren of merchants into samurai.

The urban economy as a whole was extensive, complex, and very sophisticated. Edwin Reischauer has noted that the trading in grain "futures" (commodity speculation) in Ōsaka put Japan in rivalry with similar ventures in London and Amsterdam and a century ahead of New York. Because the million people in Edo had to be fed, a huge coastal shipping industry developed, as well as insurance to protect it and banking to fund it. Trading in commodities other than rice grew rapidly as well. By the middle of the nineteenth century, Japan's commerce was nationally integrated and very healthy indeed.

The end of the Tokugawa would come for other more compelling reasons than bad economic times. But the economic woes helped to destabilize the government because of poor morale, not empty stomachs. No proletarian class rose in revolt to the bakufu. There was no great Marxian class struggle; the enemy was within. The coalition of allies that would bring down the proud Tokugawa Bakufu was made up of the ancient tozama enemies who leaped to the vanguard of imperial loyalists bent on restoring power to the emperor. The leaders of this anti-bakufu movement were the lower-ranking samurai who had lost faith with their hereditary samurai overlords. The loss of faith and confidence was gradual; and it was philosophical.

CRACKS IN THE NEO-CONFUCIAN IDEOLOGY

One must not fall into the trap of thinking that the Tokugawa were ever able to impose their philosophical will completely on all of Japan. Just because they isolated the country and had gotten rid of foreigners and Christians; just because they won the philosophical battle by making Neo-Confucianism the official ideology; just because many Zen monks became masters of Neo-Confucianism as well; just because all daimyō employed the bakufu-sanctioned ideas of government in their domains, does not mean that there were not dissenters.

There were always tiny, seemingly insignificant cracks in the Tokugawa ideological facade. Early in the seventeenth century there were men who preferred what came to be known as the *Kōgaku* or "Ancient School" of Confucianism. The argument of men like Itō Jinsai and Ogyū Sorai was that the original ideas of Confucius and Mencius encouraged "men of talent" to rise to positions according to their worth. Neo-Confucianism bound all men to their social class, and society was therefore robbed of good men who were trapped as lower-ranking samurai, or as peasants, artisans, and even merchants. There was no eternal, unchanging, natural moral law that governed society, they argued, but rather constantly evolving human laws. Man could, and must, change his laws to fit the times.

Another school of thought called the "Native School" (*Kokugaku*) thought that they had discovered the causes of Japan's social and economic problems. It lay in the foreign ideologies that ruled Japan. Men like the Shinto priest Kamo Mabuchi and his disciple Motoori Norinaga believed that the native ideas of Shinto and imperial rule were better suited to Japan than the Chinese Buddhist and Confucian philosophies. They suggested that the emperor as a living kami descended directly from the Sun Goddess Amaterasu must be restored to power. Only when the emperor and his people were one again in the land of the gods could Japan prosper. These men resurrected the eighth-century Japanese histories *Kojiki* and *Nihongi* as well as other literary classics like the *Tale of Genji* and various warrior tales. They reprinted some of the early imperial poetry anthologies and generally did much to popularize Shinto.

It was at their suggestion that people were allowed to register with Shinto shrines instead of at Buddhist temples to do the yearly fumi-e rituals to prove that they were not Christians. The followers of Nichiren Buddhism were natural supporters for Kokugaku because they too had argued that Japan was especially blessed.

A third "school" of dissenters was the followers of the sixteenth-century Chinese philosopher Wang Yang-ming (the Chinese Kanji characters are pronounced *oyomei* in Japan), who suggested that all Confucian ideas were artificial restraints on the human spirit. Man had within him basically good natural instincts for self-preservation and for peaceful relations with others. This intuition was blocked by the formalism of Confucianism. Outstanding scholars like Nakae Tōju and his disciple Kumazawa Banzan did much to popularize these ideas. Obviously this school of thought melded well with Zen Buddhism, which maintained that one's salvation was personal and from within and that it came suddenly in flashes of intuition and revelation.

The final "school" of dissenting thought was so foreign that it had no natural native allies in Japan. In fact, *Rangaku* or "Dutch Studies" was so foreign that it teetered on the edge of illegality until the late eighteenth century. The sakoku edicts of the Tokugawa were aimed at Christianity, of course, but all foreign books were suspect. Families of hereditary Dutch translators in Nagasaki were allowed limited access to carefully inspected Dutch books to be sure that there was no Christian content. Among those books were medical, cartographic, and scientific works that appealed to some Japanese, particularly some physicians. A small group of men like Sugita Gampaku, who painstakingly translated a Dutch medical book over a decade, and Otsuki Gentaku familiarized themselves with the scientific works and then began to branch off into forbidden areas such as the philosophical and political. Eventually some men learned German and English in order to further their knowledge. A few, like Honda Toshiaki and Satō Nobuhiro, would in the last half century of the Tokugawa become very influential because they represented the "modern" West to the rest of Japan.

BAKUMATSU: 1830S–1868

The last four decades of Tokugawa rule were turbulent and difficult ones. But fortunately for Japan the few battles and skirmishes that brought the Tokugawa down were mercifully short and remarkably free of casualties. That was in large part due to the fact that as much as the Tokugawa and their rivals hated each other, they all feared the West even more. Both the Tokugawa as well as their rivals were pragmatic enough to understand that if the bakufu insisted on holding onto power at any cost, the entire country would lose. If Japan was at war for any length of time, the possibility loomed large that one or more of the Western powers would meddle into Japanese domestic affairs. One only had to consider what had happened to India under similar circumstances to realize that a long-term civil war would be disastrous for Japan.

We should be careful not to fall into the trap that captures too many historians: that of looking so hard to find reasons and causes for historical events that one forgets that as Will Rogers said, "the only things that are inevitable are death and taxes." Despite the seemingly rapid and easy end of the Tokugawa, the bakufu was not at the point of collapse. The end of the bakufu was not inevitable in 1867. It could have continued on for quite a while more if it had been able to adjust, adapt, and perhaps to promote some charismatic reformers.

The name commonly given for the last two decades of Tokugawa rule incorporates the kanji "baku" (the first character in "bakufu") and "matsu" meaning "end" to be read *Bakumatsu:* literally, the "end of the bakufu." The decade that began in 1830 was a horrible one for Japan. A series of severe droughts ravaged the country for nearly three years. A national famine killed thousands of peasants and ruined many more. The bakufu mishandled famine relief badly, preferring to bleed the countryside in order to feed the samurai population in Edo and Ōsaka. Daimyō were ordered to donate "surplus" rice for famine relief, but they cried poverty and famine in their own areas.

To make matters worse, some grain merchants sought to profit from the drought by stockpiling rice, waiting for the prices to skyrocket. This caused the famine to spread to the cities as well. Peasant and chōnin riots ensued in many places as the hungry broke down warehouse doors in search of food. The worst uprising was led by Ōshio Heihachirō, a former bakufu Ōsaka city commissioner. He led some 300 desperate men on a rampage through that city in 1837 until he committed suicide when his forces were defeated.

The bakufu administrators were truly shocked at the number of deaths by starvation and by the number of peasant rebellions. A reform campaign was mounted to improve the economy. Like almost all other bakufu economic reforms, however, they were based on moralistic retrenchment principles. The same tired edicts were passed, demanding that people stop living extravagantly (hardly the cause of the famine) and that administrators and samurai "cut back" on their spending. Some rich merchants were both figuratively and literally bled white in order to raise revenue; prices were officially slashed; and debts were forgiven. As usual, the merchants responded by hiding their wealth. Because money was scarce, interest rates and prices shot upwards. Only a few effective reforms took place. A bank of surplus grain was established for famine relief; some corrupt administrators were sacked; and the worst rice profiteers had their wealth confiscated. The reforms were too little and too late.

The greatest danger to bakufu control came not directly from the economic problems but from the eroding morale of the lower-ranking samurai. All had suffered from the worst economic policies of their feudal superiors. Most had their salaries reduced or had been forced to "contribute" portions of their stipends to help han or bakufu finances "temporarily." Most were seriously in debt to the merchant class; many had taken secret side jobs to eke out a meager existence. Their resentment against the greedy merchants who hounded them for payment on past debts was surpassed only by their growing bitter contempt for the bumbling inefficiencies of their superiors.

The pledges of loyalty and honor that were the backbone of the samurai class were premised on the idea that their lords would treat them benevolently, wisely, and efficiently. But the largely ceremonial ties that bound samurai to daimyō were frayed and then severed when the superiors continually mismanaged the economy.

The situation worsened when some daimyō began to release "surplus" samurai from their oaths of loyalty in an attempt to be rid of their stipend obligations. These *rōnin* (literally "wave men" or "masterless samurai") were cut adrift in search of new employment, a new master, a new career. The rōnin would play a powerful role in the end of the bakufu.

Many samurai began to seriously question not only their incompetent superiors but also the entire philosophical system as well. How could one remain loyal to a philosophy that kept incompetent people in power and did not promote lower-ranking talented men? The unorthodox ideas of Kokugaku, Oyomei, and even Rangaku became more and more popular after 1840.

The spark or catalyst that would bring together the various elements of dissatisfied samurai, rōnin, unorthodox philosophers, and many other political elements into an uneasy anti-bakufu coalition was the threat of Western invasion. Nothing seems to bring different groups of people together like a common fear, a common enemy.

THE FEAR OF THE WEST

The fear of the West was very real in Japan in the early nineteenth century. Despite Japan's official sakoku edicts of isolation, the bakufu knew what was happening in the rest of the world. The Dutch were required to give annual reports to the bakufu commissioners in Nagasaki, and the various Chinese and Korean traders also kept the Japanese abreast of basic world developments, especially regarding the spread of Western imperialism into Asia.

As early as the 1770s, Russia had expanded into northeast Asia and had come in contact with the Japanese isolation laws. Russian admirals had tried to establish diplomatic and commercial relations but had been rudely rebuffed. Aware that the Russians were moving through Kamchatka, Sakhalin, and the Kurile Islands toward Japan, the bakufu began in the 1800s to send explorations to Hokkaido, the land of the feared Ainu.

The British also attempted to establish relations, but they too were turned away. Shortly after hearing the news that Great Britain had defeated the Chinese in what has been called the Opium War, the bakufu changed its "Don't think twice" edict that ordered the daimyō to fire upon foreign ships without a second thought. That year, 1842, the Tokugawa ordered daimyō to treat humanely foreign castaway sailors, shipwrecks, groundings, and ships badly in need of provisions. After all, if giant China had been defeated by these Western barbarians, what chance did tiny insular Japan have?

Eventually America would break the impasse, forcing Japan's "doors" open again. But even that was more of a historical coincidence than an inevitability. The fur trade in the northwest region of North America, the growing American commerce in China, and the extension of American whaling into the Pacific often brought American ships into Japanese waters. The inevitable shipwrecks and groundings put American sailors at the mercy of the Japanese.

In 1846 an American ship attempted to gain entry but was turned away by the Japanese as was another two years later, but not before the latter was allowed to carry away 15 American castaway sailors. Five years later a small armada of American ships could not be sent away.

On July 8, 1853, the four American ships sailed, not into Nagasaki where all foreigners were sent, but right into the lower reaches of Edo Bay. The small flotilla commanded by Commodore Matthew C. Perry insisted on landing in nearby Uraga and delivering a message for the "Emperor" from American President Millard Fillmore. Perry had steamed around the harbor displaying his gunners' marksmanship in artillery practice. The Japanese had heard about steamships that belched smoke but did not burn up. They had heard from the Dutch about naval guns that were accurate up to two miles. They knew that their puny shore batteries were no match for this military machine. They allowed Perry to land the message.

The message asked for humane treatment of American sailors and for the right to provision ships with water, food, wood, and coal in designated Japanese ports. It also suggested that commerce be established. Perry promised to return the next spring for an answer and then steamed away southward toward the Ryūkyū Islands.

Perry's visit and message sent Japan into a turmoil. The bakufu knew that resistance to American demands was hopeless. Factions within the bakufu counseled the shōgun to seek the support of other daimyō. This was an almost fatal mistake. The haughty tozama, almost to a man, reminded the bakufu that the title Sei-itai Shōgun meant "Barbarian subduing General." Here then were barbarians to subdue. The implication was for the shōgun to do his job. A few daimyō—most notably the Mito shimpan daimyō Tokugawa Nariaki, who (like the shōgun), was a descendant of Ieyasu—demanded that Japan fight even against impossible odds. Many fudai and even a few shimpan daimyō suggested some kind of stalling action while Japan rearm. But where was the bakufu to acquire modern guns? From the Dutch? Perhaps; at what price?

When Perry returned with eight ships, the bakufu signed the Treaty of Kanagawa on March 31, 1854, granting the Americans access to the remote ports of Hakodate in Hokkaido and Shimoda at the tip of the mountainous Izu Peninsula. There they could provision their ships, but no commerce was promised. The bakufu also agreed to a Most Favored Nation clause (discussed later) and to consider the exchange of diplomatic representatives. With that, Perry sailed away, leaving Japan in a brewing tempest.

Perhaps the bakufu could have weathered this storm, but the situation grew worse with the arrival of the American Townsend Harris two years later. The bakufu had managed to deflect the anger by rounding up the most vocal critics, imprisoning some, executing a few, and negotiating endlessly with the most powerful daimyō like Nariaki. But with the arrival of America's designated diplomatic agent, the debate flared anew.

Harris warned the bakufu that if it did not deal quickly and honestly with him, the British would not be far behind. He suggested that the Japanese could get the best "deal" with America, who, like Japan, did not want the British moving in with their hated opium like they had in China.

THE "UNEQUAL" TREATIES

The 1858 Treaty of Shimoda became the first and therefore the model for some 17 international agreements that have been called Japan's "Unequal Treaties." Although the individual treaties differed from each other somewhat, in general they contained six common characteristics.

First, they were unilateral, applying only to foreigners in Japan. Of course in the beginning there were no provisions to govern and protect Japanese abroad because the bakufu still maintained the sakoku laws of isolation.

Second, citizens of all treaty nations received the right to reside, trade, and to privately practice their religions in a few designated "treaty ports." They could rent or lease land, but they were not allowed to own property in the country. The treaty ports remained Japanese, but the Foreign Settlements, as they came to be called, actually governed themselves because all aliens were protected by extraterritoriality, as we shall see.

Third, because foreigners were accustomed to the protection of extraterritoriality in China and the Middle East, that protection was demanded from Japan as well. Actually, the legal concept of extraterritoriality could never really exist because it meant that foreigners were totally immune to Japanese legal jurisdiction and subject only to their own laws. The system called Consular Jurisdiction actually came to be a compromise that existed until the twentieth century. This allowed Japanese authorities to arrest and hold foreigners who had broken Japanese laws until the offenders would be turned over to their diplomatic consul in Japan. The consul then often became both judge and jury at the trials of these criminals.

At first the bakufu preferred this to having to deal with unruly foreign sailors and merchants who did not speak Japanese, but later it recognized the implied humiliation of this treaty clause. It suggested that Japanese laws were too barbaric and uncivilized to risk turning over foreign citizens to its jurisdiction. As more and more foreigners came to reside in Japan, they began to demand protection for their commercial enterprises and for their Japanese mistresses, children, and even their servants. The situation became even worse when foreigners began to preach Christianity (it was still illegal until 1873) and try to claim extraterritorial protection for their Japanese converts. For the bakufu, this was adding insult to injury.

The fourth characteristic of these treaties was the Scheduled or Conventional Tariff. Foreigners made this demand because of the number of internal tolls and taxes put on foreign imports in China. They feared that the Japanese would try to add such nuisance costs, so they demanded that Japan also limit the tariffs charged on imported goods to a Schedule contained in the treaty or Convention, hence the name. The usual tariff charged by Western nations on imports was 15–20 percent of the value of the good. Japan was limited to a general 5 percent thereby losing three to four times what it deserved. Most Western nations used a Protective Tariff on imports in order to make their own goods cheaper. Japan could not do that, and therefore foreign products had an unfair trade advantage.

The fifth aspect was the Most Favored Nation clause. This clause, called "the most devious invention known to man" by a foreign friend of Japan, stated that Japan had to treat each treaty power equally as if they all were "most favored." This was to avoid being pitted against each other as the Chinese had historically done in what it called "using one barbarian to fight another." Any special concessions or privileges granted to one nation were automatically given to all the others. It also worked in reverse. That is, Japan could never revise a treaty with any nation unless every other nation also agreed. At that time the Western nations could not even agree upon what time of day it was (there was actually no mutual agreement on world time until after the First World War), so the chances of Japan getting all nations to agree on any treaty were slim indeed.

The final humiliating aspect of the treaties was that they were apparently eternal. They had no real provisions for revision or termination. Some contained language to the effect that if "both nations find it mutually convenient," negotiations for revision could take place. The Most Favored Nation clause made this unlikely.

The treaties, then, contained so many unequal aspects that when the enemies and rivals of the bakufu examined them closely, they felt humiliated and shamed. How could the Sei-itai Shōgun allow the "land of the gods" to be treated so shabbily by barbarians? Why hadn't the bakufu fought? Some Japanese thought it was "better to die on one's feet that to live on one's knees." The treaties became the evidence that the bakufu must be toppled and replaced by a national government who could protect Japan's honor.

SONNŌ-JŌI: THE RISE OF JAPANESE NATIONALISM

Unfortunately for the bakufu, they had already opened the door to "public opinion" when they had sought the advice of the daimyō over the first Perry crisis in 1853. They made another mistake when they asked for the emperor's authorization for the new Treaty of Shimoda. They assumed that consent could be obtained without problems. Some of the courtiers around the emperor, however, saw this as an excellent opportunity to assert imperial authority. They convinced the emperor to withhold his sanction, and once again the bakufu was embarrassed by this public display of their ineffectiveness.

At that moment, the fudai daimyō Ii Naosuke became head of the Council of Senior Advisors and swung the bakufu back towards real authority. He swiftly imprisoned many of the bakufu's critics and forced Nariaki into house arrest. He had the most vocal critics executed and indicated that he would brook no further interference into the affairs of the bakufu. He paid for this with his life. A number of Nariaki's lower-ranking samurai waylaid Ii in 1860 and assassinated him before they committed suicide themselves.

Thus began a decade of bloody politics. The bakufu for its part tried to reassert its lost prestige and authority by arresting and executing as many of their critics as they could catch. Many tozama daimyō saw their opportunity to bring down the haughty Tokugawa and ranged themselves against the bakufu as much as they dared.

The chief enemies of the Tokugawa were the four southwestern tozama daimyo of Tosa, Hizen, Satsuma, and Chōshū. All had a long historical hatred of the Tokugawa. It is said that the samurai of Satsuma determined in which direction Edo lay every night so that they could sleep with their feet pointing in that direction to symbolically show their contempt for the Tokugawa. The ancestors of all of these daimyō had been vassals of Hideyoshi, and all had reluctantly sworn loyalty to Tokugawa Ieyasu just before or immediately after the battle of Sekigahara in 1600. All four had instituted significant economic and administrative reforms in their domains during the previous decade, and all professed now to be loyalists for the emperor.

During the next eight years they would jockey for advantageous position among themselves. The only thing that kept them from exerting more power was that they remained divided. Indeed, the only other things they had in common other than their hatred of the Tokugawa were their suspicions and jealousies of each other. For a time Satsuma actually cooperated with the bakufu in a punitive expedition against Chōshū. It was not until late 1866 when the two finally made an alliance against the Tokugawa.

The center for anti-bakufu activities was the emperor. A rather shy and re-tiring man, Kōmei was at heart a conservative man who did not really understand or care for politics. His elder advisers were similarly uninterested in the dangerous game of national intrigue, but some younger courtiers like Iwakura Tomomi quietly slipped into this political vacuum to influence the emperor. Secret discussion took place in Kyoto between representatives of the major tozama daimyō and these courtiers. Chōshū was represented by such men as Kido Takayoshi; Satsuma by Ōkubo Toshimichi; Tosa by Sakamoto Ryōma; and Hizen by Ōkuma Shigenobu.

The Chinese-style four-kanji slogan for the period became *Sonnō-Jōi* or "Revere the Emperor—Expel the Barbarian." A curious mixture of seemingly mutually exclusive ideas was cobbled together to create a new philosophical basis for Japanese nationalism. From the Kokugaku or "National School" of thought came the idea that Japan's native ideas, institutions, and customs were superior to all things foreign. Included in this foreignness were Neo-Confucianism and Buddhism. Never mind that their "foreignness" had been altered and adapted by some 10 centuries of experience in Japan. The recent national problems, they argued, came because the Japanese had been separated from their natural emperor by Neo-Confucian bureaucrats, Buddhist priests, and the shōgun himself. The perfect remedy was to honor the emperor and restore him to his rightful natural place in society. Naturally Shinto ideas were resurrected and Buddhist concepts rejected by this nativist thought. After all, the basis for the emperor's legitimacy was his unbroken lineage from the Sun Goddess Amaterasu, the country's ancestral kami.

Wedded to this antiforeignism were the ideas of the Rangaku or "Dutch Studies" school of thought. Unbelievable as this may seem, the antiforeign nationalists decided that because Neo-Confucianism, a foreign political philosophy, was to blame for Japan's military inferiority and technological backwardness, one must use the new foreign secrets to protect the country. In other words, one must restore Japan's ancient ethos by using foreign science. Curiously, this same idea was being tried in China in its "Eastern Ethics–Western Science" Self-Strengthening Movement at this exact moment. It would be an abject failure in China, but a brilliant success in Japan.

The bakufu had already made a decision to learn from the West, at least in terms of science, technology, and military ideas. It had formed a bureau to "investigate barbarian books" and had commissioned many of its interpreters to translate Western scientific books. In the late 1850s and early 1860s it sent a number of men to study abroad, the most famous of whom, Fukuzawa Yū kichi, wrote a national best seller about the West.

The Sonnō-Jōi group had similarly begun to use Western military technology to their advantage. The tozama han of Hizen had developed its own Western-style reverberatory iron furnace; both Satsuma and Chōshū had purchased Western guns and warships. Many of their samurai including Itō Hirobumi and Inoue Kaoru also studied abroad. Chōshū had begun to experiment with peasant militias and mixed peasant-samurai rifle regiments. Ironically, many of the guns they bought and used in Japan's brief civil war in 1868 had already been used in the American Civil War.

The Sonnō-Jōi movement was nothing like a coherent and unified revolutionary movement. Many within its camp wished to kill as many foreigners as possible right away; others advocated waiting until Japan had learned their military secrets. Not a few greatly admired the West, but they kept quiet about it because many of the most antiforeign loyalists began to attack anyone who seemed to be too friendly toward foreigners. In fact bands of assassins who called themselves *shishi* ("men of spirit") roamed around cutting down each other.

The shishi were able to play an influential role because of their willingness to kill almost indiscriminately. Because most were masterless rōnin, they could not be controlled through their daimyō like other samurai. They may be compared to the ultrapatriotic young military men (who also called themselves shishi) of the turbulent 1930s. Their wild use of violence allowed other military men to threaten political moderates. Several score of Japan's most brilliant young patriots died in this senseless slaughter.

One such victim, Sakamoto Ryōma, who was from Tosa, had gathered a number of patriots around him in the early 1860s first in Kyoto and then in Nagasaki. Many of these men were actual or self-styled rōnin. They had run away from their homes to symbolically cut themselves off from their feudal loyalties. They claimed their only loyalty now was to the emperor. Of course only they could determine what their new national symbol wanted them to do, because the Emperor Kōmei was not particularly interested in them or in their cause.

Sakamoto had experimented with a Western-style joint-stock trading company that secretly obtained guns in Nagasaki for many of the western tozama han. Within Sakamoto's group were a number of men who would become influential in later years including the future Foreign Minister, Mutsu Munemitsu. Unfortunately, Sakamoto too had used violence and threats of attack to force his rivals into silence. He was assassinated at the eve of the Restoration by a band of shishi. He lived by the sword; he also died by it.

THE FINAL CRISIS

The bakufu's end came as a result of its inability to unify the country against the foreign threat. The shōgunal ministers tried several different policies to bring the country together and thereby preserve the bakufu. They tried to bring the emperor and the shōgun together by a marriage of the shōgun to the emperor's sister. They attempted to win over the antiforeign element by promising to expel the barbarians "as soon as possible." They wooed the court; they tried to play one tozama daimyō against another. Nothing worked for very long. One crisis after another seemed to cut the ground out from under the bakufu.

A number of antiforeign incidents embarrassed the Tokugawa by showing their weaknesses. When the British demanded that the bakufu punish some Satsuma samurai for the murder of an Englishman, the Tokugawa seemed powerless. When Chōshū committed several antiforeign acts, including attacking and burning the British embassy and shooting at foreign ships as they passed through the Straits of Shimonoseki, the bakufu seemed to be able to do nothing. The foreigners, seeing that the bakufu seemed unable to punish these antiforeign zealots, took matters into their own hands. The Americans, British, French, and even the once friendly Dutch took turns bombarding and destroying the gun emplacements at Shimonoseki and also at the Satsuma stronghold of Kagoshima. Curiously, these Western punitive campaigns worked to bring the tozama and the West together.

When the tozama had their guns destroyed, it allowed more moderate and pro-Western factions within the han to gain in influence. They were able to convincingly argue that the han must learn from the West in order to defeat it. Among these were Kido Takayoshi, Itō Hirobumi, Inoue Kaoru, and Yamagata Aritomo—all in Chōshū. The four would become among Japan's greatest leaders within a decade.

In Satsuma men like Ōkubo Toshimichi, Saigō Takamori, and Matsukata Masayoshi sprang up to heavily influence national politics. These men became acquainted with the British consul Harry Parkes and his chief interpreter Ernest Satow. The Englishmen, hoping for better trade relations with Japan, secretly began to advise these Satsuma and Chōshū samurai on ways to destabilize the government.

In the meantime, the French, who had seen the British gain influence among the tozama, began to court the bakufu. A French school was established in Yokohama, and a naval shipyard was founded in neighboring Yokosuka. Clearly the two European nations were trying to ingratiate themselves with the two sides. The danger for Japan lay in becoming too reliant on foreign aid.

The final crisis came after the bakufu had promised to expel the foreigners. The imperial court issued a secret edict urging this action, but only Chōshū obeyed by attacking the British embassy. The bakufu responded by mounting a second punitive expedition against Chōshū (the first had been only a limited success) in August 1866. This time, however, Satsuma did not join.

Sakamoto Ryōma had secretly convinced his friends within both Satsuma and Chōshū finally to cooperate. The forces of Chōshū badly embarrassed the bakufu forces who then used the deaths of both the shōgun and the emperor as an excuse to end the shameful debacle. Now Sakamoto together with Tosa countryman Gotō Shōjiro convinced their daimyō Yamanouchi Yodo to intervene with the new shōgun, Tokugawa Yoshinobu. Ironically, the last shōgun was the son of the bakufu's nemesis from Mito, Tokugawa Nariaki. Yoshinobu agreed to resign and to restore power to the new 13-year-old emperor, who took the auspicious name Meiji or "Enlightened Rule."

Perhaps the issue could have ended peacefully there, but that would have left the Tokugawa with their huge private estates intact. The Tokugawa would have played a very influential role in subsequent politics. But Saigō Takamori secretly hired some shishi thugs to create one disturbance after another. The Tokugawa responded by attacking the combined Satsuma and Chōshū forces, and a brief civil war ensued.

In mid-January 1868 the Tokugawa forces were badly defeated at Toba-Fushimi close to the site of Hideyoshi's sixteenth-century castle. The shōgun surrendered his forces, and the adolescent emperor Meiji was "restored" to power. The political settlement that followed, called the Meiji Restoration, seized most of the Tokugawa lands and the four chief tozama han of Satsuma, Chōshū, Tosa, and Hizen pledged their loyalties to the emperor by combining their forces into the Imperial Army.

This brought to an end not only the Tokugawa Bakufu but also the nearly seven centuries of feudal government in Japan. Ironically, the last bakufu ended as had the first one, the Kamakura, with an imperial restoration.

5

The Meiji Era: 1868–1912

When the main forces of the Tokugawa diehards surrendered to the combined "royalist" forces in January 1868, it signaled the end of the Tokugawa era and the beginning of the Meiji. But the change in era names signified much more than the exchange of one government for another. It was also the end of divided regional political power in favor of a truly national government. For many it symbolized the end of feudalism, the end of an oppressive political philosophy, the demise of artificial controls over personal choice and livelihood, the end of national seclusion, the end of economic stagnation.

It was the end of an era, to be sure, but the changing of era names is not like flipping a light switch. Feudalism did not disappear overnight to be replaced by a new and "modern" social-political system. The year 1868 is not really the end of that way of life. The continuities were more important than the immediate differences between the two periods. The national ethos continued on almost unaltered for some time.

For the first few years the only changes were really cosmetic and superficial. The new imperial government existed only on paper. The national army was merely an amalgam of the combined feudal samurai forces of Satsuma, Chōshū, and a few other han. In the countryside, the daimyō continued to administer their domains as they had for centuries; to collect taxes, to keep the peace, to render justice, and to rule as if nothing had changed. The samurai continued to serve loyally their feudal lords; the peasants continued to farm; the chōnin went about their bustling commercial activities; the rice boats continued to lumber their way into Edo Bay to feed the huge population there. For a while it was "business as usual" for Japan.

Within three months of its creation, the new government issued a general statement of its intent for reforms. The Charter Oath of April 1868 promised

1   An "assembly widely convoked" to discuss matters of state.
2   A unity of all classes to promote the "economy and welfare of the nation."
3   All people "shall be allowed to fulfill their aspirations, so that there may be no discontent among them."
4   "Base customs" would be abandoned, and government would be based on "principles of international justice."
5   "Knowledge shall be sought throughout the world and thus shall be strengthened the foundation of the Imperial polity."

For nearly three years, however, very little seemed to change in the country except that the corridors of power shifted from Edo castle to the Kyoto Imperial Palace. And even then, the power would return to Edo at the head of a grand imperial procession as the young emperor transferred the throne to the recently renamed "Eastern Capital" (Tokyo) transforming the Shōgun's castle into the new Imperial Palace in 1869. But within that new palace the Meiji government struggled, muddled, and puzzled its way along on the way to becoming a real national government.

It experimented with not one, not even just a few systems of government. In fact more than twenty political reorganizations, creations, deletions, alterations, and other changes were tried. Ministries were created, altered, and dissolved virtually overnight. Men were appointed, transferred, promoted, demoted, and dismissed even more rapidly. It was a time of experimentation. It was an exciting and exhilarating time because Japan was "reinventing" itself. And yet the trial and experimentation was done self-consciously as the West loomed large on Japan's horizon. The reforms would be done with twin objectives in mind: strengthening Japan to keep her independent, and ridding the nation of the humiliation represented by the hated Unequal Treaties. The two goals were interdependent. Neither could be attained without the other.

SOCIAL AND POLITICAL REFORMS

The final decade of the Tokugawa Bakufu had been an exciting one. Although the social instability had been dangerous for the country, the fluidity of the politics had created a sense of common purpose as well as a feeling of almost unlimited potential in the country. The young lower-ranking samurai who had brought down the shōgunate shared a sense of camaraderie and national mission that had long been missing in Japanese life. Now, with the passing of the bakufu, they had to turn their focus toward another dangerous and exciting decade.

The four most significant and most wrenching changes in Japanese life were accomplished simultaneously between 1871 and 1875:

1 The creation of a national land tax
2 The abolition of the four-class social system, especially the samurai class
3 The creation of a national conscripted military
4 Haihan Chiken ("Abolition of Domains, Establishment of Prefectures")

The end of the decade witnessed other changes as well, but these were probably the most important and long lasting.

The four great changes were interdependent and could not have been accomplished independently. But of the four, perhaps the most fundamental was the land tax because it created the fiscal foundations for the new government. Various reform proposals for the creation of a regular revenue base were received by the fledgling Meiji government, but the three most influential were submitted by Mutsu Munemitsu, Inoue Kaoru, and Ōkuma Shigenobu. All three shared responsibility (and blame) because they all served within the new Finance Ministry that engineered the tax scheme. Inoue of Chōshū and Ōkuma from Hizen had the foremost responsibilities because their han connections in the upper echelons stood them in good stead. Mutsu, who was actually from the Tokugawa Shimpan han of Kii, had attached himself as a rōnin to Tosa han through Sakamoto Ryōma and Gotō Shōjiro and therefore was something of an outsider.

The three squabbled and cooperated in turns in order to create a sensible and equitable revenue system on which to base the national budget. The final scheme involved the first thorough national land survey since Hideyoshi's survey of 1587. It assessed land productivity, confirmed ownership, and assigned tax rates. The tax was based on average yields and grain prices. The peasants were now responsible for selling their produce and paying their assessed taxes in money instead of in rice as had been the custom.

These heavy and unfamiliar responsibilities were made more attractive to the average peasant by the fact that the percentage of the crop to be paid in tax was actually lowered in average years. Of course when grain prices fluctuated, and when drought or other natural disasters damaged the crops, the peasants were still liable for their annual taxes in cash.

Clearly the financial burden for the budget was placed squarely on the peasantry. Commercial taxes were levied too, but the government depended most heavily on the land tax for its revenue. By 1873 when the taxes finally went into effect, the government could rely on the regular revenue on which to base its other national economic reforms. The lot of the farmer would continue to deteriorate and would result in brief peasant uprisings occasionally. For the most part, however, the peasants suffered in silence.

The abolition of the Neo-Confucian social system, along with the creation of a conscript military were tied together and received the greatest resistance from the samurai class. The young lower-ranking samurai who had created the new government had criticized the bakufu for not recognizing and promoting men of talent. What they meant by this was that the old system did not promote *them*. But if the new society was to prosper, it must recognize that talent lay not just within the samurai but below them in the other classes as well. Every man must be allowed to rise or fall according to personal ambition, aptitude, education, and performance. Therefore, one must create a system of social mobility. But that would also cause social and political instability.

The peasants were not the problem of course. The sheer overwhelming labor kept all but the most talented and ambitious in the fields. A few merchants probably would rise to contend for power; the richest national merchants were proof of that. The greatest problem was the samurai class itself. Most samurai, by virtue of their access to education as well as their previous experience in administration, would naturally make the transition to the new system easily. They would merely transfer their loyalties from an individual feudal lord to a new bureaucratic superior.

But what of all the other samurai? Certainly the "downsizing" from some 270 feudal han governments to just a few provincial and one national bureaucracy would (thankfully) limit the number of bureaucrats needed.

One must remember that by 1868 the samurai population was nearly seven percent of the national total. Most "modern" governments need no more than perhaps from two to four percent of its population involved in government bureaucracies. They are a drain on the economy because they are not productive, they are administrative. They create nothing but order. Some could, of course, make a similar transition to the military or police forces, but that still left hundreds of thousands of samurai without jobs. And, without jobs, they lost their hereditary stipends and their social prestige.

A scheme was devised whereby the samurai who did not quickly find employment could receive commuted stipends in the form of government bonds. They could rely upon this decreasing revenue for a short period or could commute the stipend into a lump-sum payment. Many took the latter opportunity; some to personal benefit like those who pooled their bonds and formed banks or businesses. Many others quickly lost this money because they had almost no commercial experience and were at the mercy of the experienced wily merchants.

Socially, the abolition of the classes was also a samurai issue as well. Very little except residence distinguished peasants from chōnin. And the distinctions between artisans and merchants had long ago blurred away. The greatest problem was samurai pride. The two physical distinctions of the samurai—the male "top-knot" hairstyle and the double swords—were first made optional and finally were phased out altogether within a decade.

The hairstyle had become a time-consuming affectation anyway. And because the new Western styles made the samurai hair seem quaint and dated, the custom quickly disappeared except among the old diehard conservatives and among Kabuki actors. But the sword was another greater problem. The cult of Bushidō had idealized and sanctified the sword, making it the symbol of the samurai soul. Military and police officers managed to incorporate the long sword into their uniform regalia, but the rest of the samurai population had to pack away their treasures, and with the swords went a symbol of samurai haughty pride.

The shift from a samurai to a conscript military was similarly psychologically wrenching for the old samurai class. The new government readily understood that the individualized and personal warfare of the samurai was a thing of the past. When Tokugawa Ieyasu had "frozen" society in 1600, the importance of the individual mounted samurai in warfare had already been surpassed by ashigaru pikemen, archers, and ultimately arquebusers and cannoneers. The new style of warfare depended on the careful coordinated movement of thousands of troops. The old system that allowed samurai to roam the battlefield in search of a suitable opponent appropriate to his rank and fame was a thing of the past. Japan's choice to give up gun warfare during the Tokugawa era is an indication that society wished to idealize the samurai. But now, three centuries later, the samurai were an anachronism. Their style of combat was outdated.

The most powerful "modern" armies of the West relied on conscript militaries. They were led by a professional military aristocracy, of course, but manned by common citizens who did not question orders but merely obeyed. That did not describe the samurai.

Various men had advocated a conscript military, but the man given most credit for its implementation was the Chōshū samurai Yamagata Aritomo called the "Father of the Japanese Army." His argument carried the day, and ultimately all healthy adult males were liable for active and reserve military service. Many samurai rushed to join the military, and most who did so became officers. But some peasants and chōnin rose to such positions as well. Occasionally former samurai found themselves taking orders from their former social inferiors. That naturally created many problems for samurai pride. Many former samurai refused to serve in such a force. Some died rather than do so, as we shall see.

The final of the four essential Meiji reforms, Haihan Chiken, was in many ways the most easily accomplished. On paper, the abolition of the old domains (and with them, the daimyō as well) and the creation of the new administrative units called prefectures seemed to be in 1868 the most politically dangerous. Great care and planning went into this reform announced in 1871 lest the daimyō fight this reform.

The four main tozama daimyō of Satsuma, Chōshū, Tosa, and Hizen set an example for the other daimyō by turning over their feudal land tax registers to the emperor and resigning their hereditary positions. Provisions were made for each daimyō to receive a generous pension. Many were urged to accept positions within the government, some as governors of the new prefectures. The offer was sweetened when the Meiji government assumed all han debts. The government also assumed responsibilities for the samurai stipends. In effect, the daimyō received generous personal pensions and were relieved of their astronomical debts, their continuing fiscal responsibilities, and their administrative headaches. A decade later, the government made the former daimyō part of the new nobility as well.

Henceforth, all local, regional, and national positions were to be imperial appointments. Most top han administrators lost their positions to be replaced by younger men who, of course, were fiercely loyal to the emperor. Those former han bureaucrats who managed to catch on with the new prefectural governments had to make adjustments. The greatest change, of course, was that the positions were no longer hereditary. By the end of the century only those men who had passed rigorous civil service examinations were allowed to serve in government.

As a whole, therefore, the new Meiji government did remarkably well in their transition from a feudal system to a more "modern" one. With few exceptions, the adjustment was free of serious resistance from the potential enemies of the state. This is in part due to the exceptional wisdom and patience of the reformers.

Much of the peaceful transition can also be attributed to the fact that in the main, the Japanese as a people accepted the need for change. They, like their leaders, feared the threat of Western intervention. In order to avoid Western imperialism, Japan would accept many wrenching changes.

Finally, we must also consider that most people got much more from the new system than they surrendered. They got the right to determine who and what they could become. If some samurai fell in social status, many more rose and prospered. The peasantry, although they now were saddled by an uncertain grain-to-tax conversion, at least had a rational and dependable system to protect them. And they had title to the land. A greater psychological burden was their new military obligation, but many used this to their social, economic, and political advantage as well. The merchants seemed to have gained the most. Their social status soared along with their wealth, but more significantly they were able to enjoy something of which they could only have dreamed: that their sons and daughters could rise through education to the very pinnacle of society.

"TOP-DOWN" ECONOMIC REFORMS

Fairly early in the Meiji period an official embassy was sent abroad by the government. Lead by the courtier Iwakura Tomomi, the embassy had a three-fold mission:

1 To "show the flag," to demonstrate to the rest of the world that Japan had changed systems of government
2 To attempt to revise the hated Unequal Treaties
3 To observe firsthand how the West functioned

The final goal of the mission had the greatest effect on Japan because the leaders came back convinced that Japan was too far behind the West to risk anything but concerted efforts at social, political, and economic reform. The members of the Iwakura Mission returned in time to quash a military expedition to Korea (discussed later) that might have been ruinous to Japan's independence.

The members of the Iwakura Mission returned from America and Europe impressed with the West's military, legal, and political systems, but most of all with the modern industrial and economic systems. They understood that if the military could be said to be the muscles of a nation, the economy was its backbone. They witnessed the complex interdependence between the military and commercial networks. One fed the other. If Japan was to remain free and independent, if it was to become powerful, it needed more than just a strong military. It needed a powerful economy.

One of the Chinese-style four-kanji slogans for the period (like Sonnō Jōi or Haihan Chiken) was to be *Fukoku Kyōhei* ("Rich Country—Strong Military"), another was *Bunmei Kaika* ("Civilization and Enlightenment"). The Meiji modernizers knew instinctively that they could not afford for the economy to grow slowly like grass roots by ordinary private commerce as it had in Western nations during the Industrial Revolution 50 years before. The economy had to be created from above by the government. This "top-down" approach was financially and politically risky for three primary reasons.

First, it would require the government to spend huge amounts to create what has been called infrastructure: the framework on which to build private industry. Banks, railroads, shipping companies, iron and steel foundries, postal and communication systems, as well as chemical, coal, electric, and other vital industries were very expensive. Where was Japan to get such funds? To be sure, it could not make the mistake that China had made: borrow abroad and mortgage its future. The money had to come from Japan's agricultural sector. But would the peasants sit still for this? They might become natural allies with discontented samurai.

Second, where was Japan to get the technical expertise to do this? It could not follow China's example of allowing foreigners to control private commerce. But how to obtain the needed expertise without foreign help? Would the West grant it without attaching some kind of "strings" as the French had hoped to do with the Tokugawa Bakufu? Japan had no precedent to follow. No other nation had industrialized and reformed itself at such a rapid pace. Every other national economy had evolved over many decades. Only Germany had done this in less than 50 years. Could Japan manage to keep the Western powers at bay while it did so?

Third, how could the government convince the merchants to invest in the risky new commercial ventures? Three centuries of feudal rule had conditioned the merchants into very cautious and conservative men. Why would they risk their capital on uncertain industrial and commercial ventures when they could depend on a steady return on their money through traditional moneylending? Japan had learned from the West that the secret was in luring conservative capital into risky entrepreneurial schemes.

The first problem of funding was solved by placing some of Japan's most able men into the Finance Ministry. The road to political power in most developing nations runs through the military and through the Foreign Ministry. In Japan the early years of the Meiji Era saw people like Ōkubo, Inoue, Ōkuma, Mutsu, and Matsukata handling the country's finances. They watched over the land tax system with great care. They tinkered, altered, and adjusted it to Japan's reality. They managed to alleviate the peasant's worst fears and to cope with natural catastrophes like droughts, floods, typhoons, earthquakes, and fires. Through it all they kept the revenue constant and dependable. Commercial taxes had to be carefully watched as well. One had to be careful not to smother new businesses and industries with overtaxation (the mistake of China and many African and Latin American nations at similar points of economic growth). Bankers and rich merchants had to feel that the government finances were secure enough to warrant their trust. If the national treasury looked sound, then the wealthy would continue to keep their money in the banks. The Finance Ministry managed well enough. Japan took out only two modest foreign loans during the first half-century.

The second problem of expertise was solved through an ingenious scheme called ōyatoi ("Honorable Employees"), which referred to foreign experts hired by the government. Members of the Iwakura Mission were consulted to discover which nations excelled in particular industries. Japan then hired the best foreign technicians from those nations available for lucrative short-term (typically three years) contracts.

These men and women were government advisers and were forbidden to own Japanese property. Japanese learned the languages of the instructors and then in turn taught other Japanese what they had learned. For instance, Germans taught Japanese soldiers, physicians, chemists, and many other scientists; the French taught Japanese legal systems; the British instructed Japanese sailors, textile workers, and steelmakers; Americans taught elementary teachers the newly reformed educational system.

Because the ōyatoi did not speak Japanese (they were helped by interpreters), because they were in the country for only a short period (and then only as instructors and advisers), and because they were not allowed to own Japanese property, they did not build up personal cliques. All of Japan's modernized sectors were nationally controlled and free of foreign influence. The instructors were, after all, only "honorable employees."

The third problem, that of attracting investment capital, was the most difficult. In many sectors, the government had to create pilot industries to demonstrate new techniques and to create new markets. For instance, the government invested in British silk reeling machinery to show that the Japanese traditional handicraft could be mechanized. They bought iron foundries, shipyards, railways, and other industries to show Japan's entrepreneurs the way. In so doing, it also decreased the amount of risk for investors. A decade later, the government sold many of these pilot ventures to private investors.

Also, because Japan's new army and navy required much in the way of food supplies, uniforms, weapons and ammunition, as well as transportation and communication, the government contracts for these goods and services created a huge economic market and a boost for the new industries.

The building of the economic infrastructure was a collaborative effort between the government and private capital. In fact, the relations between members of government and the private economic sector were very cozy indeed. Lucrative government contracts went to friends and relatives of the bureaucrats and political leaders. Several of these "sweetheart" contracts led ultimately to scandals, but even those that did not were dangerously close to "insider" favoritism.

The era saw the foundations of many of Japan's greatest economic giants, most of them tied closely with friends and allies within the government. The financial-industrial clique Mitsubishi received outright gifts of merchant ships from the government; Mitsui and Sumitomo received generous government contracts in the industrialization of the island of Hokkaido based on favoritism and partiality. The Furukawa combine was allowed to poison an entire region of farmland with the tailings of the Ashio Copper Mine.

These financial cliques (zaibatsu) helped Japan industrialize rapidly, but not without considerable future cost to both the economy and to the political

structure as well. The unhealthy ties between the government and private industry seriously limited the development of a more open economy, and, more
dangerously, it made a more open political process very difficult as well.

ARMED REBELLION AND THE END OF AN ERA

Members of the government who had remained in Japan while the other
leaders were abroad on the Iwakura Mission had decided to punish Korea for
its arrogant treatment of Japanese diplomats early in 1873. When the Iwakura
Mission returned, however, the planned expedition was quashed. Those leaders who had been abroad understood that Japan needed to concentrate on
social, political, and economic reforms before becoming involved in foreign
adventures. In response, several leaders like Saigō Takamori, Itagaki Taisuke,
Gotō Shōjiro, and Etō Shimpei resigned in protest.

The Meiji reformers tried to channel this discontent by mounting a much
smaller expedition to Taiwan to punish the natives there who had murdered
some Japanese sailors. Saigō Tsugumichi, the younger brother of Takamori,
was placed in command in hopes that this would siphon much of the samurai
discontent. The expedition was a debacle. Although it resulted in China paying an indemnity and Japan receiving control over the Ryūkyū s, more Japanese died of tropical disease than Taiwanese died of combat wounds. Worse,
most of the discontented samurai refused to enlist, and their wounded pride
continued to fester. Talk of armed rebellion filled the air.

The first revolt was lead by Etō Shimpei of Hizen. This Saga Rebellion was
put down rather easily by the Imperial army, partially because Saigō Takamori
and the Kyushu samurai did not join Etō and his ragtag army. A few years
later Saigō joined other samurai in opposition to the government in what has
been called the Satsuma Rebellion of 1877.

Many samurai felt that this was an opportunity to cancel the government's
reform policies and to show their mettle against the conscript army. Saigō and
many others saw it as a chance to stop the wholesale social and political reforms that had destroyed the samurai way of life.

It hurt him to see so many samurai stripped of their pride and self-worth.
The recent reforms had left hundreds of thousands of them without jobs, without livelihood, and without self-respect. Even if the rebellion could give them
only an honorable death, it was worth it to most of the discontented samurai. Saigō committed suicide when the rebellion failed. Thousands of samurai
died as well; over 2,700 more were executed, and several thousand more were
imprisoned. A way of life died with them. This then, rather than the Meiji
Restoration a decade before, can be called the end of the feudal era and the
beginning of a new Imperial one.

The end of the first series of economic reforms came in 1881 when the government found itself in serious economic straits. The government had assumed the crushing weight of financial obligations owed by the various daimyō including han debts and samurai stipends. In an average year the government spent almost half of its revenue to pay these alone. In the mid-1870s the government had taken a European loan to help cover the samurai bond commutations. Added to this huge obligation were the costs involved in setting up pilot industries and creating the rest of the economic infrastructure of the new state. The "final straw," however, came when the government was forced to defend itself in the various rebellions at the end of the decade. The government had been forced to take another European loan to cover these expenses. It was very dangerous business to mortgage the nation's future to foreign bankers.

The government had temporarily paid their bills in the late 1870s in much the same manner of the Tokugawa Bakufu: by currency manipulation. They had simply printed more paper money. Before very long, however, this caused a huge inflationary spiral. The price of rice nearly doubled in two years. The government found it necessary to raise the tax rates to compensate, and before long, commodity prices and interest rates skyrocketed. The government was very near financial collapse.

The financial remedy for this economic illness was a very bitter pill to swallow. The new Finance Minister Matsukata Masayoshi had studied European economic theory and thought he had the classic solution: government deflation. This entailed cutting government expenses, tightening up the currency, lowering interest rates, and raising taxes. The first order of business was a fire sale of government-owned enterprises. The theory here was that if private investors would buy these companies, they would assume the huge financial obligations such as materials, labor, transportation, and insurance. Not only would the government be rid of those expenses, but now it could begin to collect commercial taxes on the now privately owned companies as well as on their employees.

Matsukata knew that no one would buy these companies at anything close to their actual worth. The huge start-up costs that had been paid by the government had to be forgotten. What was most important was to get them off the government's back and on to the tax rolls.

Matsukata and the Meiji reformers have been criticized by many historians for "giving away" these companies to their zaibatsu friends. But in reality, there were not many takers at even the ridiculously low prices at which they were offered. Many government leaders had to cajole their friends within the business and financial communities to take the chance. They argued that it was the patriotic duty of these former samurai to help their nation in this time of trial. The harsh reality is that only the zaibatsu could afford to take on such huge financial obligations. None of the companies sold in 1881 made a profit for many years. Many required continued government subsidies in the form of assured contracts, guaranteed low-interest loans, and temporary tax rebates. Eventually the zaibatsu would profit handsomely from these newly acquired industries, but in 1881 they were not an attractive short-term investment.

The Matsukata Deflation, as it is called, managed to save the Meiji government from financial ruin. But the price was a huge one, and it was paid primarily by the peasantry. When the price of rice skyrocketed, the peasantry did not benefit. In most cases they had sold their crops even before they were planted in order to meet other annual expenses. Nearly one-third of the farmers did not even own their own land anyway. Many had lost whatever they had in mortgage foreclosures or through forced land sales to pay their taxes. So, when interest rates and other prices shot skyward, the peasants lost even more. The numbers of farmers renting land (very often their own former land lost to moneylenders) increased dramatically so that by the end of the 1880s nearly 40 percent were tenant farmers.

Land rents were often more than 50 percent of the crop, so chances for economic prosperity for tenant farmers were grim indeed. The situation was made worse because many of the owners of these lands were absentee landlords. At least in the Tokugawa era the daimyō had a moral obligation to adjust their taxes in bad economic times. These new landlords never saw the plight of the farmers. All they wanted from them was their rent, even if it meant starvation for the peasants. Millions went to bed each night unfed. Peasants sold whatever they had, sometimes even their children. The brothels of Tokyo and Ōsaka teemed with farm girls who had been sold into the slavery of prostitution by their starving parents. The military was full of farm boys who could neither read nor write and who received their first pair of shoes and first "square" meal in their barracks.

A number of peasant revolts rose in protest, but for the most part, as historian Mikiso Hane has so eloquently phrased it, the peasants "starved to death in silence." Every revolt was quashed harshly by the government, who feared a general peasant rebellion. The Matsukata Deflation in many ways was the ruin of Japan's farmers. The nation was saved from bankruptcy; national industry and the zaibatsu prospered; but the peasantry suffered horribly.

INTELLECTUAL AND RELIGIOUS DEVELOPMENTS

Along with the social, economic, and political reforms of the early Meiji period, Japan experienced many fundamental changes in intellectual and religious life. The philosophical foundations and institutions were adapted to new realities.

Foremost among the intellectual currents was the rising nationalism that had helped destabilize the Tokugawa Bakufu. At the heart of the Sonnō-Jōi imperial restoration movement was the idea that native morals were superior to foreign ones. The main legitimizing principle for the new Meiji state was the special relationship that existed between the people and their emperor. The emperor was declared to be the one-hundred-twenty-third direct descendant of the Sun Goddess Amaterasu. Actual history was ignored and the Shinto lineage of the eighth-century *Kojiki* and *Nihongi* accepted as fact.

The believers of Kokugaku in the mid-nineteenth century had argued that the emperor was semidivine and therefore must rule. They had claimed that the foreign Chinese Neo-Confucian ideas of natural law had clouded the Japanese mind and that only a complete imperial restoration would save Japan from her foreign enemies. These ideas continued to have intellectual value among many in the early Meiji period. In fact, the first Meiji government included a Board of Shinto Ritual that was the equal to any other ministry.

In the early years Buddhism was either actively attacked or at best barely tolerated by these nationalists. Hundreds of temples were dismantled and Shinto shrines established in their places. But before very long, Buddhism began to make a comeback. This was due to the fact that most of the common people continued to believe in Buddhism, but it is also due to the fact that Shinto continued to have serious deficiencies as a national religion.

First, Shinto had long celebrated the rural communal passing of time. It celebrated the changing of seasons, the phases of the moon, and the agricultural seasons of planting and harvesting. These village festivals were more involved with celebrating and encouraging communal cooperation than they were in actual religious ritual. They were well suited to the rhythms of a rural countryside, but not very appropriate to the new urban population in Meiji Japan.

Second, Shinto still did not have a canon of holy scriptures like Buddhism enjoyed. It is difficult to create a political philosophy without a written theology. The *Kojiki* and *Nihongi* were primarily genealogical and historical in nature and were therefore ill suited as holy works. Not even the written commentaries of the Kokugaku school were appropriate because they were not "holy."

Third, Shinto did not have a moral code of conduct. Shinto dealt with that which was considered ritually polluted and inappropriate, but it had no firm ideas about sin or about punishment. How could a political philosophy be based on a religion that had no system of morality? The Western legal systems were all based on Christian principles of morality. The traditional Japanese system was based on Neo-Confucianism. But Shinto had no such principles.

Finally, Shinto did not have a national organization. Priests were really only hereditary caretakers of regional shrines without any real religious schooling and with no hierarchy of either religious or secular authority. Each shrine was autonomous in funding and administration. As noted previously, Shinto was actually more an expression of Japanese cultural community than it was a religion. It was a combination of many indigenous local cults, not a national faith.

The Meiji modernizers soon realized these problems. Within months after the establishment of the new government, they discovered that the Shinto Board of Ritual really had nothing to do. It served no administrative function. Yet they searched for some kind of native culturalism that could bind the nation together in the manner that Christianity served in unifying the various nations of the West. Because Neo-Confucianism was still associated with the decrepit and corrupt Chinese and with the failed Tokugawa Bakufu, they shied away from this familiar philosophy despite the fact that it would later be found to be eminently suitable for Japan.

The solution was to invent a new Shinto. This was accomplished by separating the secular and cultural aspects away from the religious aspects of Shinto. The religious was designated as Sect Shinto, and the national aspects were now called "Shrine" or "State" Shinto. The main imperial shrines at Ise, Atsuta, and Izumo (where the Imperial Regalia of mirror, sword, and gem were separately stored) were appropriated for State Shinto; the small local shrines were left to Sect Shinto.

The basis of the new State ideology was the semidivinity of the emperor. He was declared to be "sacred and inviolable," and any criticism of him was now considered to be treason. Indeed, by the end of the period, criticism was defined as questioning, and finally even discussion of the emperor's nature or limits of power bordered on treason. This madness, of course, made it simple work for his advisers and ministers to issue laws and edicts in his name because any resistance to an Imperial Edict or Rescript could be punished as treason. As we shall see, this would establish dangerous precedents for future governments.

Curiously, this Shintoist emperor would in 1889 grant a secular constitution. He would also issue an Imperial Rescript on Education that was fundamentally Neo-Confucian in nature, and he would also announce a Rescript to Sailors and Soldiers that denied them any political voice whatever.

The Rescript on Education would bring an end to liberal educational reform. The Meiji modernizers had experimented with British, American, and even Swiss systems of education. Educational ōyatoi were lured to Japan to help establish universal compulsory education. Unable to discover another social philosophy, the new Rescript now demanded that Japanese education be Neo-Confucian in content. The moral principles of filial piety and patriotism became more important than science and mathematics. Within a decade all students began the day by bowing in unison to a picture of the emperor and by reciting the Rescript. The emperor became a Shinto deity in this education.

Like his Heian imperial ancestors, this emperor had no real power. He was to be controlled by Fujiwara-like regents who were his ministers of state. The kuromaku "Black Curtain" of political puppetry descended on the Meiji emperor early in his reign.

The other intellectual schools of the Meiji era were primarily Western in origin. Partially because Japan wished to revise the hated Unequal Treaties, many of its political philosophers advocated Western-like ideology. If Japan resembled the West, they argued, it would be impossible for the West to continue to treat Japan unfairly.

Christianity made something of a comeback after 1873. A group of "Hidden" Christians had surfaced in the Nagasaki area and had approached the Roman Catholic French. These hardy folk had hidden their religion for nearly three centuries and now asked to be reunited with the European brethren. The new Meiji government at first started to persecute and disperse them, but ultimately they decided to legalize Christianity instead in order to avoid problems with the treaty nations. Many ex-samurai embraced the foreign faith as a ready-made vehicle for political dissent. Since the ideas of Western political liberalism were rooted firmly in Christianity, many of the members of the People's Rights and Freedom Movement (see next section) were Christians. At the end of the era many Japanese flocked to the ideas of Christian Socialism as well.

The various other Western political and social ideologies had their followers in Japan as well. The French as well as the British versions of Liberalism were very popular, particularly among the political outsiders. Positivism, Utilitarianism, Social Darwinism, and even Socialism, Marxism, and Anarchism had their followers. The Meiji oligarchy preferred the German Statist ideas of constitutional monarchy and authoritarianism, as we shall see.

The period was one of political and social experimentation, but it became increasingly more conservative and nativist as the era went on. By the end of the Meiji era Japan had drifted toward a dangerously antiforeignism nationalist ideology. Like the final years of the Tokugawa it would be very dangerous for political moderates. Many political liberals lost their lives or their political voice from the threat of nativist violence. There would be a return to the days of the Bakumatsu shishi assassin. It would represent a descent into madness.

MEIJI ERA POLITICAL DEVELOPMENTS

Japan's unique political system was a creative adaptation molded by a number of social and political pressures. The widespread samurai discontent at the end of the first decade of reform was wedded to increasing rural dissatisfaction with the economic policies brought on by the Matsukata Deflation of 1881.

Also, one must consider the effect of two mutually antagonistic pressures: the need for Westernization in order to revise the Unequal Treaties pitted against the rise of conservative nationalism. We might also throw into the mix the frustration of many former reformers against the creation of a regional political clique as well. All these pressures gave rise to the Movement for People's Rights and Freedom (*Jiyū Minken Undō*) that dominated the political scene in the late 1870s through the mid1880s.

When Saigō, Etō, Itagaki, and Gotō resigned from the government in 1873 as a result of the aborted Korean Expedition, the latter two Tosa men refused to join the others in rebellion. Instead Itagaki and Gotō began a peaceful campaign for political liberalization.

Itagaki and Gotō were both from Tosa and, like Etō from Hizen, were angry that men from Satsuma and Chōshū were beginning to take over the Meiji government. They were also upset that the government was becoming increasingly conservative and authoritarian in its outlook. The Tosa men gathered signatures for a grand petition demanding an immediate move toward liberal constitutional and elected representative government. They were heavily influenced by French liberal philosophers like Rousseau and Montesquieu who insisted that people received God-given political and civil rights. The Tosa petition echoed the liberal thoughts of Thomas Jefferson's Declaration of Independence as well as the French Declaration of the Rights of Man. But it also based its arguments in the first article of the Meiji Emperor's Charter Oath that called for "all matters of state . . . decided by public discussion."

The petitioners had in mind the immediate creation of prefectural legislatures, ultimately leading to a national constitution and a national legislature. Virtually every Meiji leader also believed in the necessity of those things, but the men within the government preferred a much more gradual approach. Naturally, those out of the government wanted an immediate sharing of actual power.

Since Kido Takayoshi had resigned in 1873 because of ill health, the government had become increasingly isolated. Only Ōkubo and Iwakura remained from the original group of men who had restored power to the emperor in 1868. Iwakura had become increasingly more of a figurehead, so Ōkubo found himself alone at the top with a few of the second generation of younger men: Ōkuma, Itō, Inoue, and Yamagata. Traditional Japanese politics preferred consensus and collaboration, so Ōkubo felt very uncomfortable alone at the top. Kido, Gotō, and Itagaki were lured back into the government in 1875 at a conference in Osaka. But all three drifted out again when it was apparent that the small oligarchy did not intend to really share power.

To their credit, the Tosa men did not rally to either Etō's or Saigō's call to arms. Itagaki and Gotō formed a political party, the Patriotic Party (*Aikokutō*) instead. They traveled around the country giving lectures and organizing groups of sympathizers. Even women were encouraged to attend and to participate. The *Sat-Chō* (the first syllables of Satsuma and Chōshū) oligarchy feared these mass demonstrations and responded by passing increasingly more restrictive laws bent on suppressing this political activity. But they could not ignore the popular pressures. The confrontation came to a head in 1881. By this time both Saigō and Kido had died in 1877, and Ōkubo had been assassinated a year later by Saigō's followers. The government was now in the hands of Chōshū men Itō, Yamagata, and Inoue; Matsukata and Saigō's younger brother Tsugumichi from Satsuma; and Ōkuma from Hizen.

It was a momentous year that saw the Matsukata Deflation, the rise of rural discontent, and a shocking financial scandal involving the zaibatsu development of Hokkaido. The oligarchy hoped to deflect much of the liberal criticism by an expression of its own support for a gradual move toward a constitution. A scheme was worked out within the government whereby the emperor asked for the advice of his ministers regarding the need for a constitution. A backstage consensus was to be reached whereby everyone would express admiration for a conservative constitution like that of Germany, and then the emperor could announce the creation of a commission to draft a constitution. Perhaps a few members of the liberals could be lured into the commission to give it legitimacy. The plan fell through when Ōkuma submitted his own preference for a British liberal constitution to be instituted immediately.

The oligarchy was livid with rage. Itō especially felt personally betrayed because Ōkuma had broken the traditional faith of consensus. Itō quickly engineered Ōkuma's dismissal from the government. As a concession to Ōkuma supporters, the oligarchy announced that a commission would be created to promulgate a constitution that would be granted a decade later by 1890.

Now the constitutional battle began. The Tosa men formed the Liberty Party (*Jiyūtō*) and Ōkuma the Constitutional Party (*Kaishintō*). Unfortunately the Jiyūtō and Kaishintō spent as much time criticizing each other as they did attacking the government. Also regrettably, a number of political meetings turned violent, and the oligarchy clamped down on the movement harshly. Ultimately Itagaki, Gotō, and Ōkuma resigned from their parties in the face of this violence.

For their part, the oligarchy members preferred the conservative constitutional monarchy of Bismarck's Germany. Itō had been impressed during his visit as part of the Iwakura Mission a decade before. He spent the next year, 1882–1883 studying various European constitutions as the head of the Meiji Constitutional Commission. Many other members came to Germany and Austria to sit at the feet of Itō's conservative political gurus Lorenz Von Stein and Rudolf Gneist. Even Itō's former Tosa opponents like Itagaki, Gotō, and Mutsu were lured there to be convinced. Not surprisingly, the Meiji

Constitution that was granted to the people by the emperor very much resembled that of Germany.

A cabinet was appointed by the emperor, and it—as were the military forces—was answerable only to him. An upper house of the parliament, called the Diet, after the German legislature, was to be similarly appointed by the emperor. Only the Lower House was to be elected by a very small group of voters. Its only power was over the budget, but the cabinet had the option to renew the budget of the previous year if it could not agree with the Lower House on a new one. A Privy Council served as advisers to the emperor, but because he appointed it, it could not be controlled by the voters. Duties as well as Rights of the People were specified, but all rights, privileges, and freedoms could be suspended by the emperor in times of national crisis.

So, the fact that the constitution was granted by the emperor implied that only he could limit his own power. The fact that he could rescind all rights meant that he was all-powerful. In reality it was his ministers, the Sat-Chō oligarchy, who retained and exercised power. The government was actually controlled by a very small clique of Satsuma and Chōshū men who were known as the "Senior Statesmen" (*genrō*). Most of the genrō either served in the government, alternating within the various ministries, or in the Privy Council. They saw the emperor as the legitimizing figurehead.

Also in 1890, the government issued a series of police security regulations. Article five of those regulations removed women from all political activity. "Activity" was later expanded to include not just political activities, but simply meeting in public. The very discussion of the Article was also considered to be illegal. So women were caught in a double-bind: They could not change the law because they could not even discuss it.

In 1898 a new Civil Code was enacted that established the family, not the individual, as the lowest legal unit. A "contempt for women," as historian Sharon Sievers has noted, "was now reemphasized, with official approval." Women were stripped of all legal rights and were in effect made the property of their male protectors. Women could not inherit or own property, they could not vote, they could not serve in political office. They could not divorce even criminal or insane husbands. In short, they lost all civil rights. The oligarchy had reestablished a feudal control over the female half of the population in the name of traditional family values. They only wished that they could control the male half as easily.

From time to time various leaders like Ōkuma, Itagaki, Gotō, and Mutsu from the political parties would be lured into the government as individuals, but for all intents and purposes, the new constitution and the government were Sat-Chō creatures. The political parties tried their best to harass and embarrass the government, primarily on the floor of the Lower House and through the press. Their primary "ammunition" for this harassment was the government's failure to revise the hated and humiliating Unequal Treaties.

TREATY REVISION: A NATIONAL CRUSADE

The Unequal Treaties were thorns in the side of all Japanese for over 40 years. They had made Japan's economic reforms difficult. The Scheduled Tariff that limited Japan's rights to impose customs duties on imports also did not allow Japan to protect its native products abroad or at home. How could Japan build, say, a steel industry if it could not raise the tariff on imported steel? Japan's new industries had to charge higher prices for its products because of Japan's huge start-up costs. The older Western industries had already paid their early costs and were now able to bring prices down to where Japan could not compete.

The economic problems caused by the treaties were significant, of course; but the psychological humiliation was much worse. At a time when Japan was turning increasingly back toward traditional cultural norms, the treaties kept reminding everyone of Japan's humiliation at the hands of the West. From very early on in the Meiji era the revision of the treaties became something of a national crusade.

As it had in the economic crisis, Japan put its greatest minds to work here as well. A number of very able men tried to revise the treaties in the early years while Japan was modernizing and reforming. After his duties in the Finance Ministry were over, Inoue Kaoru became the Foreign Minister for nearly a decade in the late 1870s and 1880s. He struggled with the problems of treaty revision and was very nearly successful in 1887, but internal domestic politics doomed his careful and laborious work.

He had skirted the reverse effect of the Most Favored Nation clause of the treaties by calling conventions of all the powers in Tokyo in 1882–1884 and again in 1886–1887. There, he could iron out the most difficult problem of revision: international jealousies. By discussing all of the needs of the individual nations, he could force them to compromise lest they leave looking like ingrates, spoilsports, and greedy imperialists. The thorniest issue was not economic. It was the problem of Consular Jurisdiction. How could the 17 nations risk submitting their citizens to a Japanese justice system that was not completely reformed?

Japan had been struggling with legal reforms for two decades, but it found that a nation's laws are closely tied to precedent and to cultural ethics. The laws reflect the nation's morality. Because Japan did not subscribe to the Christian idea of the brotherhood of man, much less the divinely inspired wisdom of the church (any church!), its laws were very different from any European or American ideal. Inoue found the solution for the problem in Egypt. The

British had instituted a Mixed Court system whereby British justices sat together with Egyptian judges whenever foreigners were tried. Japan could do the same as its laws continued to be reformed and codified. Foreign justices could sit on Japanese courts to ensure that all foreigners would receive equal justice.

The newly developed political parties, however, had seized upon the failure of the government to revise the Unequal Treaties as a political issue. Like the Sonnō-Jōi movement had criticized the bakufu twenty years before, the new parties now took the Meiji government to task for not having rid the nation of these humiliating treaties. Inoue was attacked in the press for currying favor with the West and for his alleged failure to "clear the mind" of the emperor of this shame and humiliation. The Mixed Court compromise merely ensured that Japan would continue to be treated as less than equal in the eyes of the world.

Among those who was loudest in his criticism of Inoue had been his former Finance Ministry rival, Ōkuma Shigenobu. Inoue's ally Itō Hirobumi suggested that if Ōkuma could do any better, then perhaps he should try. Ōkuma was coerced and shamed into accepting the Foreign Ministry in 1888 and very nearly accomplished the revision. In fact, he used his other Finance Ministry rival, Mutsu Munemitsu (who was now Minister to Washington), to negotiate a trial equal treaty with Mexico. As the other treaty powers were mulling over this attempt, Japan's domestic politics brought the revision to a crashing halt again.

An attempted bomb assassination by a zealot cost Ōkuma a leg and nearly his life. This return to violence in politics dangerously threatened Japan's attempts at peaceful civilian control of the population. For the next decade the threat of violence hung ominously over the country. It was not limited to Japanese politicians alone. The Crown Prince of Russia in 1890 and the Chinese ambassador, Li Hongzhang, in 1895 were both targets of assassination attempts as well. Both cost Japan dearly in terms of international humiliation.

The treaties were not revised until Mutsu became Foreign Minister in 1892. Even then it required all of his considerable intelligence as well as the backing of the entire cabinet to accomplish this national crusade of forty years. He was finally able to convince Great Britain that her best interests lay in recognizing Japan's reforms. For Great Britain and Japan shared much, including a fear of Russian expansion into northeast Asia. Mutsu finally accomplished the revision of the treaties shortly before Japan's first "modern" war with China, but not without considerable trouble with domestic politics.

Because Mutsu was also tied to his adopted homeland of Tosa, his relations with the Jiyūtō were very strong. He had been imprisoned for nearly four years because of his part in a Tosa plot against the government at the time of the Satsuma Rebellion. He had been rehabilitated by Itō and Inoue and had been sent abroad to study with Stein and Gneist. He had served as Inoue's assistant in the treaty revision conferences in the 1880s. After having served as Minister to Washington, he had been invited into the government by the oligarchy in order to compromise with the Jiyūtō within the Lower House. He and Gotō had passed along huge bribes to their friends in the Jiyūtō in order to pass budgets in the Lower House.

Mutsu then used his considerable influence in the Jiyūtō to silence much of the criticism within the House. He had used his strength within the oligarchy through his patron Premier Itō to keep the cabinet united while he negotiated in secret with the British. After some skirmishes with a number of antiforeign movements in late 1893 and early 1894, he finally concluded a revision with Great Britain in July 1894. That was just two weeks before Japan went to war with China.

The treaties were more than merely a humiliation and an inconvenience for Japan. They were the driving force for reform during the era. Many of the reforms were accomplished simply because Japan needed to change in order to revise the treaties. The treaties symbolized Japan's continued inferiority in the eyes of the world. Japan could never hope to ensure its independence until it was recognized as the equal of every other nation. The treaties had to be revised in order to do that. The next step after revision was to enter the "game" of imperialism. In order to be strong, Japan had to acquire territory for economic and political expansion. It could only do that by military means.

EARLY IMPERIALISM: 1894–1915

The next political path that Japan chose to follow was in many ways the most natural and logical choice: military imperialism. Regrettably, the nature of world politics in the late nineteenth century mandated that if a nation was not to be the "hunted," it must be a "hunter." Weaker societies and cultures were to be conquered and colonized; stronger nations benefited from the work of weaker ones. World imperialism was a game played by the "law of the jungle: kill or be killed."

The most recent scramble for colonies was really the second time that Western nations had attempted to partition the world up into empires. The first race in the sixteenth and seventeenth centuries was for territory. Portugal, Spain, England, France, and the Netherlands had acquired lands all over the world and had colonized them for their own benefit. The second race was for commercial markets and for control of natural resources. The Dutch, Portuguese, and Spanish were no longer active players; they struggled to hang on to bits of their former empires. England and France had been joined by the newly developed nations of Germany, Russia, and America. These five nations were now attempting to carve up the world into economic "spheres of influence." All sought not only the vital raw materials with which to feed their growing industries but also the essential markets as outlets for their manufactured products.

Now Japan wanted to join the game. In part this was the logical next step if it was to become a strong independent nation. It was also because the Japanese had been taught by their Western ōyatoi instructors that the world functioned by Social Darwinist natural laws of the "survival of the fittest." These ideas, made popular in Japan in the translations of the European philosopher Herbert Spencer, suggested that just as Charles Darwin's theory of "natural selection" taught that only the stronger, more "evolved" species triumphed over weaker and less well adapted species, similar natural laws governed human civilization. Japan wanted to survive and to triumph; the natural way to do this was to prey on the weak.

Unfortunately, there were not many people in Japan who disagreed with these ideas. Even Fukuzawa Yukichi, who had preached the benefits of "civilization and enlightenment" and who had been an early champion of rights for women and other political minorities, fell into line behind those who wished to colonize Asia. Itō, Ōkuma, Yamagata, Inoue, and Mutsu—who had all been dead-set against the Korean Expedition in 1873—were among the leaders who marched Japan off to war in 1894. It had not been that they were against war in general twenty years before; they had been against it because it would have been premature. Now because Japan was a mature, fully developed nation, war was an appropriate and logical step on the way to world wealth and power. Only a very few Christian Socialists and an even smaller number of pacifists spoke out against war on moral and intellectual principles.

Japan had already taken a few first faltering steps toward imperialism in 1874 in the Taiwan Expedition. It had won the Ryūkyū Islands and a large indemnity from China at that time, so it knew that the fruits of victory could be sweet indeed. But for the next 20 years Japan had bided its time and husbanded its resources.

The Sat-Chō oligarchy had carefully steered around any possible snags in foreign affairs by playing the game of world diplomacy. It negotiated whenever it could, studiously avoiding any confrontation until it felt secure enough to join the game. Japan was fortunate that the world had been involved in American and European squabbles after the "opening" of Japan in 1854. The Crimean War, the Sepoy Mutiny in India, wars in Afghanistan, the American Civil War, and the Franco-Prussian War had kept East Asia out of the limelight.

Recently, however, the stage had shifted to China. The corrupt Manchu dynasty there had nearly collapsed of its own inefficient weight. At one time in the mid-1860s two-thirds of the country was under the control of one of four simultaneous rebellions. When the landed Chinese gentry had propped up the tottering dynasty, the Western powers had rushed in to claim the economic spoils. Japan had warily stood by as Britain and France seized former Chinese territories in the various small wars and skirmishes of the late nineteenth century. It had kept its silence when one European nation after another carved China up "like a melon" into economic spheres of influence. It had avoided war with China in Korea in the 1870s and 1880s, but now the time seemed ripe for Japan to seize a few scraps before China exploded into civil war and chaos.

FIRST SINO-JAPANESE WAR: 1894–1895

The issue was Korea. Japan had been obsessed for good reasons with the "Hermit Kingdom" for nearly 2,000 years. The two civilizations shared much in the way of cultural, religious, and even genetic origins. Korea had been a pathway for the sharing of Chinese civilization for thousands of years, and the politics of the two nations were often intertwined.

When Otto von Bismarck, the Chancellor of Germany, had told the Iwakura Mission in the 1870s that Korea was "a dagger pointing at the heart of Japan," it was not news to Japan. The Mongols had used the Korean Peninsula as a staging area and causeway for invasion attempts in the thirteenth century. Hideyoshi had reversed the conduit when he attempted to invade China in the 1590s. Japan feared that some other power might use the natural path.

Because Korea was part of China's "Tributary Empire," Japan feared that a political vacuum in China would lead to trouble on the peninsula. In the 1880s, Itō Hirobumi had signed the Treaty of Tientsin with China to ensure that Korean problems would not lead to an accidental war. In late 1893 a native rebellion forced the Korean dynasty to call for Chinese help. The Treaty of Tientsin required that China notify Japan if it needed to send troops to Korea; it did so now.

Japan saw this as an opportunity to settle the "Korean Question" to her own benefit. Premier Itō called an emergency cabinet meeting wherein Foreign Minister Mutsu convincingly argued that China might use this Korean crisis to strengthen its control over the peninsula. It was decided that Japan must send an equal number of troops to counterbalance Chinese influence. The Chinese, of course, objected, and for two months the two nations petulantly tried to stare each other down.

Both claimed that the other was threatening war, but it is clear from Mutsu's telegraph correspondence with his minister in Seoul that Japan meant to "fish in troubled waters." In the meantime, Korea quashed its domestic rebellion without help from either the Chinese or Japanese.

In the meantime, Mutsu was furiously trying to steer the treaty revision talks with Great Britain to a conclusion. It is clear in mid-July 1894 that he was prepared to compromise with the British because he feared the outbreak of war before the treaty could be revised. Revision was essential; it meant that Great Britain could not use the instability of war to extort more concessions.

The treaty was signed on July 16; Mutsu then cabled his minister authorizing him to let the war begin. Two weeks later a series of incidents drove the two nations to battle. Japanese troops stormed the Korean palace to capture the regent; Japanese ships stopped a Chinese ship on the high seas and sank it; over 1,200 men went to the bottom of the sea as well.

At its outset, most nations expected a short war, with China as a victor. China had more men and more modern military equipment, including nearly double the number of modern warships. The British Navy, which had trained the sailors of both countries, knew better. Within months the Chinese sued for peace. Japan won virtually every battle and skirmish and now threatened the very capital of China.

Historians have long argued the reasons for Japan's easy victory. Three things are clear. First, Japan was united. The southern part of the modern Chinese navy was never even involved. It was controlled by regional warlords who did not wish to risk their power in what they thought was a "northern problem." The various Chinese leaders squabbled among each other. In Japan, however, Itō and Mutsu had the solid support not only of the oligarchy but of the entire country. The Japanese opposition parties nearly fell over themselves in their haste to support the war effort. It was difficult to know who was in charge in China. Many Chinese leaders wished for defeat in order to embarrass their rivals.

Second, Japan had better military leadership. Japan had learned its lessons from the ōyatoi. It had reorganized its conscript army into a German-style staff command structure with a civilian Army Minister in the Cabinet, a military Chief of Staff over a pyramid of generals, and officers commanding a similar structure, of soldiers. The Navy employed a similar command structure following the British Admiralty model. The officers of both services had all attended military academies, and all the enlisted men had received rigorous and constant training. The Chinese forces were badly led by a ragtag bunch of incompetent imperial princes, corrupt warlords, and timid bureaucrats.

Finally, Japan was much better served by its industrial sector than China was by its. The cozy relationship between the oligarchy and the zaibatsu made the supply of the military effort quick and efficient. China relied heavily on foreign suppliers. Additionally, many Chinese merchants felt no sense of patriotism and seized this opportunity to sell inferior equipment and supplies to the dynasty. Stories are told of how Chinese artillery shells were useless because they were filled with sand instead of gun powder; or of entire shipments of rifles being worthless because they had not been fitted with real firing mechanisms. Spoiled food, corroded equipment, and other worthless supplies doomed a Chinese army that was already hopelessly incompetent.

Troop morale was understandably poor; thousands of soldiers deserted, and many more surrendered quickly, often before battles even began.

When China sued for peace, the Japanese followed the lead of the Western diplomatic protocol: namely, to the victor go the spoils. Itō and Mutsu arrogantly issued what they knew were unreasonable demands. China stalled. Ironically, after some early squabbling, China sent as its representative to the peace negotiations the very man who had signed the Treaty of Tientsin with Itō a decade before.

Li Hongzhang, who had been one of China's most powerful men for three decades, had recently been under house arrest in China, having fallen into disfavor with the corrupt dynasty. He came to Shimonoseki, the seat of Chōshū power (after all, Itō was premier, and Yamagata was army chief of staff), to try to limit Japan's demands. Tragically for Japan, a madman tried to assassinate Li, and Japan hurriedly had to apologize. The emperor sent his personal physician to attend Li's wounds.

Itō and Mutsu were forced to scale back their demands. The ones they finally won were harsh enough. The Treaty of Shimonoseki won the outright cession of Taiwan; a huge indemnity to pay Japan's war costs (China paid for the bullets used to kill Chinese soldiers!); Korea renounced its Chinese tributary status and was declared independent; and Japan was given a leasehold over the Liaoning Peninsula, gateway to Manchuria and adjacent to Korea.

The Japanese celebration was very brief. Within days, Russia, Germany, and France announced that they would not allow China to be "dismembered." Japan must not be allowed to carve away Manchuria from China; it must return Liaoning. Nothing was said about Taiwan or Korea, but Japan was counseled to demand an increase in its indemnity in lieu of Liaoning.

For a few days the public mood in Japan demanded war with the Europeans, but cooler heads prevailed. Mutsu in particular was forceful in his pragmatic arguments within the cabinet. It would be foolish, he reasoned, for Japan to enter a war with any one of those powers so soon after a war with China. It would be absolute madness to fight all three. He bitterly accepted the criticism of his countrymen for having allowed this Triple Intervention, as it was called. He died two years later with that shame instead of the praise he so richly deserved for revising the treaties and for the Treaty of Shimonoseki.

The Japanese neither forgot nor forgave. They had won Liaoning with blood, it had been lost to the European bullies by threat. It must be won again. Korea had been the cause for war with China, Liaoning would be cause for war with Russia in 1904, and unfortunately, with China again in 1931.

A DECADE OF WAR PREPARATION: 1895–1904

In the decade between Japan's first two wars, the country experienced tremendous economic growth as well as a number of triumphs in foreign affairs.

But in the eyes of many of the genrō oligarchs, it was a decade of preparation for war with Russia.

Germany and France benefited from their part in the Triple Intervention, being rewarded with extensions of their spheres of influence in China. But Russia added insult to Japan's injury by negotiating a 99-year lease over the same Liaoning Peninsula that she had helped to take from Japan. Russia built a spur off its Trans-Siberian Railroad down through Manchuria to Darien at the tip of the peninsula. There it established the first warm-water port in its empire, which was christened Port Arthur. It created a formidable armada to protect its growing mineral and commercial ventures. Japan could only watch in anger.

The end of the nineteenth century saw some surprising changes in Japanese foreign affairs. Mutsu lived long enough to help negotiate a number of revised treaties. The United States, Germany, and even Russia quickly followed Great Britain's lead, and by 1899 all of the 17 nations had renounced their extraterritorial privileges. Parts of the Scheduled Tariff continued until 1911, but for the most part the end of the century saw the end of Japan's treatment as an inferior in the world.

In 1900 another crisis in China brought Japan both some long-awaited recognition as well as additional headaches with Russia. An antiforeign religious movement in northeast China called the Boxer Rebellion swept up the coast and into Beijing as thousands of Chinese Christian converts and hundreds of foreigners were butchered and burned. The fleeing foreigners established a defense perimeter in the capital and called for help. Japan sent a brigade of soldiers that constituted over one-third of the entire international relief expedition.

Interestingly, the Japanese were the only soldiers who did not engage in the holocaust of rape, torture, killing, looting, burning, and other atrocities committed by foreign troops. Japan received much praise from Western governments, and its troops were given a place of honor in the victory parade. But the Boxer affair created more problems with Russia. Russia refused to withdraw its troops from northern China in the time specified. It tried to use this opportunity to extend its influence into Korea as well as northern China. Japan appealed to the rest of the world, but with little success.

The United States was more interested with its own problems resulting from the Spanish-American War of 1898 and the subsequent Philippine Insurrection. Great Britain was involved with its own problems with the Boers in South Africa. But the British seemed to be interested when Japan suggested an alliance against Russian expansion into Asia.

The threat posed by Russia represented by its beginning of the Trans-Siberian Railroad in 1891 had been a major reason why Great Britain had revised its treaty with Japan in 1894. Several British leaders had then expressed an interest in an Anglo-Japanese alliance. Now with Russia's moves into

Manchuria and Korea, Great Britain's interests coincided with those of Japan quite nicely.

The alliance, signed in 1902, was the first between Western and Eastern nations. It guaranteed both nations the neutrality of the other in the event of war with another nation. But, if either went to war with two or more nations, the other would become an active ally. In other words, when (not if) Japan fought Russia, Britain would keep any other nation from joining Russia. There would be no more Triple Interventions.

RUSSO-JAPANESE WAR: 1904–1905

Two years after concluding the Anglo-Japanese Alliance, after a long, frustrating series of discussions with Russia, Japan broke off diplomatic relations. On February 8, 1904, the Japanese navy attacked and sank much of the Russian fleet at Port Arthur before issuing a formal declaration of war. Japan felt that Russia had cheated in the Triple Intervention and after the Boxer Rebellion. Why, then, should Japan be bound by the niceties of an international law that Russia did not respect?

The rest of the world was sure that the Japanese had gone mad. It was one thing to challenge the weakened and divided Chinese to a fight; it was quite another to go to war with a Christian Western empire the size of Russia. Again, the Japanese proved the experts wrong. She won nearly every battle, and within months Russia began to explore possibilities for peace.

The reasons for Japan's stunning victory are similar to those of the Sino-Japanese War a decade before. Japan was united, Russia was not. Japanese military leadership was superior, Japanese supply lines were better, the Japanese military was better trained and had superior morale.

Japan's domestic sector was in better shape as well. Russia's economy was in shambles, and revolution broke out in 1905 right in the middle of the war. In Japan, the solid wall of domestic support was cracked by a growing pacifist movement, but it was still small and relatively insignificant. By and large, the political parties supported the oligarchy.

Japan's early stunning victories created a sense of euphoria throughout the country. There was wild talk of conquering all of Russia and seizing everything east of the Ural mountains. Even the more realistic Japanese expected a huge indemnity to pay the American and British loans that Japan had floated to finance the war. Japan's costs were much higher this time, and her losses were much greater than the war against China. Several of Japan's victories had been very costly in manpower. The Battle of Mukden alone cost nearly seventy thousand Japanese casualties.

The Russians had put their trust in three misconceptions. First, they knew that their troops could withstand the frigid cold better than the Japanese. When winter came in 1904, they were sure that Japan would not make much head-way in the frozen wasteland of northern Manchuria, much less Siberia. The Japanese had trained long and hard in their own winter wasteland, Hokkaido. They were well prepared and taught the Russians a thing or two about winter warfare, placing men and equipment on sleighs and skis.

Second, Russia knew that its supply lines were superior because the Japa-nese had to supply by sea and then haul materials through the mountainous Korean Peninsula. Russia would be supplied by the Trans-Siberian Railroad and by the South Manchurian Railway down to Port Arthur. Of course the Japanese cut off Russia's southern supply lines when they took Port Arthur at the beginning of the war. Because Japan controlled the seas for the first 14 months, it also managed to establish supply ports high up the coast of Korea and even along the Liaoning Peninsula a thousand miles closer.

The Trans-Siberian Railroad was a mixed blessing for Russia because it was single-track and sidings were several hundred miles apart. Long delays re-sulted when trains broke down along the way because it was impossible to go around them. All too often, locomotives had to be tipped over in order to get the following train through. Empty railroad cars sat in Vladivostok for weeks because they had to await a lull in eastward traffic to send trains back toward Moscow; all of the sidings were full too.

Third, the Russians put great store in the "relief column" of the Baltic Fleet that set sail late in the war. The 46 ships represented a formidable force supe-rior to the number of ships that Japan used to control the Yellow Sea around Korea and Liaoning. But, Great Britain kept its word. It did not allow the Bal-tic Fleet to sail through the Suez Canal, forcing it to spend nearly two months circling Africa. Neither did Great Britain allow the Russians to provision or repair in South Africa, India, Singapore, Hong Kong, or any of its colonial ports along the way.

Worse, the Russian admiral, Z. P. Rozhdestvensky, made a fatal mistake of entering Japanese waters in the fog. He hoped to slip through the Strait of Tsushima between Korea and Kyushu on his way to Vladivostok instead of circling Japan eastward on the high seas. But the Japanese fleet under Tōgō Heihachirō sat waiting patiently in the fog. Within 90 minutes the Japanese had sunk or captured half of the Baltic Fleet. This famous "crossing" of the Russian "T" formation of May 27–28, 1905, was over in 36 hours. Only 12 Russian ships escaped; 34 were sunk or captured. Nearly 5,000 Russians were killed, another 6,000 captured. Japanese losses: 3 ships, 116 men killed.

But again, the Japanese celebrations were short lived. The negotiations for peace dragged on endlessly during the summer of 1905 in Portsmouth, New Hampshire, where the American President Theodore Roosevelt urged the ne-gotiators to settle. The Russians clearly were stalling for time in hopes that their government could recover from the 1905 Revolution and rearm. The Japanese became quickly exasperated by Russian stubbornness.

Worse, their host, Roosevelt, although more sympathetic to Japan than to backward Russia, did not wish to have Japan emerge too strong a force in Northeast Asia. He hinted broadly that the "world" wanted a quick end to the war and urged the Japanese to accept whatever they were offered.

On paper, the Treaty of Portsmouth seemed to have granted Japan all it had demanded at the beginning of the war. Japan received Liaoning and Korea. It won the South Manchurian Railway, the southern portion of Sakhalin, and the Kurile Islands. But there was no indemnity and no Russian territory.

Violent protest erupted in Japan, and the Portsmouth negotiators were nearly ripped apart when they returned. Japan felt cheated again. The negotiators made it clear that they had felt threatened by Roosevelt, so the Americans became the scapegoats for this new humiliation. Not that the Americans did not deserve much of the blame for a worsening of Japanese-American relations within the next decade.

JAPAN COMES "OF AGE": 1906–1915

American newspapers were full of anti-Asian paranoia. The threat of the combined Chinese-Japanese "Yellow Peril" rang even in the American houses of Congress. Months after Japan had donated huge amounts to help the survivors of the San Francisco earthquake, it was rewarded for its kindness by the School Board there that passed laws against allowing Japanese immigrant children to attend school with "normal" children. A vicious antialien movement (ironically, lead by a recent Irish immigrant) swept California attacking Chinese, Koreans, and Japanese, hoping to drive away their cheap labor.

The American government bullied Japan into signing what is ironically called the Gentlemen's Agreement (a British humorist said he failed to find any Gentlemen in the Agreement) in 1907. Japan promised to discontinue most Japanese immigration to the United States and Hawaii and to prevent Japanese laborers already in Hawaii from coming to the American mainland. That same year Roosevelt sent a thinly veiled threat in the guise of a "friendly" visit by America's Great White Fleet. Visions of Commodore Perry danced in Japanese heads.

In 1908 the United States announced to the world its intentions to maintain a strong military presence in the Pacific by establishing a naval base at Pearl Harbor in Hawaii. Many Japanese thought that this was as provocative as Russia's Port Arthur. One newspaper wondered how Americans would feel if Japan established a naval facility in Cuba?

In the meantime, Japan consolidated its position in Asia. It assumed control of Manchuria and began to fill the railroad cars of the South Manchuria

Railroad with iron ore, coal, and other natural resources wrenched from its rocky soil. In Korea, Japan established a "protectorate" and began to bleed the peninsula of agricultural and mineral riches. In 1910 Japan dropped all pretenses and annexed Korea as a reprisal for the assassination of Governor Itō Hirobumi by a Korean patriot. Koreans were treated very harshly by their Japanese "brothers." It would only get worse.

In Taiwan, Japanese administrators had been "civilizing" that island since 1895. Japanese plantations and industries abused Taiwanese labor. Even the administration of the "enlightened governor," Gotō Shimpei, rivaled the arrogance of any Western colonial power. Taiwanese children were educated, but not in their own language or in their history and culture, but rather those of Japan. Much was made by the Japanese of their improvements in hygiene, public works, and industry. Most of these humanitarian projects, however, were for the benefit of the few thousand Japanese colonists and administrators.

Unfortunately for the people of Japan's new empire, the Japanese had learned how to be imperialists from the West. The Taiwanese, Koreans, and Manchurians were no better off than the people of India, Burma, Algeria, Vietnam, Puerto Rico, or the Philippines (or the Indians of America for that matter).

Japan spent the final years of the Meiji era adjusting to its new world environment. As the world slipped down towards a world war, Japan dabbled in Chinese continental affairs. Many people in Japan sympathized with the various Chinese reformers and revolutionaries who made Tokyo their home in exile. Sun Yat-sen, who would become the "Father of Modern China," based his Nationalist Party or GMD (Guomindong) there and gathered many like-minded men around him.

When the revolution finally toppled the Manchu dynasty in October 1911, Sun continued to receive support from Japanese friends. But when the new Republican government was captured by the warlord Yuan Shikai in 1912, Sun and many of his GMD followers returned to Japan in exile. Japanese foreign policy toyed with Yuan. Japanese bankers rushed to wallow in the spoils with financiers from all over the world. He needed lots of money to "modernize" China and was only too willing to mortgage Chinese mineral and natural resources to get it. A new scramble for concessions ensued. Japan joined the rest of the world at the trough.

When war broke out in Europe in 1914, Japan honored the Anglo-Japanese Alliance (it had been renewed in 1911) declaring war against Britain's enemies. For its part of the war, Japan attacked the German base in China's Shandong Peninsula and then held the captured territory as spoils of war.

Because Japan was protecting British interests in China for the duration of the war anyway, it assumed the unofficial role of Protector of Allied interests there. In 1915, as a "logical extension" of that task, Japan issued what have been called the Twenty-One Demands to Yuan. Basically, these demands required that China surrender almost all sovereignty to Japan until the end of the war. Yuan would not be allowed to make any treaties, agreements, or arrangements with any foreign power without Japan's consent. This was to prevent giving aid and comfort to the enemies of the Allies, but in reality it was an attempt to extend Japanese control and influence over the whole continent.

The wily Yuan knew that he did not stand a chance of resisting Japan's demands alone. He appealed to the Allies, and when they did not seem overly sympathetic, he sprang a surprise on the Japanese. He declared war against the Central Powers, and in one brilliant stroke of genius, he became an ally of Japan. What need was there of a "Protector" now? China had joined Great Britain, France, Italy, and Russia, so it would protect their common interests without Japanese help.

The Allies tempered Japanese demands, asking it to cooperate with Yuan in their common war efforts. Stung by this masterful ploy, Japan seethed but had to play along. Japanese commercial interests had rushed into the vacuum created by the war anyway, and now Japan was China's greatest trading partner. Japanese goods replaced British, French, and American products in China's markets. Japan rode out the war making millions but biding its time regarding extending political control on the continent.

6

Prewar Japan

Domestic politics in the three decades after its first war held much promise for Japan. The time saw the maturation of the political parties and a lessening of power for the Sat-Chō oligarchy. Various methods of power-sharing were tried, and by 1920 the idea of "party cabinets" had lost its novelty; it was the order of the day. Difficulties in trying to control the growing independence of the military services plagued the period, but in general, the future looked bright for parliamentary government. By 1925 Japan was at the forefront of the world's democracies, being one of only a handful of nations that allowed all of its adult males to vote.

The road toward true parliamentary government was a rocky one. The political parties that controlled the Lower House of the Diet had struggled with the oligarchy from the very first. It seemed to be an unfair fight because the constitution severely limited the power of opposition parties, leaving only the budget to its control. But the parties used this power effectively to extort concessions. It became nearly impossible for the oligarchy to function on the previous year's budget, the loophole provided by the constitution. Growing government expenses demanded an equally expanding budget.

The first few Diets had been managed by the oligarchy primarily by the liberal use of bribes. When that no longer proved to be effective, the government

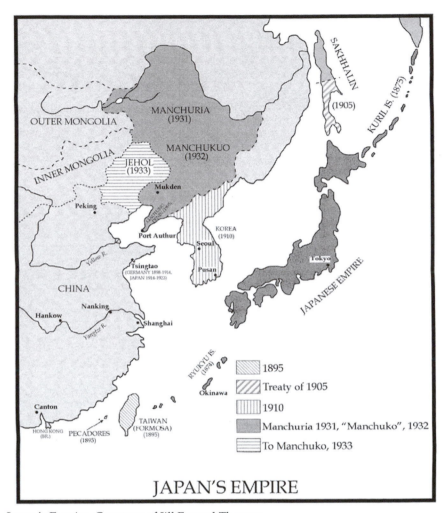

Japan's Empire. Courtesy of Jill Freund Thomas.

resorted to physical intimidation, dissolution of the House, and disruption of political rallies and elections; none to very great effect.

Through this period the parties had used the growing power of the press to embarrass and attack the government primarily over the issue of treaty revision. The oligarchy had tried early on to siphon off some discontent by bringing members of the parties into the cabinet. Gotō and Mutsu were prime examples of this practice.

A major stumbling block on the road to true parliamentary government was the Meiji Constitution. This document was the result of nearly a decade of consideration led primarily by Itō Hirobumi, who has been called the "Father of the Meiji Constitution." The conservative oligarchy wished to preserve order in a gradual transition toward a wider sharing of power. The genrō distrusted the party politicians and feared any form of government that had to take the whims of the landless, uneducated, common people into consideration. The constitution reflected this fear of the "rabble."

There were five constitutional problems. First and primary was the problem of choosing a premier. A fiction was created that the emperor alone chose his premier; nowhere in the constitution was there a provision for how it actually worked. The reality was that the Sat-Chō genrō collectively determined who the man was to be and then the emperor legitimized that choice.

In the early years it was easy because the genrō merely "shuffled the cards" and alternated in the cabinet posts themselves. When Itō was not premier, perhaps Yamagata would be. Some members did not rise to the pinnacle, but all seven served in one post or another. These Genrō Cabinets usually worked well enough because all the members had the same general goals in mind. Even the political opposition would grudgingly admit that the genrō were patriots with the future of the country as their primary concern.

The second basic problem was with the genrō concept of "transcendental cabinets." The idea was that whatever cabinet ruled, the basis for its decisions had to "transcend" politics. Government had to ignore all personal, regional, and political considerations to act for the good of the entire country. There should be no favoritism or prejudice in the minds of the ministers—every decision must "transcend" politics. The cabinet must "float above the clouds" was Yamagata's favorite metaphor.

Of course this idea was hypocritical. It was used to criticize the actions of politicians and to keep them from forming party cabinets. Every one of the genrō personally benefited from their government service, and every one of them favored friends and allies when it came to granting government contracts. Inoue was sometimes known as the Mitsui Clerk because he served as that zaibatsu's paymaster to other genrō and as the conduit for political bribes.

All of the genrō accepted gifts and favors from zaibatsu, as did the leaders of the political parties. The difference was that the genrō thought these things to be legitimate perquisites (privileges) of power. They, after all, were transcendent in their decision making. They did not have to curry favor with anyone; they did not have to run for elections. When the politicians accepted gifts and favors, however, these became bribes intended to elicit favoritism.

A third constitutional problem was the succession of the genrō. Because they appeared nowhere in the constitution, there was no machinery for their replacement. Because they had rotated in cabinet offices, a real vacuum arose when they began to retire due to ill health or when they died. By 1910 half of them were dead, and by 1915 only Yamagata was still in full control of his mental faculties. Ōkuma would have been a possible addition had he not been ousted from the government in 1881 and had he not formed his own party. Mutsu was another, but he died in 1897 as had Gotō. Who would be the new genrō?

A fourth problem was the growing influence of military leaders in domestic politics. All of the genrō were ex-samurai with military experience, but with the exception of Yamagata and Ōyama, all considered themselves to be civilians by 1890. The problem arose when the third generation of Meiji leaders came to the fore. These were Sat-Chō protégés, active or retired military men who had served previously within the cabinets as vice-ministers. Before long, they became ministers in their own right, and naturally became candidates for premier as well.

Because the constitution placed the military cabinet ministers under the control of the emperor, technically they were independent of all other ministers including the premier. As long as the premier was a genrō, however, the chance of an Army Minister approaching the emperor directly was unthinkable. But what would happen if such a minister disagreed with a cabinet decision enough to resign his post? The cabinet would have to be reconstituted with another military minister. If enough military men refused to replace him, government could be held ransom until military demands were met. A cabinet could not be formed without one of the military ministers.

The final problem was, Who controlled the emperor? Until 1922 or so it was clear that the genrō did. But Yamagata died in that year, now who spoke for the emperor? Even before that, Japan's preference for collective consensus made it difficult to continue with just a few men. Who chose the new premier? Who issued imperial edicts? The constitution had established two institutions to protect and serve the emperor: the Imperial Household Ministry and the Lord Keeper of the Privy Seal. The first managed the finances of the Imperial House, but also the extensive lands granted to the emperor. The Privy Seal was to guard the actual seal that the emperor used to legitimate laws, edicts, rescripts, and other documents. But when a charismatic man held either office, he could control access to the emperor, and thus influence politics immensely. The problem was magnified when the Emperor Meiji died in 1912 and was succeeded by his sickly son. Toward the end of the Emperor Taishō's life his son Hirohito (the Emperor Shōwa) became a teenage regent.

All five problems that we have just examined boil down to two things:

1. The idea that the emperor actually ruled was a complete fiction and genrō, military ministers, Privy Seal, Privy Council, and Household Minister had too much extraconstitutional power. The early leaders had left too much unwritten; too much assumed; too much without constitutional checks and balances.

2. there was too much to be "read between the lines" of the Meiji Constitution. The *genrō*, military ministers, Privy Seal, Privy Council, and Household Minister had too much extraconstitutional power. The early leaders had

left too much unwritten; too much assumed; too much without constitutional checks and balances.

TWO DECADES OF PARTY STRUGGLE

By 1898 the parties had gained so much strength in public opinion that they
totally controlled the Lower House and brought the budget process to a complete halt. The oligarchy hit on the idea of allowing Ōkuma and Itagaki to
form cabinets—not of their own men but of people chosen by the oligarchy.
Ōkuma and Itagaki were required to resign their membership within their
parties before they were allowed to form a cabinet. This did not work very
well either, and before very long the government returned to its old system of
forming cabinets. It was a cumbersome system that required a great deal of
haggling and compromise.

Yamagata never really lost his contempt and distrust of party politicians. He
preferred bribes, intimidation, and repression as means to control them. Itō,
on the other hand, believed that these men were fundamentally patriots who
truly had the best interests of Japan at heart. The difference between them and
the genrō was in methods.

Therefore, fairly early on Itō began to court the leaders of the parties and by
1898 had become convinced that they could be trusted to lead the government.
He preferred to control them by forming his own party and then inviting them
to join. This infuriated Yamagata and the Satsuma side of the genrō. They used
the considerable influence of the emperor himself to stop Itō from carrying out
his plan for a government party. The use of an imperial edict, however, set a
dangerous precedent: Anyone who controlled access to the emperor could use
that power for his own purposes.

By 1900 it became apparent that Itō would have his way and form a party.
Former Jiyūtō men flocked to him in the formation of the *Seiyūkai*. Among them
were two of Mutsu's political protégés, Hoshi Tōru and Hara Takashi. Hara in
particular would inherit both Mutsu's and Itō's mantles of leadership.

Yamagata thought that he could counter this power by passing legislation
that specified that only the top two active duty ranks in the military could
serve as the Service Ministers in any cabinet. This would severely limit the
pool of candidates. He could control them and thereby heavily influence the
formation of any cabinet. Within a decade the resignation of a Service Minister would bring down two cabinets and prevent a third from being formed.
Yamagata also used his power within the Home Ministry to severely repress
the rights of the parties to campaign, to publish newspapers, and to hold political rallies. Police were used to break up even peaceful political meetings on
the pretext that they represented a threat to "civil tranquility."

Finally, Yamagata sought to limit the power of politicians to reward their followers with government jobs. All but a very few positions in the bureaucracy

were to be filled not through political patronage, but through competition in the Civil Service Examination system. He correctly reasoned that this would create a conservative bureaucracy that would support the government rather than the parties.

By 1900, however, Yamagata had grown tired of the rough-and-tumble of government and wanted to pass on these distasteful tasks to his protégés. Among them was Katsura Tarō, a former general from Chōshū. Katsura was too independent minded to be completely controlled by Yamagata, but he always sought the older man's advice and showed him the respect that he deserved.

The other "Younger Genrō" (an oxymoron since genrō means "Senior Statesmen") was Saionji Kinmochi—who, being from a noble house, was the only genrō not from Satsuma or Chōshū. He and Katsura would alternate as premier for nearly a decade in much the same manner that Itō and Yamagata had taken turns a decade before.

The various political parties functioned by making deals with one of the two men. Without the support of the parties, neither man could have governed. They had to accept party men into their cabinets in return for their support. And so it went until 1918.

In addition to the two main parties, which changed names but remained much the same as the parties originally founded by Itagaki and Ōkuma in the early 1880s, there were a number of smaller parties and political movements. The most influential, though never really very powerful, were the various socialist parties. The Christian Socialists led by Katayama Sen preferred to work within the political system. Another, more radical faction led by Kōtoku Shūsui advocated "direct action," which meant demonstrations and labor strikes. The even more radical groups such as the anarchists and communists were quickly suppressed by the government almost as soon as they could form a new party.

All of the socialists were branded with the disloyal and unpatriotic notoriety of the more radical members. For instance, in 1908 when two flags were raised at a socialist rally reading "Anarchism" and "Anarchic Communism," it scandalized the country. In 1911, police discovered a plot to assassinate the emperor. Twelve socialists, including the clearly innocent Kōtoku, were executed, and many more were sentenced to life imprisonment in the so-called Great Treason Incident.

Police were given a free hand by Yamagata to arrest, harass, intimidate, and even kill leftists. Among them were a number of women who had allied themselves with the socialists. The most famous were Hiratsuka Raichō, Yamakawa Kikue, Yosano Akiko, and Itō Noe. They had been at the forefront of the budding feminist movement and had published a feminist journal called *Seitō* (or "Bluestockings" after the famous British feminist suffrage movement). Along with a more conservative faction called the Women's Reform Society, Seitō worked to repeal laws that limited the rights of women. They also led the way in a number of social reforms such as the Japan Women's Christian Temperance Union, the Japan Salvation Army, the Anti-Prostitution League, as well as movements against concubinage and for birth control.

Because none of the major parties really supported the women's movement, however, many feminists sought support from leftists. But because leftists were suppressed by the government, so too were their feminist allies. Some of the women tried other tactics. Hiratsuka, who formed the New Woman's Association, lobbied long and hard for "Women's Issues," including the repeal of Article Five of the 1890 Police Security Regulations, which forbade political activities by women.

THE PARTIES MATURE

After nearly three decades of almost constant struggle with the genrō, the parties were able to finally form a true party cabinet in 1918. It very nearly was accomplished in 1915, but Yamagata intervened one last time.

In 1912 the Emperor Meiji died after 45 years of rule. The entire country was severely affected because several generations had never known another emperor. To most Japanese he *was* Japan. He represented all the positive accomplishments that were done in his name. Added to this shock was the suicide of General Nogi Maresuke and his wife in a symbolic ritual to join one's feudal lord in death. Also, Meiji's son Yoshihito was both physically and mentally weak. It fell to Meiji's grandson Hirohito to become a teenage regent for the ailing Emperor Taishō.

In the same year that Meiji died, the country was rocked by another crisis caused by Katsura, who attempted to use an imperial rescript to force his political enemies to do his bidding. The dangerous precedent started by Yamagata was used by the Service Ministers to block a new cabinet. Katsura had the emperor issue an edict to force them to continue to serve in the cabinet. The political crisis eventually brought down Katsura's cabinet and forced a change in Yamagata's rules. After this, retired officers could also serve as Service Ministers, thus widening the pool considerably.

When the Saionji Cabinet was also brought down by the resignation of a Service Minister, Yamagata could find no one to form a new government. Saionji suggested the head of the Seiyukai, Hara Takashi, but Yamagata would not allow it. Finally the aged Ōkuma was coaxed out of retirement, and the oligarchy tottered on for three more years.

These were momentous and dangerous years to say the least. Within months, the Great War (as World War I was called then) broke out in Europe. Japan honored its alliance with Great Britain by attacking and seizing German possessions in China. Then Ōkuma's plans to act as protector of Allied interests in China led him to issue what have been called the Twenty-One Demands to the Chinese government. As noted earlier, the demands would have required China to give up most of its own sovereignty.

Because Western goods were no longer being sold in China, Japan's economy quickly began to prosper. But this was a mixed blessing because the increase in Chinese trade drove up the prices of goods in Japan. The resulting inflation caused a series of disturbances in Japan as the poor sacked granaries and raided the homes of the rich in search of food. These Rice Riots of 1918 finally brought the Ōkuma Cabinet down, and at last Yamagata had to face reality. The only government that would appease the people was a party cabinet. Hara Takashi formed the first elected cabinet in Japan's history. It would become the order of the day for the next decade and a half.

For all his claims of being Japan's first commoner Premier (he refused offers to become a noble), Hara was a traditionalist and basically politically conservative. He refused all attempts to pass universal manhood suffrage because he still distrusted the common people. He thought it would be too easy for demagogues and charismatic adventurers to rise to power at the head of a rabble. Also, he felt that Japan's destiny lay in acquiring economic colonies on the Asian mainland.

It was under Hara's control that Japan attempted to keep the former German possessions in the Chinese Shandong Peninsula as part of the Treaty of Versailles that ended World War I. Despite Japan's bribery of corrupt Chinese officials, the Chinese population rose up in an anti-Japanese demonstration that matured into the nationalist May Fourth Movement in 1919. Anti-Japanese boycotts embarrassed Hara's government. A few years later Japan was coerced into returning Shandong as part of the 1922 Washington Naval Conference (and Five-Power and Nine-Power agreements).

Hara's preferences for a Japanese economic imperialism in China fueled a rapidly expanding domestic economy. The zaibatsu industrialists benefited by the widening world economy. Unfortunately, the peasantry did not benefit equally. Many farmers became tenants on their own land when they were unable to keep up with the increase in taxes that went along with the industrial prosperity. These landless peasants became the source of continuing restlessness. Tenant strikes and rural violence increased dramatically in the 1920s. The rural discontent would create a very dangerous situation when the world depression hit Japan savagely at the end of the decade.

The bright promise of parliamentary democracy that accompanied Hara's formation of Japan's first party cabinet in 1918 was dimmed considerably in 1921 when he was assassinated by a madman. Party cabinets continued sporadically for another 10 years, but the rest of decade saw democracy slide dangerously down toward military adventurism and finally into a world war.

ON THE "SLIPPERY SLOPE"

The 1920s were turbulent years for Japan. On the whole, the period has been referred to by historians as the era of Taishō Democracy after the posthumous name of Emperor Yoshihito; but the era can also be characterized as the period when Japan moved away from democracy toward military adventurism. It was a slippery slope toward what the Japanese call the "Valley of Darkness": World War II.

The 1920s saw tremendous economic growth in Japan. The British, French, and Dutch never really regained the markets that they had lost in China during the war. Japanese manufactured goods swept onto the Asian mainland with a vengeance. With the end of the hated Scheduled Tariff in 1911, Japan could use tariffs to protect its native industries. Shipping costs from Japan were infinitely cheaper than freight from Europe.

The other major change in East Asia was the absence of a real Russian threat for nearly a decade. The Communist Revolution in 1917 had forced the Russians to concentrate on the European half of their empire. The Russian resurgence in the 1930s would threaten Japan's influence in Northeast Asia, but during the 1920s Japan dominated the area.

The portents for the future of Japan were mixed in 1922. Late that year Japan joined the other victors of World War I at the Naval Conference in Washington, D.C. It was here that Japan came as close as it ever would to being the equal of the major world powers. At that conference Japan joined with America, Britain, and France in the Four-Power Treaty, in which each signatory agreed to respect the Pacific possessions of the others. In addition, Japan signed the Nine-Power Treaty, agreeing to respect the independence and territorial integrity of China, and the Five-Power Treaty, limiting the capital ships of each power's navy to stipulated tonnage amounts. Japan also agreed to return the Shandong Peninsula to China because this was the greatest impediment to peace. When Japan joined the League of Nations, it appeared that it had at long last become an equal to the rest of the world powers.

Also in 1922, the decade-old women's rights movement had some measure of success when its supporters managed to prod the government into amending the 1890 constitution to allow women once again to attend political rallies and sessions of the Diet. Women, however, were still not able to actually join political parties or to vote. Nine years later the Lower House passed a law to allow women to vote, but it was overridden by the Upper House. Women would have to wait another 15 years before suffrage would be extended to them.

Nevertheless, with the increasing liberalization of the government, women and other political minorities seemed to be making considerable headway. The government was by the mid-1920s spending more of the budget on domestic reform programs than it was on the military. As long as Japan's economy remained robust, the promises of parliamentary democracy seemed rosy.

The period between 1924 and 1932 held much promise because each successive premier was appointed by virtue of the fact that he was the president of the dominant political party in the Lower House. Party cabinets were a huge step away from Yamagata's Transcendental Cabinets. Equally promising, in 1925 a domestic political compromise was reached that gave all adult males the right to vote. The trade-off was a harsh system of Peace Preservation Laws that made it possible to suspend the civil rights of political dissidents.

Even worse than this suppression of political thought was the behavior of the police and right-wing thugs during the devastating Kantō Earthquake of 1923. In addition to the tremendous loss of life (estimates as high as 120,000 killed, perhaps a half-million more were injured or burned, a million more were rendered homeless) from collapsing buildings as well as by the fire caused by the earthquake, the police used the opportunity to arrest and then murder a number of leftists. The right-wing thugs used the disturbance as an excuse to attack thousands of Koreans who had been lured to Japan as casual laborers. Perhaps more than a thousand were beaten to death amid the rubble of Tokyo. Neither the police nor the thugs were ever called to justice.

BEGINNINGS OF MILITARY ADVENTURISM

Despite the positive beginnings of the Washington Naval Conference, the final few years of the period saw the rise of military adventurism on the Asian continent. The army and navy were very upset that the party cabinets had dragged their feet when it came to increasing military budgets. The army saw Russia as the greatest threat and wanted very much to increase the number of active divisions in order to counter Russia in Manchuria and Northeast China. Their argument was that Manchuria had been "paid for in blood" by the 100,000 Japanese casualties in the Russo-Japanese War of 1904–1905.

The navy looked southward in its ambitions. It would have preferred to expand Japanese territorial and commercial interests toward Southeast Asia because that is where the oil and rubber needed to run its ships lay. Another difference between the services was that most of the officers in the navy were more cosmopolitan in their views than were the army officers. The navy men had spent considerable time abroad and were more familiar with foreign nations than the army men.

Both military services tried to put pressure on the civilian government to expand the budgets for them, but the zaibatsu supporters of the parties were more interested in domestic consumer goods than in investing huge amounts of money in the military. The army itself was divided into generational factions. The younger officers were not, for the most part, from old professional samurai families. They were the products of the military academies, heavily influenced by a number of "national socialist" philosophers such as Kita Ikki who argued that Japan's growing rural poverty was the fault of the zaibatsu.

Kita and others argued that Japan's salvation lay in tax reforms and in the expansion of Japan's agricultural land by annexing Manchuria for Japanese emigration. The young officers believed that the politicians had been corrupted by zaibatsu money and no longer had Japan's best interests at heart. They also thought that the top ranks of the army were corrupt as well. They wished to rid the country of all of these corrupt officials by revolution. They advocated a true restoration of power to the emperor. They called themselves advocates of the "Imperial Way" (*Kōdō-Ha*) and thought of themselves as inheritors of the late Tokugawa shishi "men of spirit."

The older generation of officers filled the top ranks of the army. They were mostly from professional military families and had attended the prestigious War College. They, too, were interested in expansion into Manchuria and also thought that the politicians and zaibatsu leaders were corrupt. Where the older officers, who called themselves the "Control Way Faction" (*Tōsei-Ha*), differed from their Kōdō-Ha subordinates was in the manner of change. They would of course prefer to remain at the top of the army—but also to take over the civilian government as well. They did not advocate revolution; they preferred a more gradual approach. Like their younger officers, they believed that Manchuria, dominated and administered by a selfless and patriotic army, could serve as a model for a New Japan—one without corrupt politicians and zaibatsu leaders.

The hotbed for the Young Officer Movement was the army division stationed along the South Manchurian Railroad, known as the Kwantung Army after the name commonly given for the region. Many of the lieutenants and captains serving in that division began to hatch plots to force their more cautious superior officers into "doing something" in Manchuria.

The first of these plots was to assassinate Japan's most loyal ally in Northeast Asia, the warlord Zhang Zuolin. The Old Marshal had cooperated with Japan in the joint administration of the area around the railroad. He provided protection for Japanese civilian employees in return for a steady supply of guns and bribes. But in late 1927 Zhang began to realize that China's new nationalist government under Jiang Jieshi offered a better deal for Manchuria. When the young Kwantung Army officers heard of a rumored alliance between Jiang and the Old Marshal, they did not wait for instructions from Tokyo. Their careful plot was hatched in 1928 when they dynamited Zhang's personal train and then blamed it on Chinese opium dealers and bandits in the area.

Because there was no proof of their involvement, the young Kwantung Army officers demanded that the government of Tanaka Giichi do something to ensure Japan's primary interest in Manchuria. Although Premier Tanaka was himself an army general, he sympathized more with the Control Way. He was caught in an embarrassing situation. On the one hand, he could not punish the young hotheads because it would embarrass Japan. On the other hand, he wished to bring them under control.

Then, to Tanaka's great surprise, the young emperor (his father Taishō died in 1926) Hirohito demanded an investigation. Hirohito's grandfather Meiji had seldom interfered in the government. Hirohito's father Taishō had been unwell both physically and mentally most of his life and had never become involved in government. Tanaka, caught between the emperor and the young officers (who ironically wanted to restore power to Hirohito!), could do little but resign.

The greatest tragedy for Japan was that except for a few of the most radical young officers who were quietly retired, the Kwantung Army officers were not brought to justice for the murder of Zhang Zuolin. This led to more plots because the Kōdō-Ha officers felt that they had wide sympathy and support within the army and the government. They became even bolder in their actions. The uncontrolled adventurism in Manchuria would worsen, and it would come home to Japan. The nation took its first step on the slippery slope toward militarism when the Kwantung Army was allowed to dictate foreign policy to the government.

The paranoia of the Young Officers was whetted by Japan's next attempt at diplomacy. The effects of the world depression seemed to threaten every country. The rise of fascism in Spain, Italy, and Germany loomed large as did the resurgence of Russian military power. The major powers hoped to strengthen the bonds among the victors of World War I by convening a new naval conference in London in 1930. Japan, like Britain and America, was once again assured of maintaining one of the largest navies in the world. Each pledged to keep the peace. In 13 months Japan would break its word, mostly because the Kwantung Army would dictate policy for the government.

THE MUKDEN INCIDENT

The Kōdō-Ha radicals within the army thought that Japan's last chance in Manchuria might have been thrown away by the corrupt politicians at the London Naval Conference. They were determined to force the government's hand. Another plot was hatched in mid-September 1931 at Mukden in northern Manchuria. The Kwantung Army hotheads exploded a charge of dynamite near the South Manchurian Railroad and claimed that the Chinese had attacked. The Japanese "reaction" to this alleged attack was as swift as it was carefully planned. Despite being vastly outnumbered by Chinese troops, the

Kwantung Army seized almost all of Manchuria in a matter of weeks, and within a month threatened Beijing.

The Japanese government at first believed that the Chinese had actually attacked. While it attempted to negotiate with Jiang Jieshi, it supported the Kwantung Army. It soon became apparent, however, that this was yet another case of military adventurism on the part of the Kōdō-Ha. The government was unable to stop the fighting, however, because the Tosei-Ha supported the goals of their rivals. They, too, wished to annex Manchuria. Also, the government had no stomach for punishing the army, because the Japanese people wholeheartedly supported their military heroes. Nothing unites domestic rivals like a common foreign enemy.

While the Japanese government stalled, Jiang appealed to the League of Nations. The League conducted an investigation led by the British Lord Lytton. After some months, the Commission reported that the Kwantung Army was at fault and recommended that Japan be forced to return to its original positions prior to September 1931. The Young Officers next engineered a Manchurian Revolution in 1932, proclaiming a new independent nation, the Republic of Manchuria (or *Manchukuo* as it is rendered in Japanese).

"Henry" Pu-yi, the last emperor of China, was lured into becoming the "emperor" of this new nation, but the Kwantung Army made him into little more than a puppet. The Young Officers dared the Japanese government to undo the independence of Manchuria, soon to become part of Japan's expanding empire. When the League of Nations criticized these actions, Foreign Minister Matsuoka Yōsuke led the Japanese delegation out of the League in protest. Scarcely 18 months before, Japan was a stalwart of the League. Now it was an international outlaw. Then when Premier Inukai Tsuyoshi criticized these actions, he was promptly assassinated.

For the next decade and a half, virtually anyone who criticized the military was cut down in similar fashion. Not surprisingly, very few men risked their lives against this increasingly popular militarist movement. Even the Tōsei-Ha generals were not safe.

In February 1936 the Young Officers staged a brutal coup at the head of some 1,400 troops in downtown Tokyo. They killed several politicians and called for the rest of the army to come to their aid in what they called the Shōwa Restoration. Unfortunately for them, the Shōwa Emperor refused to be restored and branded them as mutineers. The Tōsei-Ha generals leaped at this opportunity to be rid of these rebellious hotheads. The leaders of the coup were rounded up (some preferred to commit suicide than to be taken prisoners) and were quickly tried, condemned, and secretly executed.

But the damage had been done. The radicals had accomplished the aims of their rivals in the military. The generals were now in firm command of the government. Only those civilians who agreed with the military were allowed to serve in the new cabinets. Elections for the Diet continued, but party cabinets were a thing of the distant past. And within a year Japan would be at war with China.

By late 1936 the Chinese Nationalists under Jiang and the Communists under Mao Zedong put aside their decade-long civil war and united against Japanese expansion. In June 1937 an incident at the Marco Polo Bridge outside Beijing escalated rapidly into total war. Again, the Japanese army made initial spectacular inroads, winning nearly every battle. Tragically, this already bloody war would degenerate into horrible Japanese atrocities.

7

The Pacific War and Allied Occupation

THE CHINA QUAGMIRE

The seemingly invincible Japanese army rolled through coastal China defeating every army put in its path in 1937. The superior air forces of the navy bombed and strafed even clearly civilian areas in an attempt to break the morale of the Chinese people. The Japanese military was frustrated by the stiff Chinese resistance around Shanghai. The generals grew increasingly angrier when the Chinese refused to either surrender or compromise as they had always done before.

In December 1937 the Japanese approached Jiang's capital at Nanjing expecting surrender of the nationalist government. To their dismay, virtually the entire government packed up and left Nanjing in favor of Chongqing far up the Yangtze River. The government left Nanjing defenseless declaring it to be an "open city." Under international laws of war (surely an oxymoron) an open city was an indication that it would not be defended. The Japanese army marched into the city and began a reign of terror. The troops murdered hundreds of thousands of civilians in horrific ways. Tens of thousands of women and children were raped and tortured; the city was looted, burned, or otherwise destroyed. Even some Japanese civilians were horrified by their army's actions.

It would have been horrible enough if this had been merely an isolated incident. But as the war dragged on, the Japanese military continued to commit horrendous atrocities. Part of the blame can be attributed to the fact that the Japanese were frustrated and angry that their attempts of pacification of the countryside led only to continued guerrilla warfare primarily by the insurgent Communist forces in north-central China. The hit-and-run tactics of Mao's supporters seemed cowardly to the Japanese, and they responded by killing thousands of peasants who seemed to be supporting the guerrillas. In the 1942 Ichi-go Campaign, the Japanese brutally engaged in what has been called the Three-All Campaign ("Kill-all, loot-all, and burn-all") that killed perhaps half a million civilians and doomed another two million to slow starvation in a scorched-earth policy in central China. Destroying dikes and dams along China's rivers caused tremendous devastation to the people of central China.

By the end of the war the Japanese had caused the deaths of an estimated 20 million Chinese. Their actions in conducting despicable "scientific" experiments in biological warfare on captives and civilians in the notorious Unit 731 have only recently been discovered. Some historians add to Japan's list of atrocities the fact that it helped to destabilize Jiang's Guomindong (GMD) government, contributing significantly to the eventual triumph of Mao's communist movement. Ironically, the primary goal of the Japanese Army at the beginning of the war had been to contain the spread of communism in Northeast Asia.

Japan's actions in China finally escalated into a world war. What had begun with the Kwantung Army's adventurism in Manchuria gradually led Japan into a widening quagmire. Each step along the way seemed to drag Japan into a certain tragedy. The need for a Korean buffer for Japan led to a need for a buffer for Korea. Manchuria became the solution. And then Manchuria dragged Japan southward to pacify its borders. The southward movement ran smack into a newly united China. The need to pacify China meant that Japan had to strike even deeper into China. This used up much fuel oil and rubber, hence the move toward Indochina.

The Japanese government struggled to keep ahead of its troops in China. A new premier, Konoe Fumimaro, was found to unify the various political elements. A member of the ancient courtier Fujiwara family, Konoe was supported by the military because he seemed to share their vision of Greater Japan. Konoe tried first to negotiate with Jiang but then turned toward a collaborationist government in Nanjing in order to divide and conquer China.

Unfortunately, Japan's World War I allies, Britain and the United States, supported Jiang. A hastily built Burma Road over the Himalayan foothills was used to send arms and supplies to the GMD stronghold at Chongqing. This enraged the Japanese, who began to bomb the road until Jiang's allies began to ferry the supplies by air. A number of foreign pilots joined an American-run Flying Tigers in this heroic "flying over the hump."

France's defeat at the hands of Hitler's Germany in 1939–1940 gave the Japanese an idea by which to gain badly needed fuel oil and rubber in French Indochina. Unfortunately, this move southward would stretch Japan's already overextended military capabilities and draw it into a needless war with the United States and Great Britain.

Partially because the Soviet Union became embroiled in war fairly early on in Europe, Japan's military began to see the unofficial Anglo-American alliance as the greatest threat to Japanese hegemony in East Asia. In 1936 Japan had signed an agreement with Germany called the Anti-Comintern Pact, which served to protect Japan against Russian expansion into Asia. In 1940 Japan cemented their alliance with Germany and added Italy in the Tripartite Pact. A year later Japan hedged its bets by signing a Neutrality Pact with Russia. All of these alliances were intended to protect Japan's northern flank against Russia when (not if) it decided to turn southward in search of oil and rubber.

Because Russia was effectively neutralized by these alliances as well as Germany's attack in 1941, Japan now felt confident to deal with what many in Japan's military called the ABCD Encirclement. This was the idea that America, Britain, China, and the Dutch (hence the initials) cut Japan off from its natural spheres of economic interest. When the British and the Americans began to warn Japan about moving southward, the Japanese felt that their fears and paranoid predictions had been proved correct.

America imposed an oil and scrap iron embargo against Japan, and Japan responded with threats and ultimatums. By late 1941 war seemed inevitable between the United States and Japan. Both nations made impossible demands and too irrational steps.

On the part of Japan, it was silly to expect that the Americans would allow them to move into Southeast Asia because America had almost a half-century interest invested in the Philippines (about the same as Japan had in Taiwan and Korea). On the part of the Americans, demanding that Japan evacuate China and Manchuria as the price for resumed trade was equally inane. It would have been as ludicrous as if Japan had demanded that America return Texas, California, Arizona, and New Mexico after the Mexican War in the 1840s. This would make Japan a second-class nation. No Japanese government could survive such a move.

Among other American actions that made war with Japan almost inevitable was the complete ban on Japanese immigration to the United States after 1924, as well as the so-called Stimson Doctrine that heavily criticized Japan at the time of the Manchurian Crisis.

Negotiations broke down in November, and on December 7, 1941, the Japanese attacked the American forces at Pearl Harbor in Hawaii. A series of mistakes by typists and translators at the Japanese embassy in Washington, D.C., prevented a declaration of war before the attack. America took this as a willful "sneak attack." Within days America was at war with Japan and her Tripartite Allies, Germany and Italy.

THE PACIFIC WAR

Japan's successes in the first six months of the war were spectacular. It conquered the Philippines and most of Southeast Asia, including the supposedly invincible British fortress at Singapore. By the end of 1942 it controlled virtually the entire South Pacific and was marching toward India. But by that time the American forces defeated the Japanese navy at Midway Island and had begun a relentless "island hopping" advance toward Japan. By 1943 the Japanese were in retreat. By 1944 the Japanese home islands were being bombed daily.

Japan's fanciful dreams of a Pan-Asian coalition against America and Britain (the Greater East Asia Co-Prosperity Sphere) turned out to be a failure. No Asian people fancied the idea of exchanging Western imperialism for an equally harsh Japanese one. The Pacific War, or sometimes the Fifteen-Year War, as the war was known in Japan, made life dreary and dangerous at home. From the beginning of the China Incident in 1937, the little opposition to the war and to the militarist government was harshly stifled. Perhaps the greatest political theorist of the time, Minobe Tatsukichi, was hounded out of his academic position at the prestigious Tokyo Imperial University and nearly killed for his Organ Theory. He suggested that the emperor was an organ of the government and not the sum total of the government and nation.

Special police harassed and arrested anyone suspected of harboring dangerous thoughts. Thousands of socialists, communists, and other dissidents were rounded up, jailed without charges, and routinely tortured. Those who did not renounce their unpatriotic views often disappeared, probably murdered by their captors. By mid-war all of the various political parties were forced to disband and become part of the coalition Imperial Rule Assistance Association.

Children began each school day bowing low to a picture of the emperor and spent at least an hour drilling with mock rifles and hand grenades. The textbooks were rife with patriotic slogans and chock-full of lies about how Koreans, Taiwanese, and now Manchurians were happy to be part of Japan's Greater East Asia Co-Prosperity Sphere. Towards the end of the war, children were taken from their classrooms and organized into work details. Children were used as domestic self-defense guards and were encouraged to inform on anyone (even their parents) who did not seem to be properly patriotic.

The Japanese press was harshly suppressed in its written opinions to the extent that any story that did not condemn and vilify the enemy was deemed to be unpatriotic. By 1942 the press could not even report American World Series

World War II in the Pacific and Asia, 1943–1945.

scores to the Japanese, who loved baseball. An attempt was made to "cleanse" the language of foreign loan-words so that *rajio* (radio), *rekodo* (phonograph record), *jazu* (jazz), and other such words disappeared from the newspapers to be replaced with silly newly invented words that constantly puzzled readers. Any journalist or editor who dared to criticize the government, the bureaucracy, the military, let alone the emperor, could expect to be arrested without a second thought.

The public was exhorted to enjoy wholesome Japanese games instead of the immoral foreign pastimes. Ballroom dancing was outlawed, and decadent foreign music except for German and Italian classical music was banned from radio programs. Baseball games, now called *yakyu* ("field-ball") were enlivened with grenade-throwing competitions between innings. American, British, and French art and literature were destroyed or quickly hidden by collectors and museum curators, and foreign movies disappeared from theaters.

Serious shortages of meat (even fish!), fuel, rubber, sugar, and other domestic commodities were common and were made even worse by government rationing programs. The government attempted to punish black marketeers, smugglers, counterfeiters, and currency speculators, but the country suffered from a rapidly spiraling inflation. By mid-war electricity and fuel oil were in such short supply that very few lights shown in Japanese windows after dark. Of course by 1944 the danger from Allied bombing air raids was so great that black-out conditions swept the entire country, so there would not have been very many lights anyway.

By early 1945 the war was going so badly for Japan that the Allies began daytime air raids because they had little to fear from Japan's devastated air defenses. The Allies claimed in leaflets dropped from airplanes that they wished only to destroy military targets. But because of Japan's crowded conditions, many civilian areas were damaged as well. By March, the Americans began to firebomb civilian areas in the hopes that they could break the civilian morale (ignoring that Japan had not broken the Chinese in Shanghai and that Hitler had failed to destroy morale in London). Estimates of damages from conventional bombing suggest that perhaps 40 percent of Japan's domestic economy and 60 percent of the country's urban housing was destroyed by July 1945. Even the ripening rice fields became targets of incendiary bombing.

Clearly Japan was all but defeated by the summer of 1945, yet its government continued to stubbornly insist that Japan could win with "one great decisive battle." This military mentality was born in the last-ditch suicide charges of the Sino-Japanese and Russo-Japanese Wars. The battles of Tsushima, Port Arthur, and Mukden convinced them that Japan could not lose because of its superior spirit and morale. Suicide bomber squadrons were formed, called *kamikaze* after the "divine winds" that had saved Japan from the thirteenth-century Mongols. Women, children, and old men were formed into self-defense units armed with farm implements. Everyone was to do their duty, and to die honorably in defense of Japan.

Despite some behind-the-scenes secret overtures for peace, Japan seemed destined to commit national suicide. The Allies did not help much by insisting on unconditional surrender as part of their 1945 Potsdam Declaration. Japanese politicians hoped to salvage the monarchy, but the Allies dashed those hopes. Japan's "sneak attack" at Pearl Harbor and news of Japanese atrocities made mercy to the Japanese improbable. Of course the militarists used the demand for unconditional surrender to argue that Japan might as well fight to the death than to risk having the emperor tried as a war criminal and even have the monarchy abolished altogether.

The end of the war came sooner and more tragically than anyone could imagine. A series of body blows crippled the nation in early August 1945. The firebombing of civilian neighborhoods in Shanghai in 1937 was brought home to Tokyo in March 1945 when it was firebombed, killing over 100,000 people. The atrocities of killing civilians indiscriminately was now extended to Hiroshima and Nagasaki in horrific ways. The residents of those cities who perished immediately were more fortunate than the tens of thousands who died slowly from the effects of radioactive poisoning as a result of the atomic bombs.

Nearly 100,000 people were incinerated by a uranium-based bomb on August 6 in Hiroshima and another 75,000 three days later by a plutonium "dirty" bomb in Nagasaki. In addition, perhaps 10,000 war prisoners (primarily Korean slave laborers) died in these bombings.

Equally damaging to Japanese morale was Russia's declaration of war on August 8, minutes before Manchuria was overrun by Russian troops. The Japanese government still stalled. Only the Emperor's intervention ended the impasse. On August 15 his recorded voice was beamed throughout the country. He asked his subjects to "endure the unendurable," that is, to surrender unconditionally. The horrible war finally came to a tragic halt, but not before hundreds, perhaps thousands, of military officers committed suicide rather than surrender.

POSTWAR JAPAN

The Pacific War had caused nearly three million Japanese deaths. The political repression and the wartime hardships made the 15 years a difficult and wrenching period; in many ways, the next seven years would be equally trying for Japan.

Beginning with the unconditional surrender on August 15, 1945, Japan entered a period of political, economic, social, and even psychological revolution. The very fundamentals of Japanese society and culture were called into question as the nation paid for its "crimes against humanity." Defeat and war-time privations had discredited Japan's military regime, and with it most of its arguments that Japan was somehow divinely destined to rule East Asia and perhaps the world. The Imperial State Shinto myths about a semidivine emperor protected by the kami were shattered by Japan's defeat.

As devastating as this self-examination was for the majority, there were many who welcomed the chance to reestablish the democratic principles that had been quashed by the military regime after 1932. Japan's democratic centrist and leftist political groups jumped at the chance to return to parliamentary democracy. They were given ample opportunities to do so as long as they cooperated with the Allied Occupation regime.

American General Douglas MacArthur was the Supreme Commander of Allied Powers (SCAP) as the leader of the 13-nation military occupation that lasted for seven years. MacArthur did not believe in the need for extended punishment of Japan. Rather, he thought that his primary task was to reform Japan. He sought a legacy of a democratized country. To that end, he brought hundreds of social reformers and academics to Japan and set them to work in this "grand experiment."

If MacArthur's ultimate goal was democratization, then the necessary steps were demobilization, demilitarization, decentralization, and "demythification."

Demobilization

As physically difficult as the first phase, demobilization, would be, it would be by far the most easily accomplished. The mostly American Allied military machine had four years of experience in a grand-scale mobilization of men and material; MacArthur and SCAP merely had to shift the huge machine into reverse.

Over three million Japanese soldiers and sailors were disarmed where they had surrendered across Asia and then repatriated to Japan. Another three million civilian workers in the far-flung Greater East Asia Co-Prosperity Sphere were similarly bundled back to Japan. This huge influx of humanity quickly put a strain on Japan's economy. Within months SCAP was required to set up refugee camps to house the homeless and soup kitchens to feed starving refugees. MacArthur is said to have argued with his American superiors, including President Harry Truman, that feeding and clothing the former enemy was necessary to keep Japan from riots or from turning toward communism. "Send me food and blankets, or send me bullets," he argued.

Demilitarization

The demilitarization was more difficult. Japan's wartime military complex had been extensive and pervasive throughout the society. Added to Japan's huge active-duty military forces had been a very powerful Reservist Association that had helped to control the countryside. Also, Japan's police force had been largely paramilitary in nature, and there were several youth and women's self-defense forces that were dismantled. For the most part, Allied soldiers and sailors assumed the roles of Japan's police in the early part of the Occupation. Most of the country's military weaponry and matériel had been left to the nations of Japan's empire as war reparations, but much was confiscated and destroyed in Japan as well.

Demilitarization included destroying the overwhelming military mentality of Japan's wartime society as well. Japan's leaders had long preached the ideas of Total War: the complete militarization of the culture. The idea was that women, children, and civilian men had duties and obligations equal to those of active soldiers and sailors. All of society was regimented as if everyone was in the military.

Also part of demilitarization was purging former military men from Japan's government and bureaucracy. Perhaps 220,000 men and women were stripped of their posts and made ineligible for election or appointment in postwar governments. A polite fiction was created that blamed these leaders for "capturing" Japanese society. The reasoning was that Japan had been developing along democratic lines but had been led astray by the militarists. If this was true, then Japan could be set back on the course toward democracy by merely purging the country of its bad elements.

Unfortunately, it allowed many Japanese to avoid their own war guilt. After all, if this reasoning held true, then common Japanese citizens were every bit as much victims as were their Asian brothers who had similarly suffered under Japan's militarists. Even ordinary soldiers and sailors could be forgiven because they had been led astray and had been merely "following orders." The fact that Japan had been the victim of atomic bombs also contributed to the idea that the Japanese were "co-victims" of war.

The campaign to cleanse militarism from the educational curriculum was part of demilitarization. Physical education classes no longer included grenade-throwing, marching, and bayonet drill. School textbooks were first purged, often by inking-out offending passages, and then replaced altogether. Democracy became the new curriculum in Japan's schools.

Decentralization

The premise of decentralization was that one of the primary causes of Japan's militarism was the government's centralization of power. This had robbed the Japanese of their civil rights and had allowed a small clique of militarists to seize control of the government. If Japan could be forced to decentralize, most of the functions of government could be democratized. The trick would be to decentralize all political power out into the hamlets and villages of the country. Hereafter, virtually every local government position was to be an elected one. No longer could the central government impose its will on the country by appointing officials. Every village and town henceforth chose its own officials. Bewildered election officials muddled through because they had no experience in local elections. Some zealous rural villages even elected their police, firemen, and postal clerks. Hundreds of small political parties and thousands of candidates vied for votes as Japan learned democracy by actually practicing it.

In an attempt to destroy the power of Tokyo's large zaibatsu, agricultural cooperatives and rural credit unions were established. Trade unions were encouraged; local school, taxation, and zoning boards were established in a blizzard of local reforms. Also, the zaibatsu were "busted up" into small independent companies. Mitsui industries were forbidden to do business with Mitsui banks; Mitsubishi mining firms were enjoined from dealing exclusively with Mitsubishi chemical companies; Sumitomo banks were forced to sell their interests in Sumitomo factories. Many of these smaller companies simply withered and died because their interlocking dependencies were too deeply ingrained. But hundreds more flourished and rapidly learned to cooperate and compete with companies outside of their old "family" groupings.

Perhaps the most comprehensive change was land reform. The purpose of this sweeping reform was not to ensure the government of a sound financial base as it had been the last time land reform had been attempted back in the 1870s. The goal this time was to redistribute the land into equitable plots among the former tenant farmers who had actually farmed the land for their ancestral landlords. Farmers were not allowed to own more land than they could till without hired aid. Surplus land was bought by the government at very low fixed prices and then sold to landless peasants at extremely low time payments. Postwar inflation lowered the payments even further. It is said that an acre of land came to cost the same as a package of American cigarettes.

The idea was that if the landless tenants could become independent farmers, they would never again permit the absentee landlords to determine their fates or dictate their political will over the countryside. The goal was "those who till the soil of Japan shall have a more equal opportunity to enjoy the fruits of their labor." Millions of peasants became land owners in one fell swoop. The rural sector thereafter became the most staunchly conservative political group in the nation. MacArthur's reformers were absolutely correct: Once the farmers recovered their ancestral lands, they would defend them politically.

Demythification

By far the most difficult and wrenching phase of reform was the "demythification" of Japanese society. The SCAP reformers judged that until Japan was cleansed of the irrational myths of State Imperial Shinto, the country could never be really and completely democratized.

The first step was to destroy the myth of imperial divinity. Even before Hirohito was urged to denounce his divinity to the nation in a nationwide radio speech on January 1, 1946, he became part of the reform campaign. A picture of the emperor and MacArthur standing together was published to give the people a symbolic physical image. MacArthur, who was well accustomed to having his picture taken for publicity, slouched arrogantly in his casual khaki uniform. He towered over the bespeckled middle-aged Hirohito who squinted at the camera, stiffly uncomfortable in his diplomat's swallowtail coat. Clearly, if a godlike figure appeared in the picture, it was not the diminutive emperor.

For the next seven years the emperor was trotted out to every functionary party. He snipped ceremonial ribbons, handed out prizes, and constantly bowed to his subjects. Only months before, children had begun each morning bowing to his picture, and thousands of soldiers had died in his name. Now he was slyly referred to by some as the *Aso desuka Tennō* ("the Is-That-So Emperor"), after the phrase he often uttered when touring the country. Journalists were encouraged to write human interest stories about the imperial family. Historian Roger Purdy demonstrates that suddenly the emperor and his family appeared in movie newsreels as "people" and not the stiff uniformed monarchs on horseback of wartime footage.

Another integral part of the demythification campaign was bringing war criminals to public justice. Nearly five thousand lower-ranking military men were indicted, tried, and usually executed on the spot in the countries where they had raped, pillaged, and murdered. But 27 of the "bigger fish" were brought before a public arena to answer to charges of having brought war to a peaceful world. Two years later, seven of them, including wartime Premier Tōjō Hideki, were hanged in the dead of night to avoid any public demonstrations.

The premise, again, was that these militarists had hijacked the government away from democratic political elements. Once these bad elements had been punished, then the rest of Japanese society could be rehabilitated back to their more normal and natural democratic tendencies. In short, Japan's militarism was an aberration led by twisted and demented men who now had to answer with their lives for Japan's wartime atrocities. It was a cancer that had to be cut out of Japan in order to save the society.

Clearly, many of the legal charges in the War Crimes Tribunal were trumped up or written after the fact. After all, war had been legal in international law before the 1945 International Nuremberg Tribunal against the German Nazis had declared it to be a "crime against humanity." One historian has called it "victor's justice." Some military officers were held accountable for war atrocities of which they had no knowledge; yet others were never tried for their biological atrocities because Americans wished to gain access to the results of these "scientific experiments."

Clearly the point of the Tokyo War Crimes Tribunal was to discredit and demythify the military. Films and photographs of the atrocities were distributed widely so that everyone could witness the depravity and degradation of their Imperial Army. Many clamored for the emperor himself to be tried as a war criminal. Perhaps this would have sealed the demythification campaign, but MacArthur would not have it. He argued that if President Truman wished him to do so, then he should probably send "a million soldiers" to squash the predicted Japanese rebellion.

SCAP reformers reasoned that the most effective use of the imperial symbol was to make the emperor himself a convert to democracy. Besides, SCAP decided that the transition towards democracy was infinitely easier by cooperating with natural Japanese "democratic elements." By using the emperor, the thinly veiled fiction could be created that the Japanese themselves were democratizing. The emperor became a symbol of "Japan's democratic aspirations." His place in the new government was carefully circumscribed and controlled.

MACARTHUR PEACE CONSTITUTION

The new constitution, still called the MacArthur Peace Constitution even today, became the culmination and legacy of the Occupation. A half-century after it was announced in 1947, it remains fundamentally the same. It is often ignored and circumvented, but despite some notable legal challenges, it remains unchanged.

MacArthur had officially requested that the Japanese government write a new constitution to replace the flawed 1890 Meiji Constitution. After a few months he expressed disappointment with the results. He then ordered the SCAP Government Affairs Section to draft a "model." The result was the basis for the new constitution.

Not surprisingly, the new constitution resembles the American model in many ways; these were, after all, Americans who wrote it. It guaranteed everyone all civil, social, economic, human, and political rights as in the American Bill of Rights. It wrestled with many of the same issues as Americans had a century and a half before: national versus state's rights, separation of powers, checks and balances, and so on. But there were a few surprises.

First, the Lower House of Parliament is more similar to the British House of Commons. Premiers are elected by their peers, and become the chief executive officer. The premier appoints a cabinet that forms the government until the Lower House calls for another election. The House of Councillors, like the American Senate, becomes a counterweight to the lower house in that the Councillors represent the prefectures and the nation at large rather than the smaller parochial local districts of the Lower House.

Second, the emperor is weaker than even the British sovereign. He has no government duties and is a figurehead rather than an active member of government. He is the "symbol of the state and of the unity of the people with whom resides sovereign power."

Third, an independent Supreme Court rules on the constitutionality of laws. This becomes a check and balance on the powers of the legislature and executive branches.

Fourth, women are totally emancipated by the new constitution. Gone are all of the paternal controls of the Meiji Constitution. Women can own, inherit, buy, and sell property. They can marry and divorce without the permission of anyone. They can bring lawsuits and can testify and bear witness. They may initiate, sign, and present petitions. They may vote and run for political office. In short, they became constitutionally equal with men. Significantly, in the first election under the new constitution 37 women were elected to Parliament; by far the greatest representation in any subsequent election. A few of the early feminists from the 1920s such as Hiratsuka Raichō lived long enough to be vindicated by being elected to the Lower House.

Fifth, the constitution contains protection for laborers to unionize. Collective bargaining had evolved under the British and American constitutions, but the Japanese model expressly grants unions more freedom from government control.

Finally, the new laws were crowned the Peace Constitution because of the much celebrated Article Nine, which states that "the Japanese people forever renounce war as a sovereign right." To make sure that Japan would never invade its neighbors militarily, the military was dissolved forever. Without question, this would eventually become the most controversial provision of the new constitution. But when it was promulgated, the majority of Japanese were so tired and disgusted with the results of the recent war that virtually no one spoke out against Article Nine.

THE YOSHIDA LEGACY

As much as the Occupation years can be called the MacArthur Years, the period can also be characterized by one man: Yoshida Shigeru. He would place his personal stamp on the period.

Yoshida was a complex and difficult man who came to represent New Japan. He was arrogant, stubborn, irascible, and brilliant. He was never popular in the country except in his home electoral precinct. Most of his political followers feared him more than they idolized him. His immediate subordinates (a half dozen became premier after him) were fiercely loyal but avoided him whenever they could. Many said that Yoshida acted more like an ancient daimyō than like a political democrat. He had served in the Foreign Ministry during the 1930s but had fallen into disfavor with the government during the war, even being briefly imprisoned for his attempts to end the war in early 1945. This imprisonment had cleared him in the SCAP purge of militarists during the Occupation.

Most of the politicians who were elected in the first few Diets after the war were immediately purged because of their wartime activities. Also, because the politicians elected to replace them had very little actual experience in the government, Yoshida naturally rose to the top very quickly. Hatoyama Ichirō, who stood to become premier, was purged because of his wartime participation in government. Hatoyama personally chose Yoshida to be a caretaker premier in his place. After Yoshida was made head of the Liberal Party, however, he would not relinquish the leadership. He was appointed by SCAP as premier in May 1946.

Within months he had formed a coalition among the centrist political parties together with the conservative bureaucrats who as a group were not purged in the immediate postwar period. In 1948 Yoshida managed to unseat the socialist-dominated coalition that had ruled since the postwar election of 1947. He was to be premier for seven years of the first postwar decade.

For most of the Occupation years he was the Premier and his own Foreign Minister. MacArthur put aside his personal distaste for Yoshida and managed to cooperate with him in the governing of the country through the critical early reform years. For his part, Yoshida often disagreed with MacArthur's vision of the New Japan, but he realized that MacArthur had the power to do virtually anything; it was up to Yoshida to temper and alleviate the harshest reforms. Yoshida saw himself as the defender of Japanese tradition and culture. As such, he was a brilliant strategist.

Although he was personally against such constitutional reforms as "zaibatsu-busting," strengthening unions, women's rights, land reform, and especially Article Nine, he understood that they were inevitable. He was able later to use the reforms to his own ends during and after the Reverse Course after 1948.

THE REVERSE COURSE

MacArthur had political aspirations and wished to use the successful democratization of Japan as a springboard for the American presidential elections of 1948. Being politically conservative, his political advisers began to fear that MacArthurs's reputation as a social reformer would make him unpopular with the Republican Party back in the United States. That, and the fact that the leftist unions in Japan were calling for a nationwide strike in February 1947, turned the Occupation around. Yoshida managed to convince MacArthur that the communist-dominated unions intended to use the strike to bring down the Japanese government. He very possibly was right, but that would have meant that the newly established democratic political system would have reflected the wishes of the people. But the SCAP authorities feared that Japan was going to turn toward communism, especially because Eastern Europe was doing that precisely at this time. MacArthur was never to achieve his presidential ambitions, but Yoshida and his party managed to use them to gain much for Japan.

Coupled with these fears was the emerging specter of a communist China, because the Nationalist forces under Jiang Jieshi seemed intent on bungling their civil war on the Asian continent. Little wonder, then, that MacArthur and SCAP turned against their former socialist allies in early 1948. Hereafter SCAP cooperated with Yoshida to blunt further democratic reforms.

The old zaibatsu were gradually rehabilitated and allowed to form "rational" industrial cooperatives. Banking reforms swung Japan back to a more centrally controlled conservative fiscal economy. The unions were more tightly controlled, and strikes were quashed in the interest of national security. Eventually a new Red Purge forced communists out of the government at the same time that former militarists were rehabilitated and allowed to return. Even a few convicted war criminals were allowed to return to public life. One, Kishi Nobusuke, would rise to become premier after having served time in prison for his wartime actions.

The Reverse Course gained even greater momentum in 1949 when the communists under Mao Zedong declared the People's Republic of China and later in June 1950 with the invasion of South Korea by communist North Korea. The American paranoia of a dominolike collapse of the world toward communism seemed to be coming true. First China, then Korea; it seemed that Japan would be the next domino to fall.

Within weeks of the invasion of South Korea by communist North Korean troops, SCAP began to refer to Japan as the "bastion of democracy in East Asia" and "America's Unsinkable Aircraft Carrier." Japan became the staging ground for United Nations and American military forces as they prepared to fight the communist menace in East Asia. Japan's industries were flooded with orders to turn out the needed military matériel to clothe, arm, and otherwise supply the United Nations' military forces. Those former zaibatsu that had not already rationalized back into industrial and financial cooperatives, rushed to do so now. Yoshida called this economic surge a "gift from the kami."

SCAP wished to free American troops from their duties of policing and protecting Japan. So Yoshida was urged to form quickly a domestic military force to assume these roles. Yoshida had wisely resisted a wide-scale remilitarization as early as 1948 because he feared that his former enemies in the wartime military might rise to power again. Now, he agreed to develop a 75,000-man (less than half of what SCAP requested) self-defense force but used Article Nine as the reason why these troops could not be used in Korea or anywhere else outside Japan. Also, he used the high level of anticommunism in SCAP to purge communist "sympathizers," meaning socialists and other leftists.

Yoshida used the Korean War as a lever to wedge out most of the SCAP reforms that he did not like. He began to preach a strategy called the Yoshida Doctrine. This meant that Japan would cooperate with the United States as much as possible but would not become involved in world politics. Japan would instead strive toward economic development and would devote only the minimum funding for a small self-defense force. He arbitrarily set a ceiling of 1 percent of Japan's total governmental expenditures to be spent on the Self-Defense Forces. This became the model for subsequent premiers and was surpassed only in the 1990s.

Similarly, he used the New Partnership (as Japan's new relationship with America was sometimes called) to win substantial changes in Japan's role in the world. By 1951 virtually the entire world was ready to welcome Japan back into the brotherhood of nations. Only the Soviet Union and its communist allies disagreed.

In September 1951 Japan signed a peace treaty at San Francisco ending the war and became once again an independent nation. It was a partial and incomplete independence to be sure. Japan signed a Mutual Security Treaty with the United States that allowed an American military presence in Japan and maintained an American military occupation of the Ryūkyūs. Shortly thereafter Japan signed a separate "understanding" with the Soviet Union and China that recognized the occupation by Russia of Japan's Kurile Islands.

It was a bittersweet ending of the war for Japan. For the most part Japan was purged of its wartime guilt; it would become part of the United Nations and once again a member of the "peace-loving" brotherhood of man. But this came at a price. It would be decades more before the Japanese government could exercise complete autonomy in foreign policy. Everything that Japan did was closely scrutinized. Japan still had many war debts to be paid.

8

A New Japan

MUTUAL SECURITY TREATY: 1952–1960

Japan began a new era on April 28, 1952, the day when the Allied Occupation officially ended. The peace treaty ending the war had been signed seven months before in San Francisco, but Japan did not count itself truly independent until the Allied Occupation ended. Japan, however, was not truly independent even then. Because Yoshida had refused to rearm Japan during the Korean War, he chose to yoke the country to the United States until Japan completed its economic recovery. Japan therefore signed a Mutual Security Treaty with the United States that made Japan a dependency for another decade.

The treaty guaranteed Japan's defense under America's "nuclear umbrella" because the United States pledged to respond to any attack against Japan as an attack against America. Many Japanese objected to the irony of defending Japan with the hated atomic weapons that had destroyed two of its cities in 1945. But if Japan refused to create a real military, it needed protection.

In order to properly defend Japan, the Americans were allowed to station troops in the country and were allowed to administer the island of Okinawa for that purpose. Further, the United States was permitted to use those troops against any enemies in Asia without prior consultation with the Japanese government. Japan promised not to lease or sell land for military bases to any other nation. Japan had no say as to whether Americans would bring atomic weapons to these military bases. Also, Japan agreed to grant diplomatic recognition to the Nationalist government of Jiang Jieshi on Taiwan and to ignore the nearly one billion Chinese in the People's Republic on the mainland.

Perhaps the most galling aspect of the Mutual Security Treaty was that American military personnel and their dependents were granted extraterritoriality while residing in Japan. Many conservatives and liberals alike complained bitterly, citing this as a return to the humiliating nineteenth-century Unequal Treaties.

This was the substantial price that Japan was forced to pay for American defense. The treaty, although technically eternal because it had no length of time specified, continued only as long as the Japanese really wanted it. Yoshida confided to his political allies that this was to be a necessary "temporary burden" until the country could recover its prewar economic might and stability. Not surprisingly, after Japan regained its independence in 1952, a new crop of political leaders came to the fore. Tired of the Occupation and chafing under American military control, this new group of men and a very few women advocated a return to Japanese cultural traditions.

THE POST-YOSHIDA YEARS

This new force led by the recently rehabilitated Hatoyama coalesced in the Democratic Party, which vied with Yoshida's Liberal Party for control of the country. Hatoyama was still bitter that his protégé Yoshida had kept the premiership for himself. He engineered a new coalition in 1954 with former war criminal Kishi Nobusuke that managed to rule for seven years.

Hatoyama's party was even more staunchly conservative than Yoshida's party. It followed Yoshida's tactics of working closely with the bureaucracy, big business, and the large agricultural cooperatives in the countryside. They all wanted a stable, growing economy and had very little sympathy with social reformers, union activists, and their leftist allies.

The government passed a series of laws that extended the Red Purge against communists and other leftists out of the government and the labor unions. It gradually began to recentralize some government controls, particularly in banking and education. No overt and direct moves were made against other civil liberties, but quiet and subversive actions were taken to freeze women out of politics. Only a few token women were allowed to compete for elections within the tightly controlled party (Yoshida's Liberals did the same). Women who wished to run were forced to seek electoral spots within the socialist and communist parties.

Most of the legislation passed during this period was aimed at helping big business and the largest rural agricultural cooperatives. Hatoyama actively recruited former bureaucrats for his party and put them to work drafting legislation and lobbying their fellow Diet representatives. It was a brutally effective means of running the country. Most people went along because Japan's alliance with the United States provided it with lucrative contracts as well as reliable markets within the American sphere of influence. Trade with South Korea, Taiwan, and the rest of America's Asian allies filled Japanese coffers.

The Democratic Party managed to stay in power through three premiers because the people mostly benefited from its conservative platform and because the other parties remained jealous of each other. The various leftist parties finally recognized that the Liberal and Democratic parties managed to stay in power because the socialists remained disunited. In early 1955 a new socialist coalition was forged. This forced the bureaucrats, businessmen, and powerful rural men to demand a similar conservative coalition.

The result was the Liberal-Democratic Party (LDP). The LDP quickly became a coalition not of the two former parties but of many cliques formed around charismatic men. For the next 40 years Japanese politics would be fought within the LDP as the various factions struggled for power. The Japan Socialist Party would remain the chief political rival to the LDP, but it split into many parties over the years. For all intents and purposes, the LDP was the party of power in postwar Japan. This came to be called the 1955 System because the electoral ratio between the LDP and various leftist parties remained basically unchanged. For about six months, however, the leftist parties managed to come together over the revision of the Mutual Security Treaty.

THE TREATY DEBATE

In late 1959 Kishi, Premier since 1957, seemed poised to crown the legacy of his political rehabilitation with two great accomplishments. First, he announced that his government had successfully revised the Mutual Security Treaty with the United States. Second, American President Dwight Eisenhower would visit Japan to signify the real beginning of the country's independence.

The new treaty, negotiated in secret during September and October 1959 seemed to be an improvement over the previous one. Although American troops would still be stationed in Japan, Americans would henceforth be required to consult with Japan about the use of those troops abroad. Also, extraterritorial provisions were ended, and the treaty life was limited to 10 years. Kishi argued that Japan and the United States were now equal partners. Many Japanese disagreed.

The badly divided socialists rallied to the antitreaty campaign. Within weeks, labor unions, student groups, communists, socialists, and anti-LDP politicians of all stripes declared themselves against the new treaty. Surprisingly, many of the rightist nationalistic parties joined with their former leftist enemies in their objections to the new treaty. Their primary objections had to do with the fact that American troops were still to be allowed in Japan. All parties agreed that this compromised Japanese sovereignty.

Secondly, the Mutual Security title seemingly bound Japan to defend American Cold War foreign policy. The leftists were particularly disturbed because it apparently was aimed at isolating and destabilizing communist regimes and supported the authoritarian militarist regimes of South Korea and Taiwan.

Public protest demonstrations grew larger and larger each day. The government was caught unawares and handled the otherwise peaceful demonstrations harshly. Hundreds of protesters were beaten and/or arrested and one student was even killed; she became an instant martyr.

The protests spread even into the Lower House, where the struggle for control of the podium became violent. In May, Kishi was forced to call the police into the Diet, and while the socialists boycotted the resulting meeting, the government rammed the treaty through into legislation. In June, Eisenhower's advance planner was assailed by protesters and had to be rescued by a police helicopter. Within days the Eisenhower visit was postponed, and the American President never came to celebrate Kishi's triumph. Kishi resigned shortly thereafter and calm was restored.

THE "BUSINESS" OF POLITICS

After a time Kishi was replaced by a Yoshida protégé, Ikeda Hayato, who managed to avoid further problems for a four-year term as premier. Ikeda remained in power because he delivered on his promise to double the average wage in a decade. In fact, this seemingly impossible goal was accomplished in slightly less than four years. His pro-business policies were very popular, obviously, with the old bureaucratic, business, and agricultural elites. Even the urban workers seemed to be happy with their rapidly escalating salaries.

Other Japanese, however, began to grow uncomfortable with increases in taxes and spiraling inflation. Residents of the big cities grew tired of being shut out of the political process by the LDP. The electoral districts that had been established in 1947 were now badly out of date. Population in the countryside had gravitated into the cities, but the districts remained unchanged. The LDP had created nearly impenetrable safe seats in the rural areas by pouring money for agricultural price supports, roads, tunnels, dams, and other capital improvements into the provinces. Rice was purchased by the government at inflated prices in order to win the support of the farmers. Local patronage policies kept the same politicians, or their families, returning to the Diet every year.

Similarly, the multiseat districts in the large urban districts were tightly controlled by the LDP. In most cases, if there were three seats in a district, the LDP would concentrate their considerable finances behind two candidates. This would guarantee that they would both win; leaving the other seat for the socialists or other splinter parties.

Elections were very expensive, and therefore anyone who could contribute financial support had control over the candidates. Obviously this gave tremendous influence to big business contributors. Usually large corporations contributed lump sums to their favorite LDP faction leaders who in turn doled out the money to individual candidates. The leaders could then reliably turn out blocs of votes for pro-business legislation. Business leaders even further consolidated that power with the foundation of *Keidanren* (Federation of Economic Organizations). Funds from this organization of over 700 businesses were then coordinated to have the greatest legislative impact.

This perpetuated the power of the faction leaders. There were few if any independent LDP members, each had to choose a "boss" in order to obtain campaign financing. Once he had done so, he was bound to him for his political life. Only death released a Dietman from his obligations to his boss. The LDP was constantly evolving and adjusting to new political environments. None of the various factions was particularly ideological. None of them even bothered to advertise a political platform. As long as they delivered on local jobs and services, they continued to win.

The Communist Party was as splintered as the LDP. Factions supported various movements popular in Russia, China, and North Korea. They seemed to be as antagonistic towards each other as they should have been towards the LDP. Their only electoral strengths were within some labor and student unions.

In the mid-1960s the Buddhist sect *Soka Gakkai* ("Value Creating Society") launched the political party *Kōmeitō* ("Clean Government Party"), which won twenty-five seats in the Diet in 1967. Because Komeitō represented primarily urban centers, the LDP took notice. A rival coalition within the LDP seized on the urban discontent to oust Ikeda in 1964. He was replaced by Kishi's younger brother Satō Eisaku (Kishi had been adopted by another family).

Satō played the game of politics remarkably well. With the support of the cliques controlled by his brother Kishi and Yoshida, he enjoyed considerable support within the LDP. He parceled out ministries in his cabinets to his rivals and played one faction against the other. Unlike his predecessors who concentrated their efforts on domestic policies, Satō ventured out into the field of foreign affairs. He hosted the world's athletes when the Olympic Games came to Tokyo in 1964. He visited the United States, managing to negotiate the return of Okinawa, reputedly for an agreement not to criticize American President Richard Nixon's Vietnam War policies. He revised the Mutual Security Treaty with barely a ripple of discontent in 1970.

Satō's 1969 visit to the United States caused some problems for Japan due to a misunderstanding inherent in the Japanese language. Nixon urged Satō to impose "voluntary" limits on Japanese textile exports and Satō promised "serious consideration." When Satō found that his countrymen were not about to agree to this costly cut, he stalled and maneuvered in order to reroute some of the textile exports to other markets. In 1971 Nixon, who felt that Satō had broken his promise, imposed a 10 percent tariff surcharge on Japanese textiles. This gave Satō an excuse to force the voluntary limit. Unfortunately, Americans thereafter were convinced that the only way to do business with the Japanese was to "be tough."

This would have serious implications for United States–Japan relations. For instance, in the summer of 1971 Nixon announced that he would visit the Peoples' Republic of China. This was only months after Satō had reemphasized his support for Taiwan and for the U.S. China policy of continued nonrecognition. Satō had not been consulted and had received no prior warning from the United States and therefore was caught totally unprepared. Satō scrambled to normalize relations with China but was rebuffed by the Chinese. Normalization would be left to his successor.

When he left office after eight years, Satō engineered a successful campaign to be Japan's first Nobel Peace Prize winner. The campaign reputedly cost several millions of dollars in publicity, entertainment, and generous gifts. He was awarded the prize for his continued efforts in keeping Japan from developing or obtaining nuclear weapons and for his treaty "restricting the spread of nuclear technology."

Tanaka Kakuei, the man to replace Satō, with only one notable exception, was the last of the Big Men to become premier. After him, the premiership would be shuffled around to faceless political mediocrities in what historian Mikiso Hane has called political "musical chairs." Only one of them served longer than two years. If it was not already so prior to Tanaka, Japanese politics would be a struggle between kingmakers who fought to appoint their own flunkies to power. Yoshida and Hatoyama wielded real power until they died; other behind-the-scenes puppet masters would continue the practice for decades. With the exception of Nakasone Yasuhirō (who, like Tanaka, later became a kingmaker), the rest of the premiers were almost interchangeable faceless pawns in this political game.

Tanaka was truly a renegade and an unusual figure in Japanese politics. Unlike virtually every other premier, he had not graduated from one of the top universities in Japan. In fact, he had not even attended secondary school. He was not a former bureaucrat as were perhaps two-thirds of Japan's postwar premiers. He was a wealthy man who had made his fortune in Japan's corrupt construction industry. He was reputed to have intimate ties to Japan's *yakuza* crime underworld and had considerable support from some unions.

Tanaka had clawed his way to the top of the LDP by spreading money around lavishly in support of young candidates. He had close ties to another shadowy LDP figure, Kanemaru Shin. Kanemaru was reputedly tied to various small rightist splinter groups and was a known conduit for yakuza political contributions, particularly from Japan's lucrative *Pachinko* pinball parlor gambling interests.

Tanaka was a very visible and publicity-conscious man. Only days after his election as the youngest postwar premier, he flew off to Hawaii to meet with Nixon, and then to China to normalize relations with the PRC. He boasted that his legacy would be the rebuilding of Japan and quickly began a number of overambitious construction projects, to the benefit of his former business partners.

His projects were left unfinished after only two years, partially due to his own chicanery and partly because of the Middle East oil crisis of 1973. The oil crisis was of course beyond his control. The primarily Arab-controlled Organization of Petroleum Exporting Countries (OPEC) first limited and then stopped the export of oil to countries like Japan who supported Israel. Japan, who imported virtually all of its oil, made a sudden about-face in its foreign policy. This was not enough, however, because the 10-fold increase in oil prices crippled Japan's oil-reliant heavy industries.

Tanaka was brought down also because he was implicated, and ultimately convicted (though he managed to avoid the prison sentence), for "influence peddling." It was discovered that he had demanded huge bribes from the American airplane manufacturer Lockheed in return for his support for a multimillion-dollar sale of jets to Japan's Self-Defense Forces.

Tanaka resigned in late 1974 in favor of the LDP reformer Miki Takeo. Despite the fact that the Lockheed Scandal and trial dragged on for over 15 years, Tanaka continued to be reelected to the Diet (ultimately replaced by his daughter) and continued to wield considerable backstage power as a kingmaker. No one expected him to be punished because the entire top level of the LDP was saturated with leaders who accepted such bribes. Even after conviction, his sentence was never carried out on the basis of his "debilitating illnesses."

To characterize Miki as a reformer is an indication of the nature of Japanese politics. He, like every other faction leader in the LDP (and some would argue within all the other political parties as well), found it necessary to collect money from various sources and then mete it out to his followers during elections. The movement of vast amounts of money was never to be fully documented in the ebb and flow of parliamentary elections. The LDP was embarrassed during the Lockheed Scandal and found it necessary to create the fiction that it was cleaning up and reforming itself. Miki became the compromise candidate between two other faction leaders because he had a reputation as a clean and uncorrupted politician.

Miki began to take his reformer reputation seriously, and actually managed to push some political reforms through the Diet. When he tried to have Tanaka indicted as part of the Lockheed affair, however, Tanaka's supporters quickly rallied to call for Miki's resignation. Miki tried to win support for his reforms by calling for a parliamentary election in December 1976. That election confirmed that the Japanese public was disgusted with the LDP corruption. For the first time in two decades, the LDP did not gain an absolute majority in the Lower House. The two leaders whose infighting had led to Miki's election in 1974 now settled their differences and agreed to alternate as premier.

The first, Fukuda Takeo, was an old-style LDP politician. A former bureaucrat, a graduate of Tokyo University, and a follower of Kishi, he was from the conservative nationalistic wing of the LDP. Despite his rightist leanings, Fukuda will be remembered as the Premier who finalized the diplomatic normalization with Communist China. It was not that he had any great admiration for communism, of course, but rather because it was in Japan's best economic interests to do so. Fukuda and Ōhira Masayoshi, who succeeded him as premier (as well as every other premier), put Japanese economic interests ahead of their personal political beliefs. They normalized relations with communist regimes because it filled Japanese coffers. Their support, after all, came primarily from business interests.

The 1970s were the height of the country's economic upturn. It was during this period that Japan ceased to be a debtor nation and began to export heavily to the rest of the American-dominated Free World. The balance of payments swung in Japan's favor, primarily because of Japan's manufacture of small economical cars and miniaturized radios and television sets.

The Japanese government focused its attention on helping private companies to capture market share in the world. The powerful Finance Ministry and the growing Ministry of International Trade and Industry (MITI) gave Japanese companies as much assistance as they needed to improve Japan's economy. It was during this period that foreigners, primarily Americans, began to characterize the entire country as "Japan Inc." The implication was that the government was acting more like the directorship of a huge national corporation than the head of a sovereign nation. American businessmen, particularly those involved in the stagnant and bloated American automobile industry, accused Japan of monopolistic and other unfair trading practices.

The primary accusations had to do with Japan's restrictive markets, which made foreign imports too costly to compete with Japanese domestic products. The greatest discontent here was in agricultural products. Because Japan subsidized domestic rice and imposed huge tariffs on foreign-grown rice, it made it impossible to import this food staple.

Overly restrictive import inspections, quarantines, and tariffs disadvantaged foreign manufacturers as well. Certainly Japan was exacting economic revenge for the Unequal Treaties of the nineteenth century.

Also, Japan was criticized for "dumping," which implied that Japanese goods were being sold abroad below manufacturing costs in order to drive foreign domestic manufacturers into bankruptcy. The idea was that the government of Japan was subsidizing these unfair practices in order to capture market share. The primary evidence usually cited was Japanese steel, which routinely sold for cheaper prices abroad than it sold for in Japan, even cheaper in Pittsburgh than American steel. The Japanese argued that Japanese products were cheaper because of more efficient Japanese methods; Americans argued that it was because Japan wanted to destroy competition.

A Shift to the Political Right

When Ōhira died in the middle of the 1980 national election campaign, Japanese politics took a decidedly nationalistic turn. The next two premiers reflected Japan's growing dissatisfaction with its status in the world. Increasingly, the Japanese had grown tired of being dictated to by American presidents. The so-called Nixon Shocks in the 1970s had embarrassed and even enraged many LDP leaders. The nation's growing economy had put it into serious rivalry with the United States; the Japanese were therefore feeling more self-confident and independent.

The succeeding governments, starting with that of Suzuki Zenko, attempted to take advantage of Japan's increasing economic power. The right wing of the LDP reasoned that this power would force the rest of the world to accord Japan more respect in the political realm. This was the period when Japan's burgeoning financial power seemed to be the future of the new world economy. Pundits were referring to "Japan as Number One," and of "Japan in the Passing Lane" as if the nation were about to surpass Great Britain, the Soviet Union, and even the United States.

Increasingly the LDP began to "float trial balloons" to see what it could get away with. There was talk of converting the Self-Defense forces into an actual army and navy in order to flex Japan's international muscles. Not surprisingly, the leftist parties reacted in a predictable way, railing against these alleged "returns to fascism." What surprised the LDP, however, is that the centrist parties sided with the Socialists and Communists. Political polls showed that the nation's electorate did not sympathize with these neo-nationalist ideas. Suzuki came under attack when he publically visited the Yasukuni Shrine (see continued discussion in Chapter 9) on the thirty-fifth anniversary of the end of World War II. He came under immediate attack by not only the leftist-centrist coalition, but also from the governments of China and Korea.

Suzuki continued to stagger under the criticism but seemed to rally only to be toppled, over a disclosure that American ships in Japanese waters routinely carried atomic weapons. Suzuki had grown tired of dealing with opposition from both the left and right. He did not run for reelection in November 1982.

His successor, Nakasone Yasuhirō, was even more nationalistic and more conservative than Suzuki. Nakasone was a protégé and staunch defender of Tanaka Kakuei. His election is an indication of just how powerful Tanaka remained despite the Lockheed Scandal. Nakasone hit off a first-name friendship ("Ron-Yasu") with the new American president Ronald Reagan and quickly began to change the Japan–United States relationship. He bolstered Japan's Self-Defense Forces, buying sophisticated planes and weaponry from the United States. He announced that Japan would become much more active in its own defense and signaled his resolve by allowing American ships stationed in Hokkaido to openly carry nuclear weapons. Further, he agreed to hold joint naval exercises with the American fleet as a response to the deployment of Russian nuclear submarines off Japan.

He openly worshiped at the Yasukuni Shrine and appointed a number of archconservative nationalists to his cabinet. During his administration, Nakasone followed the lead of his American partner Reagan by leading a campaign to privatize formerly government-owned utilities and railroads. Like Reagan, Nakasone was a believer in supply-side economics. He cut back on government spending for social welfare programs and dramatically increased defense spending past the magical 1 percent of the budget. The resulting brief economic surge, coupled with his overt and brash conservatism, won him wide support in the 1984 elections, becoming the last premier (until Koizumi) to win reelection.

His handpicked successor, Takeshita Noboru, continued Nakasone's policies after his election in 1987. Indeed, Takeshita engineered a substantial change in the income tax structure that benefited his business supporters. Late in Takeshita's term, the nation was rocked by the lingering illness and finally the death of Hirohito, the Emperor Shōwa.

While the emperor lay dying, the country was shocked to hear several leftist politicians openly criticize the imperial institution as well as the emperor himself. The mayor of Nagasaki suggested that the emperor bore much responsibility for the war, especially because hundreds of thousands of Japanese had died needlessly after Japan's surrender was a foregone conclusion. The mayor paid for his frank opinions when a member of an ultraconservative splinter party tried to assassinate him. This did not silence the critics. Many in Okinawa in particular used the death of the emperor as an opportunity to raise serious issues about atrocities committed by Japanese soldiers at the end of the war.

Many of Hirohito's critics raised the issue that Japan had never really come to terms with the magnitude and scope of its war crimes. The death of Hirohito was a messy end to the wartime generation. Many questions seemed to have been left unanswered. The death of Hirohito in 1989 brought many of these questions to the forefront of the national consciousness. The death of the man who had been born a "god" and died as the symbol of Japanese democracy brought back many bad memories and provoked a reexamination of Japan's history. Many of these issues and questions have been raised in anthropologist Norma Fields' evocative book, *In the Realm of a Dying Emperor*. The questions remain unsolved.

9

Turbulent Politics

The Heisei era has been a politically turbulent one characterized by domestic political realignment; domestic corruption and scandal; international crises caused by domestic politics; and two Middle East wars, neither of which were of Japan's choosing. There were also several constitutional crises that arose when neo-nationalists in the Diet attempted to amend Article Nine of the 1947 Constitution. In all cases, Japan was able to weather these political storms.

Takeshita's government fell in 1989, due in part to the Cosmos Recruit scandal in 1989. The latest financial scandal involved stock manipulation that allowed several LDP leaders (including Nakasone and Takeshita himself) to reap huge financial windfalls. There was nothing particularly surprising about politicians benefiting from private financial deals, it had been going on since the early days after the Meiji Restoration. What was now different was the public cry of outrage.

The growing number of small private newspapers did much to heighten the awareness of the common people to the shameful affairs of politicians. This growth in the influence of the press had happened twice before in Japanese history. The first time, as shown by historian James Huffman, was in the 1870s and 1880s when the opposition political parties had used the numerous small papers to criticize the genrō-led government. The government at that time had responded by passing a series of restrictive press laws to limit the power and influence of the press. The second time that the press gained significant power was in the period right after World War II. The release of so many political prisoners by the Allied Occupation government had given rise to the birth of many small, mostly leftist newspapers. The "Reverse Course" taken by the SCAP administrators and the Yoshida government after 1947 led to the suppression of many of these publications.

By the 1960s, many of the small independent newspapers had gone bankrupt or had been absorbed by the huge corporate giants including the *Yomiuri Shimbun*, which at 10 million daily copies printed is the largest nongovernment newspaper in the world (the *People's Daily* in China is technically larger). In the late 1980s a new jumble of specialty papers abounded. They were mostly sensationalist tabloids, and a few were devoted to sports or women's issues. These all vied for readers, and together with a few television news systems, they seemed to focus on the seemingly daily scandals that popped up in government.

The press was aided immeasurably, if unintentionally, by the bumbling ministers of the LDP. Because many of these men were political hacks or former bureaucrats, they were not used to the crush and pressure of a news conference. Almost weekly one minister or another would say something incredibly foolish, and the media would gleefully run off to publish or televise the latest brewing scandal. Other ministers were then asked to comment on the previous silliness, and before long the original minister would be forced to apologize or to resign, sometimes both. The favorite topic was World War II, the second most common was personal finances.

So when the Takeshita government resigned in 1989, once again the LDP turned to a "reform" premier. Uno Sosuke, who had served as Takeshita's foreign minister, was himself soon the focus of yet another scandal that brought down his government after only two months. Uno was caught in a sexual affair with a geisha who sold her life story to one of Japan's many news tabloids. Such extramarital affairs were usually not only tolerated but expected by the public. Many businessmen and politicians openly kept mistresses, and Noble Peace Prize winner Satō even admitted that he had occasionally beaten his wife. But in this instance the scandal served as an indication that women voters were gaining power and influence.

MORE SCANDALS

Perhaps Premier Uno Sosuke was made an example for his sexual improprieties and was singled out unfairly, but his political demise was also due to a number of other political coincidences. The Recruit scandal was still fresh in the minds of the electorate, and many of the LDP factional leaders were themselves tinged. Tanaka had suffered a stroke, leaving a considerable political vacuum in the leadership of the LDP. Uno was sacrificed in the interest of peace and was replaced by the very model of the faceless LDP premier: Kaifu Toshiki.

Kaifu was a very attractive, youthful looking, former bureaucrat who vaguely resembled a popular television actor. He had done so little in the Diet that he had not offended anyone. His chief attribute was that he sported polka-dotted neckties when all the other LDP men wore somber blue ones. Kaifu was not even the leader of a political faction within the LDP. His chief function was to announce decisions made by the real kingmakers in a round of American-style news conferences.

Surprisingly, the kingmakers found that this system worked rather well. Kaifu remained premier even during the Persian Gulf War of 1991 when Japan came under considerable world criticism for its actions. Japan refused to contribute soldiers to the United Nations' forces, citing Article Nine of its Constitution. Japan did, however, make a huge $13 billion contribution, which opened the doors to international criticism for its "mercenary conduct" of war.

In November 1991, Kaifu was replaced by Miyazawa Kiichi, who apparently had recovered from his part of the Recruit scandal. It was widely rumored that he had been selected because of his fluency in English and his friendship with American President George H. W. Bush. Miyazawa's tenure was tarnished by two unfortunate incidents, only one of his own making. In a cabinet news conference, he suggested that the Americans themselves might be responsible for the negative Japanese–American imbalance of payments because they were lazy and did not work as hard as the Japanese. Obviously, Americans did not take kindly to such characterizations, and Miyazawa was forced to apologize hurriedly.

That same year President Bush came to Japan accompanied by the leaders of America's three largest automobile manufacturers intent on forcing open Japan's automobile trade barriers. In the middle of a state dinner Bush became ill, and the world was treated to television coverage of Bush vomiting into Miyazawa's lap! Political jokesters had a field day, mostly at the hapless Miyazawa's expense.

Miyazawa's government suffered from yet another financial scandal, this one involving the actions of the "shadow" kingmaker, Kanemaru Shin. It was common knowledge that Kanemaru could incite or stifle the vociferous attacks of black vans bristling with ear-splitting loudspeakers used by the militarist parties to denounce politicians. A cordon of these vans parked around any building could drown out the business inside. Companies made it a point to contribute large sums of money in exchange for "gifts of silence." Yakuza thugs would also disrupt stockholders' meetings in similar extortion schemes.

It was common knowledge that Kanemaru received large campaign contributions from these extortionists. He used the money to buy legislative influence. Every LDP kingmaker respected and feared his power.

In 1992 a courageous newspaper published the story that Kanemaru had received over $4 million in illegal campaign contributions from the Sagawa Kyubin financial group. The public had at long last grown tired of this corrupt system. Kanemaru was convicted (and fined a paltry few thousand dollars), but the news coverage of the Yakuza-LDP links forced a number of LDP politicians to distance themselves from the scandal.

One group led by Ozawa Ichiro (who replaced Kanemaru as the ultimate behind-the-scenes power broker) and Hata Tsutomu even went so far as to break with the LDP and form its own short-lived political party, the Japan Renewal Party (Shinseito). Another politician, Hosokawa Morihiro, formed his own party; before long the LDP and its 1955 System splintered. Hosokawa formed a coalition with the Socialists and Kōmeitō in 1993 and became Japan's first non-LDP (though he had been a longtime LDP member) premier in over 40 years.

Hosokawa, the grandson of the Fujiwara clan wartime premier Konoe Fumimaro, attempted to use his new power to dismantle the 1955 System through a series of election reform bills. Instead of the multiple-seat districts that had kept the LDP in control, he sought single-seat districts. He tried to impose stricter campaign finance laws and to reapportion Diet representation. These reforms, although popular with the public, were inconvenient to virtually all Diet members who were comfortable with the old corrupt system. Ironically, Hosokawa's government collapsed when Hosokawa's own shady financial past was uncovered.

NEW COALITIONS

A new coalition, led by Hata Tsutomu (with Ozawa's support), replaced Hosokawa but was short lived. Two months later the coalition fell apart and a new government led by the socialist Murayama Tomiichi took its place. The Socialist triumph was also short lived. The coalition that brought Murayama to power included so many former LDP members that he had great difficulty pushing through any significant political reforms.

Murayama was also unfortunate that on January 17, 1995, a huge earthquake (called Hanshin) rocked the Kobe-Ōsaka area, causing over 6,000 deaths and billions of dollars in damage. The tragedy was made worse by the government's bungling of the relief efforts. The Customs Service refused to allow the import of relief supplies and food from abroad and demanded that the special dogs used by the Swiss Army to sniff out survivors in such wreckage be quarantined for the usual 90 days! The Self-Defense Forces did not particularly distinguish themselves in the disaster relief either. They sealed off the area to prevent looting, but they also hampered ambulances and other emergency vehicles. Nearly eight months after the tragedy, thousands of residents of Kobe were still living in temporary shelters, and the rubble had not yet been removed from the area.

Of course earthquakes are endemic to Japan, occurring an average of 1,000 times per year, and cannot be blamed on the government. Most are of the minor variety, but even the large ones are expected by the public. The major problem with earthquakes and other natural disasters is not the loss of life or the destruction of property, it is the government's handling of the crisis. It is expected that the government will respond with quick and assured measures to ameliorate the losses; it is part of the so-called Social Contract. When the government fails to do so, it can cause a major political disruption. Heads of governments (national, prefectural, or municipal) are expected to resign in apology, to be replaced by governments that promise to do better.

A related danger is the threat of nuclear accidents caused by earthquakes. Seismic disturbances wreak havoc on the production of nuclear energy. Eight times between 1997 and 2007 such accidents in Japan have caused some political instability. None of the accidents were catastrophic on the order or the 1979 incident at Three Mile Island in Pennsylvania much less the 1986 catastrophe at Chernobyl, but three caused the loss of life. In 1999, 70 people were irradiated and two men were killed at Tokaimura. In 2004, five were killed in Mihama, and in 2007 eight more killed after an earthquake in Kashiwazakai caused a radioactive water leak.

The year 1995 ended with the government of Murayama showing signs of instability. The old socialist stalwart showed signs of wear and tear as the political situation began to fray at the edges. One of the more ironic problems for poor Murayama was his earlier statements regarding the constitutionality of the Self-Defense Forces. In the 1970s and several times in the 1980s Murayama had led the charge of the leftist opposition parties to criticize the government by claiming that Article Nine of the constitution made any Japanese military illegal. Like the opposition parties a century before had castigated the Genrō government for failure to revise the Unequal Treaties, the leftists had found the Self-Defense Forces issue a convenient club with which to beat the government ministers at every turn.

Murayama had also taken the government to task for allowing American nuclear-powered ships into Japanese waters. He railed constantly that government officials did not even ask if those ships were armed with nuclear weapons. He knew that the very words raised the hackles of the various anti-war movements, and he must have known also that the rightist parties would jump into the fray for somewhat different sovereignty reasons. When Murayama became premier, however, he was assaulted by newspaper and television reporters as to what he intended to do now that he was in charge.

After an embarrassing series of attempts to stall and evade the issue, Murayama in late 1995 mumbled something about the fact that "perhaps the Self-Defense Forces cannot be said to be wholly unconstitutional." It was hardly the battle cry of the political left. In January 1996 a visibly tired and aged Murayama resigned and was replaced by the LDP stalwart Hashimoto Ryūtaro.

THE LDP COALITION GOVERNMENTS

Hashimoto was considered by many to be a "new style" political leader. He was used to the rough and tumble of inter-faction LDP politics, and differed significantly from his predecessors in that he wielded a wry sense of humor. He was adept at news conferences and proved to be rather "telegenic." He appealed to many people in that he rarely mumbled and had mastered the art of looking at the television camera seemingly in earnest.

He managed to "muddle through" a series of bank failures as well as the collapse of several housing loan companies. The Japanese stock market reeled from the financial blows. Many other scandals, public and private, seemed to rock the nation. Several prefectural governments were found to have been wasting billions of yen in entertainment expenses. Several others had funneled public construction money into privately held firms. Most disturbingly, the Green Cross Corporation, which controls the supply of blood in Japan, was found to have ignored the contamination of blood products with HIV. Thousands of hemophiliac patients were thereby infected with Acquired Immune Deficiency Syndrome (AIDS).

Uncharacteristically, Hashimoto stumbled when he responded to a reporter's question regarding international trade in mid-1997. He was asked to comment at the end of a long economic briefing about the fact that the Bank of Japan used ownership of American gold securities in order to cushion fluctuations in currency exchange. Hashimoto was quoted as having said that Japan could cause tremendous damage to the American dollar if it ever chose to demand payment on those securities. It was an obviously unlikely hypothetical situation that no world leader would even contemplate. Not only would the American dollar be in trouble if that were to happen, but so would virtually every national economy in the world, especially Japan, because 80 percent of the world's currencies are pegged to the dollar.

Several anti-LDP newspapers suggested that Hashimoto had intended the remark as a threat to force the United States into economic concessions. Hashimoto spent the next week explaining himself. He had wisely telephoned President Clinton and virtually every world leader to explain that he had been misquoted, but he was forced to muddle through the political fire storm for his verbal slip.

The Hashimoto government several times seemed at the point of collapse in early 1997, but each time the LDP banded together in a united front against possible competing coalitions. Hashimoto announced that he would visit the United States in the late summer of 1997 and invited American President Bill Clinton to Japan as well. Hashimoto also promised that an election would be held in 1998, but he refused to speculate as to whether he would stand again for election. When his faction did poorly in the elections, he resigned and was replaced by another faceless faction leader Obuchi Keizo.

Obuchi's coalition LDP government did not particularly distinguish itself and seemed headed toward another political crises when Obuchi suffered a stroke and fell into a coma in April 2000. He lingered on for a month before he died, but he was replaced as Prime Minister by his long-time rival Mori Yoshiro.

Mori's government was falling in public support when he received a bit of a reprieve when the Empress Dowager Nagako died just as the Diet had voted no-confidence in the government. Hirohito's widow died scarcely a week before former Prime Minister Takeshita died as well. In a spirit of conciliation, two weeks later the LDP managed to form a coalition with two other parties and Mori was allowed to continue as Prime Minister.

Mori weathered two attempts at a vote of no-confidence as well as an official censure before he announced he would resign in April 2001. Before resigning, however, he managed to conclude a compromise treaty with Russia regarding the Kurile Islands.

The Kuriles had been seized by Russia at the end of World War II and had been part of a *modus vivendi* settlement in 1956. Technically Russia and Japan remained at war until 1956 despite the 1951 Peace Treaty with the United States and its allies. Now 55 years later, Russia agreed to return the two southern islands of Shikotan and Hakomai to Japan, but retained the northern two islands of Etorofu and Kunashiri. In February of that year an American nuclear submarine the *U.S.S. Greenville* collided with a Japanese fishing trawler the *Ehime Maru* near Hawaii. Nine people on the Japanese ship, including some high school students drowned as the ship sunk in minutes. Despite the American apology Mori announced he would step down as Prime Minister, in part to apologize to the nation.

THE KOIZUMI YEARS

Koizumi Junichiro became Prime Minister in April 2001 and continued with an almost unprecedented popularity for five years. Something of a maverick, Koizumi built a coalition with other minor parties in order to keep his rivals in the LDP at bay. Curiously, Koizumi seemed to build national support despite a series of economic set-backs. The Nikkei stock market index fell to new lows; Toshiba and Hitachi announced plans to lay-off nearly 20,000 employees; and the unemployment figures rose dramatically. Koizumi's support came in part because of his staunch support of the George W. Bush American government in the wake of the September 11, 2001, terrorist attack of the World Trade Center in New York City.

Koizumi overrode the opposition of pacifists by pledging to send Japanese Self-Defense Forces to support the UN effort in Afghanistan and also three years later to help the American in Iraq. In both cases he claimed that Article Nine of the Constitution did not apply because Japan was really not sending armed troops abroad. In 2001, he sent two destroyers and a supply ship to the Indian Ocean to help lend logistical support to UN troops. In 2004, he sent troops to southern Iraq on a humanitarian mission to help rebuild the domestic infrastructure and supply water to that war-torn area.

He also brazened annual visits to the Yasukuni Shrine (see the following section "The Yasukuni Controversy") and allowed neo-conservatives within the LDP to try to revise school textbooks (see the following section "Textbook Controversy"). In both cases, he had to back-track a bit when public opinion clearly demonstrated that these were unpopular moves. He visited China and South Korea to try to ease tensions caused by his neo-nationalist policies. During his September 2002 visit to North Korea the issue of kidnapped Japanese arose (see the following section "Asian Foreign Relations"). He managed to build some public support by managing to return with a few of those captives.

During his tenure he managed to pass legislation through both houses to privatize the postal service, a notoriously corrupt and inefficient government bureau. The postal savings bank, a copy of the British system, was rife with LDP nepotism and patronage, controlling an enormous (over $2 trillion) source of cheap capital for Japan's large corporations.

Koizumi maintained coalition support within the Diet despite a series of economic setbacks, but finally had to resign in September 2006 when it became clear that his public support was eroding. He was replaced by Abe Shinzo, the first prime minister born after the war. His grandfather, Abe Kan and father, Abe Shintaro, were both politicians. His mother, Kishi Yoko, is the daughter of Kishi Nobusuke, prime minister of Japan from 1957 to 1960.

Abe lasted scarcely a year, badly misjudging the popularity of continuing the neo-nationalist ideas of Koizumi. Abe had campaigned on promises to revise Article Nine to allow Japan to become more self-assertive in the world. He had argued that if Japan were able to mount a token military commitment, it could become a permanent member of the UN Security Council. The new coalition Democratic Party led by Ozawa Ichiro mounted a more traditional pacifist campaign to retain Article Nine and to recall Japanese troops from the Middle East. Ozawa managed to seize control of the Upper House, which elected him Prime Minister in September 2007. The Lower House, however, preferred Fukuda Yasuo. After a brief constitutional crisis, Fukuda prevailed.

Fukuda, in a classic LDP coalition move, seized Ozawa's thunder and allowed the law allowing troops in Afghanistan to expire, recalling the troops in November. Fukuda and Ozawa maintained a kind of *modus vivendi*, cooperating on minor issues in order to allow the government to muddle through.

These were hardly auspicious actions to usher in what some Japanese earlier had characterized as the New Japanese Era. Japan appeared to have entered the twentieth-first century as it had entered the previous, growing in self-confidence but plagued with self-doubt. One would hope that this time the democratic elements in the country will be strong enough to withstand any competition from the antiforeign, ultranationalist factions within Japan.

REAPING THE WHIRLWIND

Without question Japan's political leaders performed many wonderful services for the nation. By and large, they guided the society through turbulent waters. They steered a careful course between the Asian evils of communism (Vietnam, Laos, North Korea, and China) and neo-nationalism (Indonesia, Pakistan, Philippines, South Korea, and Taiwan) by forging a stable and prosperous coalition with the more conservative sectors of society including the bureaucrats and the rural small landowners. They created and nurtured a highly educated and patriotic workforce that came out of Japan's excellent educational system. But if the politicians can be credited with Japan's long postwar history of prosperity and stability, then it must also shoulder the blame for many of Japan's Postwar problems as well.

In the early 1990s, Hosokawa's government had been rocked by a series of foolish statements by cabinet ministers to the press regarding World War II. One cabinet minister was forced to resign for stating that the Nanjing Massacre was a "Chinese fabrication." Another had to apologize for having said that Japan had not really fought a "war of aggression" in China. Even a member of the rival Democratic Socialist Party demonstrated that the LDP did not have a lock on stupidity when he stated that, in his estimation, in the fighting around the Nanjing Massacre, the killing of "only 2,000–3,000 people was permissible."

Also, Murayama had to suffer the embarrassment of more cabinet ministers being caught by the press in foolish statements about the war. The tabloid-style newspapers had field days. One minister stated that Korea had become a Japanese colony willingly. When Murayama was asked about it, he compounded the mistake by saying that the 1910 Japan–Korea Treaty had been "legally valid." A day later he hastily made apologies. Another minister claimed that Japan had done a number of "good things" in their occupation of Korea and China, referring to the building of roads, sewers, dikes, and the like. When North and South Korea and China took umbrage, Murayama was forced to again apologize. One political wag suggested that Murayama should make a tape recording that he could play again and again.

When the Showa Emperor died in 1989 the post–World War II generation was faced with a number of national questions that had been left unresolved. First among these questions was the extent and nature of collective guilt and responsibility for war crimes committed by the State and individuals during World War II. The Tokyo War Crimes Tribunal had convicted only a very few men for these wartime actions. The overwhelming majority of men who had raped, pillaged, burned, butchered, maimed, tortured, and conducted viciously inhumane "scientific experiments" on prisoners of war and helpless civilians were left unpunished. A few hundred of these men (and a few women) had confessed their crimes in public and had tried to make some kind of restitution or atonement. The thousands who had never confessed or even acknowledged that such crimes had been committed left the rest of the nation unwilling to broach the subject. After all, who could be certain that one's own fathers, brothers, and sons had not also been involved?

The Asian neighbors that had suffered from Japanese invasion and oppression continue to castigate Japan for its lack of sincerity. In some ways, Japan has handed its neighbors a convenient club with which to beat it. Any time its neighbors encountered social, political, or economic problems with Japan, they could revert to the topic of wartime atrocities in order to force the Japanese into a corner. Japan has chosen to deal with wartime atrocities piecemeal and incompletely. Veiled and qualified apologies have been insufficient to placate Japan's victims. Japan has refused to enumerate and specify its crimes, preferring to hide behind a very general admission of war guilt contained in the 1951 Peace Treaty. Whereas Germany has admitted the guilt of the Third Reich and has tried to set up individual reparation programs, Japan refuses to recognize that its victims continue to suffer.

International victims of biological experimentation, forced prostitution, slave labor, torture, murder, and other crimes have been told that Japan settled those claims with the national governments of its former enemies. Technically, Japan is correct in that the 1951 Treaty requires foreign nationals to apply to their own nations for recompense and reparations, but to hide behind the letter of the treaties has been ill advised. Germany has set up special courts and financial funds to deal with its wartime victims. German leaders have pointedly visited the sites of former concentration camps in East European nations and have gone to Israel to apologize for German wartime atrocities and have set up schemes to recompense domestic and international slave laborers. Japan has chosen instead to stonewall its victims. Naturally, their victims continue to appeal to the international press and electronic media so the graphic depictions of their sufferings are a constant source of embarrassment for Japan.

Also Germany has passed laws making denial of the Holocaust a crime as well as acting to severely suppress neo-Nazi literature. Contrast those proactive actions with the almost annual fiascos of Japanese government ministers or bureaucrats denying Japanese war atrocities. These blunders have caused Japan tremendous embarrassment abroad. Each time it has happened the governments of China, the two Koreas, and other Asian nations have complained bitterly and Japan's national government must once again deal with their discontent. It appears to the world that Japan is trying to simply wait until their victims die rather than deal with its national guilt comprehensively.

"COMFORT WOMEN" CONTROVERSY

Japan still had questions regarding national responsibilities for war reparations to individual victims. The 1951 Peace Treaty had seemingly settled the issue regarding reparations owed to the various nations that had suffered from Japanese aggression but made no real stipulations for individual reparations. Chief among the groups that demanded official Japanese government apologies and reparations were the so-called Comfort Women who had been forced into sexual slavery by the invading Japanese armies.

Thousands of these women had been sexually brutalized as they were forced to give "comfort" (hence the euphemism) to Japanese soldiers and sailors throughout Japan's far-flung wartime empire. Most of these poor women had returned to their homes too ashamed to speak out about their vicious treatment. Most were considered "unclean" by their own families, and very few were able to assume anything remotely resembling a normal life after the war. Most of the victims were Korean and Chinese, but there were Filipinas, Dutch, Indonesians, and several other nationalities as well. For its part, the Japanese government at first refused to even acknowledge the crimes committed against these women, and then refused to make apologies or offer some compensation.

The Japanese government also claimed that prostitution, still legal during the wartime, had been a privately run business to "comfort" Japan's military. It argued that prostitutes were willing, "independent agents" who should seek reparations from their employers, not from the Japanese government. Historian Yoshiaki Yoshimi, however, has proved conclusively through official documents that it was the government that had initiated and controlled the various brothel companies. He also proved that it had helped kidnap and enslave Korean, Chinese, Dutch, Thai, Indonesian, Malayan, Filipina, and other women, forcing them to serve as prostitutes.

Despite this conclusive evidence, the government refused to meet with survivors, to offer them official apologies, or to pay any reparations. Instead in 1995 it established the Asian Women's Fund, a privately funded philanthropic organization to pay survivors. Private Japanese companies were urged to contribute money, several did. In 2007 it dissolved after it provided 285 women in the Philippines, South Korea, and Taiwan two million yen (US$17,800) each in compensation, helped set up nursing homes for Indonesian former sex slaves and offered medical assistance to some 80 Dutch former sex slaves. Unfortunately, many women who claimed to have been victimized during the war, died before they could receive any compensation. Regrettably, the government has refused to make any official apologies to any of the women until their "individual cases can be investigated." By so doing, it has put the burden of proof of these collective atrocities on each individual victim.

THE OKINAWA CONTROVERSY

A third unresolved question is what is Japan's responsibility for the treatment of Okinawans? The primary problem is that many residents of Okinawa claim that the Japanese military committed wartime atrocities against Okinawans who were considered second-class citizens. They claim that thousands of Okinawans were coerced or forced at gunpoint into committing mass suicide during the bloody final days of the war. Okinawan women were raped, they claim, or were forced into becoming Comfort Women. The issue would come to a head in the mid-1990s along with many other problems regarding the continued status of Okinawans.

In the torrid summer of 1995 the country exploded in rage over the rape of a young Okinawan girl by three American servicemen. The extraterritorial-like provisions of the Status in Force Agreement (SOFA), part of the Mutual Defense Treaty, angered many when Japanese police were not even allowed to arrest the culprits. American President Bill Clinton apologized for the actions of the men who were surrendered to Japanese justice, but it did not quell the outrage. A revision of the Security Treaty was called for, particularly by the Governor of Okinawa Prefecture.

As disgustingly vicious as this rape case was, the national crisis that ensued was out of proportion. For instance, in that same week four Japanese boys attacked a homeless man, beat him senseless, and then set him on fire. The news media paid scant attention to this vicious homicide and filled their news reports with the Okinawan rape instead.

One of the reasons for this is that the Okinawans seized the opportunity to give voice to their anger over what they considered national discrimination of Okinawans in general. They raised several interrelated complaints. First, they felt that they have been discriminated against in civil service employment, placement in national universities, appointments as officers in the Self-Defense Forces, representation in parliament, and even in tax assessment.

Okinawans remain outraged that Japan took so long to "recover" administration to Okinawa from the United States (1951–1972). They felt that they were sacrificed as war scapegoats by the national government for two decades in order to ensure American defense of Japan from its Asian neighbors. They argue that Okinawa should have been part of the country in the 1951 Peace Treaty. It was only because the Japanese "main islanders" consider themselves to be superior to the backward Okinawans that this happened.

Also, nearly one-fifth of Okinawan land is "leased" by the national government for use by the Japanese Self-Defense Forces and by American military forces. Owners of the land have no choice as to who may lease the land or as to who rents. These leases are part of Japan's Mutual Security Treaty with the United States. Not even the Governor of Okinawa Prefecture has any say whatsoever. Not surprisingly, because the largest number of foreign military persons are in Okinawa, the natives there have disproportionately suffered from racial and violent incidents. Okinawa annually leads the nation in reported rapes, murders, and other violent crimes. Even Tokyo with 10 times the population has fewer such crimes.

There are roughly 50,000 U.S. troops based in Japan; the broader American military-related population in the nation totals some 96,000 people. Of that number, almost 60 percent (54,000) are stationed in Okinawa. The population of Okinawa is roughly 1.4 million. During 1995–2007 there were 2,621 violent crimes reported in Okinawa; 856 were committed by Americans. So that means that almost one-third of the crimes were committed by four percent of the population. Obviously, the Okinawans say, they are saddled with the "American problem." Japan needs the United States to maintain a military presence there to provide security for Japan. Okinawans feel that they must pay the price to maintain the American Nuclear Umbrella.

Okinawans point to these and other indications that they are treated as second-class citizens. There has been a small but very vocal grass-roots movement for Okinawan independence. The two most recent governors have artfully used this threat in order to win concessions from the national government.

TEXTBOOK CONTROVERSY

Shortly after the war the American Occupation administration forced Japan to discontinue use of wartime history textbooks that were deemed to be fascist in content. New textbooks were written as early as 1946 explaining how Japan had invaded its neighbors and describing Japan's war atrocities. As early as 1953 elements within the Japanese government began to try to rewrite school history textbooks to lessen the effect of written criticism about Japan's war crimes. In that year the Education Ministry tried to force one author Ienaga Saburo to change his new manuscript. Ienaga refused and instead began a series of lawsuits against the Ministry (the textbook was published unchanged). The lawsuits dragged through the courts until 1997 when the nation's Supreme Court found partially in his favor, but awarded him no monetary damages. For his courage, Ienaga was nominated for the Nobel Peace Prize by American academic Noam Chomsky, but died in 2002 before it could be awarded.

In 1982 the *Asahi* newspaper disclosed that the Ministry had tried again to force a new author to change a phrase that said "Japan invaded Northern China" to have it read "Japan advanced . . ." instead. The Chinese and South Korean governments vehemently protested this attempted censorship and the Japanese government issued a statement to the effect that it was "keenly conscious of the responsibility for serious damage that Japan caused in the past . . . through war and deeply reproaches itself." The apology and promise to revise its textbook authorization system seemed to calm the furor temporarily.

In 2000, however, a group of right-wing academics calling itself the Japanese Society for History Textbook Reform attempted again to change a new junior high school textbook. Again, domestic and international dissent sprang up in many quarters. The government tried to pacify the controversy noting that the new textbook was designed to be used only by private and not public schools. Despite this, huge anti-Japanese public demonstrations erupted in China and South Korea.

In the middle of the controversy it was disclosed that a former education minister had privately bragged in a 2007 meeting of the LDP that his government had succeeded in removing references to "wartime sex slaves" in high school history textbooks. In that same year the Okinawa Prefectural Assembly officially demanded that the Ministry of Education stop its attempts to remove references in a new junior high school history textbook that the Japanese army had forced Okinawan citizens to commit mass suicide in 1945.

In both instances, the government was embarrassed by the disclosures and had to publicly apologize again. The issue continues to instigate controversy and is indicative of Japan's government refusal to face up to Japan's sordid history officially and conclusively.

THE YASUKUNI CONTROVERSY

Another national controversy revolves around the Yasukuni Shrine. The shrine, founded by the Emperor Meiji in 1879, served as a focal point for honoring militarism during the war. Because the Japanese do not routinely bury, but instead cremate their dead, Yasukuni was to the country something like Arlington National Cemetery is to Americans. The American Occupation had forbidden a continuation of ceremonies honoring the war dead in hopes of demystifying Japan's military.

The shrine was "privatized" in 1946, severing its official relation with the government and "returning" to the independent Shinto religious sector. By 2004 its *Book of Souls* lists the names of 2,466,532 soldiers and sailors who died in service to the nation. In 1979 at the 100-year anniversary of its founding, the names of 1068 convicted World War II war criminal were secretly added to that roster. The Showa Emperor (Hirohito) had visited the shrine eight times prior to that, usually at the commemorative service held each year on the August 15 anniversary of the end of the war. When he heard of the secret addition of the war criminals, he stopped attending. His son the Heisei Emperor has never visited.

Since 1975, starting with Miki Takeo, various prime ministers have visited the shrine as private citizens on August 15. After the secret inclusion of the war criminals was leaked, the Chinese and South Koreans vigorously protested these semiofficial visits to the commemoration ceremonies as a signal of Japan's rising nationalist sentiments. From 1985 to 1992 government ministers ceased to come, but then Miyazawa secretly visited in 1992 and then Hashimoto did so publically in 1996. Each time Koizumi visited (six times in 2001–2007) during his term in office, the Chinese and South Koreans government protested, forcing Koizumi to visit those countries to apologize. Evidently he believed that the support of the right-wing political parties was worth the annual castigation from Japan's East Asian neighbors.

Another problem arose when Yasukuni began to "consecrate" the spirits of soldiers and sailors who had died while on active duty in the Self-Defense Forces after World War II. They did this even though they were not really "war-dead" because Japan could not be at war according to the constitution. One Christian widow sued to have her husband's name removed from the list of "consecrated war dead" on the grounds that this Shintoist ritual violated her constitutional religious freedom. The furor that resulted from this lawsuit escalated into a public firestorm. She was joined by members of several New Religions and even some mainstream Buddhist sects. The political right sprang to action in opposition. She received death threats and a flood of hate mail for her "unpatriotic spirit." As usual, the Supreme Court muddied the issue by issuing a ruling that is nearly incomprehensible to even the finest legal minds. It suggested that both the state as well as the woman were "probably within their constitutional rights."

Also, because 27,863 Taiwanese and 21,181 Koreans are on the Yasukuni list, having died in service to the empire, the controversy has remained an international problem as well. In June 2005 a group representing Taiwanese aborigines attempted to visit the shrine in order to remove the souls of the Taiwanese dead. The group was turned away by security guards, but not before they were photographed by television and print media, creating yet another embarrassment for the government.

A documentary film titled "Yasukuni" by Chinese director Li Ying, a 10-year resident of Japan debuted at the Pusan International Film Festival in 2007, was shown at the Sundance Film Festival in 2008 and won the best documentary award at the Hong Kong International Film Festival in 2008. It had earlier received 7.5 million yen (about US$70,000) from the Japan Arts Council in fiscal 2006 as a production subsidy. Liberal Democratic Party lawmaker Inada Tomomi led a coalition of right-wing parties that threatened the theater that was about to show the movie in Tokyo in May. The film was shown later in the month despite continued threats by right-wing groups.

RELIGIOUS ISSUES

In June 1994 a radical religious cult called Aum Shinrikyō sprayed the poison gas sarin in the town of Matsumoto, causing several deaths. Nine months later, while the origins and culprits were still being investigated, the cult released another sarin attack, this time in the Tokyo subway system killing another a dozen and injuring thousands more. This outrage brought the issue of religion to the forefront of public opinion for a brief time.

The nation had been struggling with religious issues since the Occupation and even before. At the beginning of the twentieth century a number of religious movements had sprung up to compete with the state-sanctioned Shinto and Buddhist sects. These so-called New Religions were usually clustered around a charismatic shaman and were often a combination of Shinto and Buddhist beliefs. As long as they did not actively disturb the peace, most of them were left alone to practice their private customs. A few, however, ran afoul of the law by preaching that the state had no right to demand that citizens participate in Shintoist ceremonies. These "anti-patriotic" groups were harshly suppressed by the police; many religious leaders were arrested, tortured, and even killed.

In the early postwar liberalism hundreds of new religions resurfaced or were founded. The new constitution guaranteed religious freedom and granted tax-free status to religions that had been "institutionalized and registered." This was interpreted to mean that any group professing to be a religion could register with the government and gain release from taxation. Of course many opportunists and criminals used the new laws for personal gain. By the late 1980s there were over 180,000 tax-free registered religions. By comparison, the United States had granted such status to about 14,000 religious groups.

The national government tried several times to tighten up restrictions on what would be considered legitimate religions but was met with wide-scale protest at every turn. These protests came from the religions themselves, of course, but also from civil libertarians who feared any assault on the civil rights guarantees of the constitution. The issue was before the parliament again in 1995 when the Aum Shinrikyō incident struck. In fact the police had been investigating this particular group for over 18 months before the sarin attack. The religious recognition issue remains a controversy even as the perpetrators of the gas attack are tried in court.

The Nichiren Buddhist sect of Soka Gakkai continued to struggle in Japan despite its huge numbers of believers. Part of the problem had to do with its rather controversial conversion (some say by coercion) methods. They took on the status of a dangerous religious cult during the 1960s. Another part of the problem is that they formed a supposedly "nonreligious" political party in the middle 1960s called Kōmeitō ("Clean Government Party"), which threatened every other existing party, of course. In the 1990s Komeitō split with Soka Gakkai, and the members of the party were actually excommunicated from the religion for having criticized the latter's controversial leader.

ZAINICHI PROBLEMS

Japan has not deal adequately with its *zainichi* (foreign residents) population. Generally speaking, the relatively small percentage of aliens living in Japan have caused problems disproportionate to their numbers in Japan. Japanese do not look kindly upon them, especially the Asian ones. Part of problem is that most Asian aliens are poor and tend to live in squalor compared to the Japanese. Crime and poverty rates are high among them as are disease and mortality ratios. In the main, they are in Japan for economic reasons. Many were drawn to Japan to work in low-paying low-status positions. But many are in Japan because they were forced to come by the Japanese themselves.

Many Koreans were brought to Japan as slave laborers during World War II, and others were dragooned into the Japanese military. About 5.4 million were conscripted and about 670,000 were brought to Japan. Perhaps 60,000 of them died in what amounted to slave labor. By the end of the war there were nearly 2.5 million Koreans in the Japanese islands. Most returned to Korean at the end of the war, but many feared that they would be ostracized as collaborators if they returned to their homes. Many others had lived their entire lives in Japan and really had no homes, land, or property in Korea to return to even if they had wished to do so. So by late 1946 there were still almost 650,000 who remained in Japan.

A lesser number of Taiwanese were also brought to Japan as laborers, perhaps 100,000 of them were in Japan at the end of the war. Most returned to Taiwan, but a significant number remained in Japan. Also, offspring of mixed racial unions in Japan's empire have been allowed to "return" to Japan and settle there. Thousands more Chinese have come to Japan to study or work. According to Immigration Bureau data, the number of registered foreigners in Japan set a record high of about 2.08 million in 2006. Among them, permanent residents have continued to grow, reaching 837,000, or 40 percent, of all registered foreigners in 2006. They now make up about 1.7 percent of Japan's population of 127.8 million. There were 606,889 Chinese residents and 593,489 Korean residents in Japan. Brazilians and Filipinos are Japan's third- and fourth-largest foreign groups. Americans accounted for just 2.4 percent of foreign residents. Chinese-speaking residents—from the Chinese mainland, Hong Kong and Taiwan—accounted for 28.2 percent of Japan's 2.15 million registered foreigners, while Koreas dropped to 27.6 percent.

These statistics are somewhat misleading because almost 290,000 naturalized citizens of Japan are of Korean ancestry. Also, of the some 600,000 Korean resident aliens, almost 97 percent of them were born in Japan and have lived their entire lives there. Many speak only Japanese and are not fluent in Korean. Unlike the United States and many other industrialized nations, being born in Japan does not entitle one to citizenship. Some 90 percent of Japanese-born Koreans were born to Korean parents who were themselves born in Japan. That means that they are second, and sometimes third generation noncitizens in the country where they were born. Until recently, they could not vote, own property, or avail themselves of free education, medical care or unemployment insurance and retirement programs because they were not citizens of Japan. They were forced to register with the national and local municipal governments as aliens and to carry special identification. They were of course denied Japanese passports to travel abroad. They could "return" to Korea (either one), but they were not assured that they would be allowed to return to their homes and families in Japan.

There are nearly 300,000 Brazilians of Japanese ancestry currently living in Japan. In the early part of the twentieth century many Japanese emigrated to Brazil for economic reasons. Many settled there permanently amounting to upwards of 1.3 million living there in 2007. Beginning in the 1980s many were allowed to "return" to Japan to work in Japan's burgeoning industrial economy. Most intend to return to Brazil once they have made significant savings. While they are in Japan they remain outsiders to the society. Many do not speak Japanese fluently, and many are of mixed race. They tend to reside in economic ghettos where they are treated with mixed bemusement and racial discrimination by the Japanese.

An almost equal number of Filipinos live in Japan. Most have come to work there, but not a few are the descendents of mixed race marriages and liaisons. The number of Filipinos are disproportionately female, having come to Japan to work in "entertainment" districts as bar hostesses and prostitutes. Interestingly, many Filipino nurses were lured to Japan to work in nursing homes and aged care facilities. Generally speaking, their contracts did not allow them to bring spouses or dependents, but many have done so illegally. Many have married Japanese men. A Supreme Court ruling in June 2008 finally allowed for citizenship of children born to Japanese fathers and Filipino mothers, even if the parents were not married.

ASIAN FOREIGN RELATIONS

Japan's relations with its East Asian neighbors during the last half-century have been fractious at best. Much of the instability is a direct result of Japan's horrendous history of atrocities during World War II, and some of the recent frostiness can be blamed on the ineptitude of its politicians. The bumbling of its leaders in relation to textbook and war crimes denial controversies alluded to above need no further elucidation except to say that each controversy continues to feed the paranoia of its East Asian neighbors.

Other causes have more to do with Japan's continuing close foreign relations with the United States than with anything else. The fact that Japan continues to allow a significant American military presence on the islands alienates the Peoples' Republic of China and communist North Korea. No one need remind those nations that Japan has served as America's "unsinkable aircraft carrier," in deterrence to communist expansion for half a century. Also, Japan has been a staunch ally to the United States in the United Nations. But then one could say the same, until recently, about South Korea and the Republic of China on Taiwan.

To be charitable, one should note that Japan has been relatively successful in steering a middle course between the United States and its Asian allies (Taiwan and South Korea) on the one hand and the unpredictable actions of North Korea on the other. The regimes of Kim Il Sung and his son Kim Jong Il has been the bane of Japan's existence. The invasion of South Korea in 1950 needs no clarification, but one must also consider the North's bomb attack of South Koreans in Rangoon in 1983 and the destruction of the KAL airliner off the coast of Burma in 1987, and the North Korean nuclear threats as well. Add to those provocations the North's bellicose actions towards Japan itself.

There have been several incidents of North Korean incursions against Japanese sovereignty including attack boats in Japanese waters. Also, several Japanese citizens were kidnapped and taken to North Korea in order to help train sappers and saboteurs speak Japanese. Some were forcibly married to Koreans (and even one to an American military deserter). Their children served as hostages to keep the captives in Korea. Until recently North Korea has refused to provide an accurate, or even consistent, accounting of the number of Japanese captives still alive in North Korea. Finally, the North Korean government has used its developing nuclear industry as leverage to force Japan and the United

States to provide badly needed economic assistance. In the 1990s, when negotiations had reach an impasse, the North Koreans "test fired" missiles over Japan as a warning. The Koreans have tested Japanese patience with many such acts. Also they have stirred up *zainichi* Koreans living in Japan from time to time. All in all, one must admit that Japan has been relatively patient and tolerant of its northern neighbor.

DOMESTIC POLITICAL MINORITIES

Japan has reaped a whirlwind because of its treatment of domestic political minorities. It has made some rather callous decisions to ignore huge sectors of its society by denying them any significant political voice. In ways reminiscent of its LDP political coalition building, it has behaved as though those minorities did not exist until those policies backfired. When social problems arose due to poor retirement benefits, student suicide, bullying in schools, environmental pollution, or sexual harassment, the government suddenly swung into muted response and did the very least necessary to ameliorate the excesses. These reactionary policies seem to work to its advantage in terms of keeping the LDP in control for most of the Postwar era.

When minor political parties seemed to be gaining ground on any social or political issue, the ponderous LDP would swing in that direction. Factions of the LDP that seemed more sympathetic would gain a temporary ascendency until the issue was muted or the crisis passed, then the party would gradually absorb the new policies and move on. Three political minorities continue to be neglected: women, the *Ainu,* and the *Burakumin.*

THE WOMEN'S MOVEMENT

The Women's Movement had gathered considerable strength due in part to its alliance with the feminist movement in the United States. "Office Ladies" (shortened to "OLs") in Japan were increasingly dissatisfied with low-ranking and poorly paid positions in Japan's workforce. They demonstrated substantial influence primarily in the Green or environmentalist movements. A number of women rose in the ranks in the leftist political parties. One, Doi Takako, became head of the Socialist Party in 1986, and several others even cracked the male-only ranks of LDP cabinets.

Because many women controlled the purse strings of their own household budgets, their economic power forced even the conservative LDP to sit up and take notice. A national law to stop employment discrimination and sexual harassment was pushed through the Diet, but it has still languished, poorly enforced, for several years. Part of the problem was that in the economic depression that hit Japan in the early 1990s, women employees suffered disproportionately. The usual response of Japanese companies in times of economic downturn is to honor their rigid code of promotion by seniority. Therefore, the "last hired–first fired" were usually women.

Also, the usual hiring practice of Japanese large companies is to hire women as temporary workers because they would inevitably marry and quit work in order to care for their children. Not surprisingly, women's wages and fringe benefits, such as medical insurance and retirement packages, lagged far behind those for permanent employees—men.

Some of the other problems perceived by feminists are the fact that Japanese law almost totally forbids women to use their natal names after marriage; low-dosage birth control pills are still illegal (though abortion is not); medical and law schools accept very few women; pornography and prostitution are still very common in Japan. Thousands of foreign women are imported as bar hostesses and entertainers, and many travel agencies advertise special men-only "culture tours" to the sex spots of Southeast Asia (Bangkok and Manila primarily).

The Women's Movement gained considerable strength and influence because of the rising consumer and environmentalist movements. The environment had long been a prickly issue in Japanese history. After the Matsukata Deflation of 1881 the Furukawa chemical zaibatsu had been allowed to pollute an entire agricultural region with the poisonous tailings of the Ashio Copper mine. Furukawa Ichibei himself had only agreed to compensate and clean up the pollution after a national peasant movement had marched on Tokyo.

In the 1950s a new chemical poisoning called Minamata Disease killed hundreds and poisoned many more when mercury was spilled into the fishing waters near Minamata. Women who had given birth to deformed children or had been forced to care for their stricken relatives came to the fore in protest movements. These women gained experience in politics, and many of them became famous in their campaign to gain reparations. Unfortunately these individual legal cases dragged through the courts for literally decades until many suits were consolidated into a class action suit. Even then, full compensation was not forthcoming until the mid-1990s when the Supreme Court ruled in favor of the plaintiffs. In actuality, an out-of-court settlement had been arranged that paid the victims less than $25,000 each. As late as 2008 there were still many victims who had not been fully recompensed.

Women had been active in pacifist movements as early as the Russo-Japanese War in 1905. They had participated in socialist and proletarian groups as well as in the Communist Party during the early part of the twentieth century. They came to the fore, however, in the antinuclear bomb and pacifist movements after World War II.

Many young women had also participated in the anti–Vietnam War student movement in the late 1960s and 1970s. A few notable women became notorious as members of the Red Army terrorist activities as well. Most of the women who became involved, however, were law-abiding women who could no longer bear the idea of sending their men off to war. They were in the vanguard of the movement to enforce Article Nine of the Peace Constitution. They resisted every attempt to revise the constitution.

Some women became active in public life as members of PTAs, school boards, and consumer cooperatives. Activist women often tired of lip service from male politicians and began to seek office on their own. Some of these women parlayed their experience in these and other primarily women's organizations into national politics. The LDP made this very difficult so that the majority of women who sought political office did so as members of other political parties.

THE AINU

The term *Ainu* refers to a small minority of indigenous people that reside primarily in Hokkaido and the Kurile Islands, though they seem to be related to the people of Sakhalin and the Maritimes in Russia. There are perhaps 150,000 people left, though their numbers are uncertain because many either are unaware of, or deny their heritage due to racial discrimination among the Japanese.

They are physically distinct from most Japanese, with hairier bodies, wider foreheads, lighter-colored skin, and sometimes different eye color. Long thought to be of proto-Caucasian extraction, recent DNA studies can find no real biological affinity. They have been present in Japan since the prehistoric *Jomon* times (1500–200 b.c.e.). They are present in ancient Japanese folk tales and are mentioned in the first Japanese written histories (*Kojiki* and *Nihonshoki* of the eighth century c.e.). They were ancient enemies of the Japanese, raiding the northern periphery for centuries. Distinct in their social and religious customs, they remained hunters and gatherers into the late nineteenth century. They fought a series of wars against the Japanese, the most notable ones in 1457, 1669, and 1789. They were pushed increasingly northward until Meiji times when the new government isolated them into enclaves on the island of Hokkaido.

The Meiji government began a century-long campaign to "civilize" and "modernize" them in much the same brutal cultural genocide practiced by Euro-Americans on indigenous peoples in North, Central and South America and Australia. The Ainu were denied their homelands and culture, being forced into sedentary agriculture. They were forbidden to speak their native language, their young being forced to study Japanese in schools. Indeed, the language nearly died out except for the efforts of some enlightened Japanese.

The language did not even have a systemized Ainu-Japanese dictionary until the late twentieth century.

From 1899 until 2008 the government did not recognize the Ainu as a distinct racial, cultural, or political minority. In fact, in the mid-1980s Nakasone Yasuhiro, the then prime minister, declared that Japan was a homogenous nation with no minorities. The government behaved as if all Japanese were of a common racial, linguistic, and cultural background; a nice sentiment, but one that had negative consequences for the Ainu.

Because Japan had signed the United Nations Treaty in 1979, it came under considerable international pressure to honor the International Covenant on Civil and Political Rights (ICCPR). In 2008 the government finally designated them as a separate culture, providing national funds for the preservation of their society. In a report to the Lower House of the Diet Chief Cabinet Secretary Machimura Nobutaka said, "Our government solemnly accepts the historical fact that the Ainu people were discriminated against and suffered poverty in the process of our country's modernization." Unfortunately, the Diet's recognition of the Ainu was in a nonbinding resolution. It created an eight-member committee to recommend further steps for the government to take, but only one member, is Ainu. Many Ainu doubt that the government will officially apologize—as Australia and Canada did recently to their native populations for past policies—pay compensation or grant access to land for hunting or fishing.

During most of the twentieth century the government allowed them a certain amount of social autonomy, but they were under Japanese political and judicial jurisdictions. They were allowed to vote only if they had succumbed to Japanese political customs (name, language, and registration). It remains unclear how they will be allowed to administer themselves under the new laws. An indigenous organization has sprung up in Hokkaido to press for legislation to allow for more Ainu cultural programs such as alternate language instruction for their children in elementary schools.

BURAKUMIN

The word *burakumin* is a euphemism that means something like "hamlet folk," and connotes a kind of special category set aside from regular or normal citizenship. Despite the exceptionalism that connotes abnormality, the term is somewhat better than the previous *eta*, which translates as "abundant filth." The origins of the caste-like status are unclear at best. They are racially, linguistically, or otherwise indistinguishable from the rest of society. Historians believe that they originated from the ritual impure tasks that were assigned to poor people in the feudal period.

Because the society was predominately Buddhist during the period, those tasks that were considered impure, if not "sinful," such as those dealing with death and dirt, were probably assigned to criminals, immigrants, and other socially inferior people. There was probably a Shinto stigma of *kegare* or filth impurity involved as well. Jobs dealing with disposal of dead animals including leatherwork were relegated to remote parts of villages. Also executioners and people that had to dispose of unwanted human bodies (the Buddhists themselves were involved with cremation of "normal" people) were also shunned. The religious and social stigma attached to the tasks were then transferred to the people themselves. The people were ostracized socially to the margins of society, very often physically as well as socially. They were made to live in dangerous and nonproductive areas of the country such as dry river bottoms, the edges of forests, swamps, and the like. They became something like the untouchable caste in Indian society.

During the Tokugawa era (1600–1868) society was divided into four official Neo-Confucian classes ranked according to professional tasks and their contribution to society at large. At the top were the warrior/bureaucrats *samurai*; below them the peasant agriculturalists; then the artisan/craftspeople; and finally the merchants. Ranked below them were all sorts of nonproductive (necessary evils) folk like entertainers, vagabonds, prostitutes, and criminals. Curiously, Buddhist and Shinto priests were not part of the four classes, but were treated with some respect because of the philanthropic works that they performed in society. The *eta* were outside the normal village administration and were not accorded social rights, nor saddled with duties, obligations, or even rice tax. The Tokugawa allowed them a kind of autonomy among themselves as long as their leaders kept the peace.

The new Meiji government designated them as *shin-hinin* ("new citizens") when the four classes were dissolved in 1871. Later they were relegated to special districts (*toshoku buraku*) that ended up branding them with the new term *burakumin*. Government tried to remove the pejorative connotation, but society itself refused to accept them. They were not allowed into polite society and were discriminated against in every way. People refused to allow them to integrate by profession or marriage. The special districts received little government funding for education, police protection, and the like. Landlords refused to rent or sell property to them and they were ostracized from every aspect of social and political life.

Some attempted to assimilate into society by leaving their homes and immigrating to new areas, including going to the newly settled areas such as Hokkaido, and even going abroad to Hawaii, Brazil, and the United States. The ones who remained in the *buraku* special districts fared badly. When parents sought mates for their children, special detectives were hired to ferret-out anyone with "impure blood" including former *burakumin*. In the early 1920s a leftist organization called "the levelers" (*suiheisha*) tried to force the government to legislate their socioeconomic improvement. After the war, various social agencies tried to help, mostly through education and professional training. In 1969 a Special Measures Law for Assimilation Projects was enacted to help *burakumin* to assimilate into society at large. The law focused on building better housing and municipal services such as hospitals, clinics, libraries, swimming pools, and the like. The law terminated in 2002 after billions of dollars had been spent.

The Socialist and Communist parties have continued to work with these unfortunates. It is indicative that the LDP has made no concerted effort to garner their support. A number of their community have been elected to municipal and even national legislatures. A 1993 survey found 298,385 households with 892,751 members in the country, but their unofficial numbers probably range higher than three million.

Part of the problem why the social stigma and discrimination continues is that many *burakumin* have become involved with the *yakuza* organized crime groups. Sociologists argue that because the *yakuza* have accepted nearly anyone who wishes to join (foreigners, *zainichi*, etc.) it is natural that some *burakumin* youth gravitated there.

SUMMARY

Without question, Japanese society has had a rocky ride in the Heisei Era; not as disruptive as the previous Showa period of course. Japan seems to have weathered the storms of international and domestic politics. The few serious problems outlined above will certainly challenge the nation in the months, years, and decades to come. Problems that have arisen will have to be dealt with in order to avoid them growing into real crises that might threaten the culture as a whole.

Japan seems to be capable of meeting most challenges, both domestic and foreign. The political system, despite its flaws, seems to be readily capable of adjusting to new realities. Political factions within the dominant LDP have evolved into a flexible system for addressing pressing issues. The electoral system has continued to meet the needs of society. Japan has needed to change from time to time without compromising its constitutional foundation. It does not seem to be unreasonable that it will continue to do so. Nothing succeeds like success.

10

Society in the Twenty-First Century

This chapter is meant to provide a glimpse of the Japanese society in this new century. It is by no means intended to be comprehensive nor authoritative; one should consult recent books by sociologists, journalists, or political scientists (or anthropologists for that matter) if one seeks a more systematic and academic treatment of Japanese society.

Another caveat that should be noted is that much in this chapter appears to examine the exceptional and exotic nature of Japanese society; that is, that which is different or unique about Japan. The reason for this is that Japan *is* exotic and exceptional. It is unlike any other society on earth. But then, so is every other society with which we are unaccustomed. In many ways Japan is more similar to America and Northern European nations because its political, technologic, and economic systems are conscious emulations by the Japanese. But in its social, religious, and agricultural (gustatory as well) systems, Japan is much more like its Asian cousins.

A final caveat is that there is in Japan a particular (and peculiar) strain of thought that argues that Japan's exceptionalism is precisely what makes it better than other societies. This is called *Nihonjin-ron*; the argument that Japanese exceptionalism is an essentialism as well. They contend that Japanese intestines are more suitable for vegetarianism; that the Japanese diet is more conducive for pacifism or that Japanese women are suited for hand-eye co-ordination tasks because of the shape of their eyes. Proponents have been labeled racists, neo-nationalists, chauvinists, and jingoists. Their arguments are reductionist and silly at best.

With those caveats in mind, we may now proceed to examine some aspects of Japanese culture that are perhaps different, but not better or worse than the Western examples.

THEATER AND CINEMA

In terms of the performing arts, traditional forms of Japanese theater fared very well in the Postwar years. Part of this success can be attributed to the fact that Kabuki, Noh, Bunraku, and the even older genres had lost political relevance in the eighteenth century. That is the period when most of the dramas had been written. None of the theater forms had been tainted by militarism as had the cinema, which had become the propaganda arm of the military during the war. Therefore, the Occupation authorities heartily encouraged the revival of the old morality plays. Within months after the beginning of the Occupation, theater troupes were doing a thriving business as people sought inexpensive release from their drab lives.

After the Occupation, the national government mounted a concerted effort to preserve and encourage the theatrical art forms. Famous actors, musicians, and puppet masters were designated National Living Treasures and given generous stipends to subsidize the theater. National theater troupes were formed, and sumptuous new buildings were constructed.

The newer, more Western-style theater troupes managed to eke out a meager life until the 1960s when they became increasingly more popular. One theater form that did amazingly well was the Takarazuka Revue. This form of musical theater, which has been the focus of study by anthropologist Jennifer Robertson, was based on the reverse of Kabuki convention. Namely, women portrayed all the roles on stage. It had been popular in the wild permissive days of the 1920s as a showgirl revue. It had been largely suppressed during the militarist period, but came back with enormous popularity in the postwar period.

Japanese cinema came into its own in the postwar era. Because of Occupation censorship as well as the high cost of film, the immediate postwar era has been called the "Director's Age." Cinema giants like Kurosawa Akira, Mizoguchi Kenji, and Ōzu Yasujiro produced many of their classics during this period. The 1960s and 1970s saw Japanese cinema rise to great heights, and it has not slowed down since then. Critics had once suggested that Japanese films were too derivative of Hollywood influences, but before long Kurosawa's films became the focus of Western "remakes." Sergio Leone's "spaghetti westerns"

Japan Today.

that made Clint Eastwood a cinema star were remakes of Seven Samurai, Yojimbo, and Sanjuro. In the 1980s the films of Itami Juzō (Tampopo, Taxing Woman) became very popular throughout the world.

THE MARTIAL ARTS

The martial arts took on a new popularity in postwar Japan. *Judo, jujitsu, kendo, aikido, karate,* and even *sumo* became familiar to Westerners as well. Most participants became involved with these forms as exercise and sport. By the 1960s the Zen Buddhist underpinnings of the disciplines became increasingly more important. *Judo* and *jujitsu* eventually became Olympic sports, which helped provide Japanese athletes a world presence. When *karate* became very popular in the United States in the late 1960s, it helped to revitalize the sport in Japan as well.

Sumo had always been a distinctly Japanese sport because it is so heavily imbued with Shinto ideology. It was difficult for non-Japanese to understand, let alone appreciate, the esoteric rituals that are part and parcel of the sport. Beginning in the early 1960s, however, a number of Asian Americans from Hawaii began to filter into *sumo*. The pioneer was Jesse Takayama who, after he retired from a decade of wrestling, opened up his own "stable" of young Hawaiians who took to the sport with a vengeance. The mountain-sized Konishiki (a Samoan born Saleva'a Fuauli Atisano'e, at one point he weighed 564 pounds!) very nearly rose to become a Grand Champion (*yokozuna*) in the sport. He complained that only racism kept him from that honor. Eventually his stablemate Akebono (the Hawaiian-born Chad Rowan) managed to force the Japanese to grant him that honor by winning a succession of tournaments. He was later joined by countryman Musashimaru (born Fiamalu Penitani in Samoa). In the 1990s there were no fewer than a dozen Americans in the top echelons of *sumo* and perhaps twice that many moving up through the lower ranks.

Since the late 1990s *sumo* has been beset with another invasion, the Mongolians. For centuries Mongolian society nurtured a wrestling culture similar enough to *sumo* that during World War II the two systems influenced each other. Japanese soldiers stationed in Outer Mongolia facilitated the symbiosis by staging *sumo* matches during times of peace. They brought back some of the wrestling holds learned from the Mongolians after the war. With the advent of the American grand champions, some Japanese entrepreneurs began to bring over Mongolian wrestlers to Japan. Several of the Mongolians rose rapidly through the ranks until two mastered the system to become *Yokozuna*. Several other wrestlers were moving up the ranks so that by 2008 at least seven had reached the top three ranks (*Sanyaku*).

Similarly, several East Europeans joined *sumo* in the early part of the twenty-first century. At one point in 2008, 60 percent of the *sanyaku* were non-Japanese. Not surprisingly, the old conservative ranks of *sumo* enthusiasts voiced alarm that the sport was being inundated by aliens.

LITERATURE

Japanese literature deserves a historical volume of its own (there are several, the best by Donald Keene) because it took on an importance in postwar Japan that continues to climb. International recognition of such giants as Kawabata Yasunari and Oe Kenzaburō rose to such heights that both would receive the Nobel Prize for World Literature. Many more authors became wildly popular in Japan as well as in the rest of the world largely due to the excellent translations of such people as Keene, Edward Seidensticker, Helen McCullough, and Ivan Morris. The notoriety of avant-garde writers like Mishima Yukio and Abe Kōbo helped to popularize Japanese fiction throughout the literary world as well. A whole new generation of authors like Yoshimoto Banana and Murakami Haruki have become familiar to readers all over the world.

The traditional forms of literature enjoyed a rebirth of popularity. Haiku and other traditional forms of poetry gained new admirers and aficionados. Classics like Tale of Genji, Tosa Nikki, Confessions of Lady Nijō, and the various warrior tales received new attention. The prewar works of Tanizaki Junichirō, Natsume Sōseki, Dazai Ōsamu, and others were reprinted and sold millions of copies.

ARTS AND CRAFTS

Japanese art became wildly popular in the rest of the world, and the Japanese were forced to reconsider it after a brief pro-Western period when Japanese art was underappreciated in Japan. Most of the works that became popular were the old styles of *sumi-e, ukiyo-e,* and *Yamato-e.* Newer genres and contemporary artists struggled as they do in perhaps every society. The more avant-garde forms of art prospered in their own small communities, but when one thinks of Japanese art, one tends to think of the traditional ones.

The same could be said about architectural styles. The old Sino-Japanese Buddhist styles still held great currency, however, more modern and progressive ideas took hold, particularly within the commercial sector. Japanese architects gained international notoriety for their "earthquake-proof" designs, particularly in the 1960s.

Traditional styles of sculpture continued to be popular, though a generation of artists went abroad to study in Paris, New York, Vienna, and other centers. Quite a few Japanese became famous in the classical and avant-garde genres. Japanese pottery took on a new popularity in the world due mostly to the number of pieces that left the country during the Occupation. Hundreds of foreigners came to Japan to sit at the feet of Japanese pottery masters. One could say the same about a number of Japanese folk arts such as kimono, silk brocade and embroidery, paper making, and miniature carvings. Art collectors descended on Japan after the war to buy ancient Japanese swords and armor. The manufacture of these samurai equipment was revitalized as well.

The traditional Zen arts of flower arranging (*ikebana*), tea ceremony (*cha-no-yu*), miniature plant husbandry (*bonsai*), and the various forms of rock and moss gardening enjoyed rebirths when people began to have more leisure time. Virtually every Japanese above the age of 40 pursues one of these arts as a hobby. Clubs and associations for these and other leisure arts abound.

Japanese dance forms enjoyed a revival in the 1960s. The popularity of Kabuki and Noh helped to revive the traditional dance forms. Amateur dance troupes helped to revitalize other dance forms such as *gagaku*. It also helped that Japanese mothers somehow decided that an essential part of their daughters' social education had to include some kind of dance training. Millions of little girls spent part of their afternoons plodding away at learning at least one dance (usually "Sakura") for an ultimate dance recital. It became a "coming of age" ritual and therefore helped to preserve the traditional forms and styles by providing performers and teachers with a real livelihood.

POPULAR CULTURE

If the traditional cultural forms are alive and well in Japan, popular culture can be said to be absolutely thriving. Japan is arguably the hothouse for virtually any fad that comes along in the rest of the world. The Japanese watch a lot of television. Among the most popular shows are those that show how the rest of the world plays, eats, and amuses itself. The Japanese therefore know what is popular almost anywhere in the world. They quickly emulate what they see. If women are wearing berets in Toronto on Monday, by Tuesday Japanese women are demanding berets at the trendy boutiques along the Ginza in Tokyo. Department store buyers now routinely are allowed to preview television shows so that they can have the trendy new items in supply. The large department stores have been known to bribe television producers to show Westerners wearing whatever the stores have in large stock.

The same may be said about popular music, films, and television. Most of what becomes popular in the United States becomes the rage within a few weeks in Japan as well. The Japanese are well acquainted with international film and television celebrities who populate Japanese television and print commercials.

"JAPLISH"

In terms of advertising, the Japanese are enthralled with foreign words. In the same manner that Americans pay more for products if they have French names, the Japanese attach English names to virtually everything in the hopes it will seem more trendy. Often their understanding of the words is no better than Californians who refer to El Camino Real Highway or El Rancho Ranch. Foreigners will erupt in glee to some of the unfortunate malapropisms like the coffee creamer called "Creap," the premoistened towelettes called "My Wet," or the isotonic drink called "Sweat."

Japanese have created a gaggle of thousands of words that are called *gairaigo* or "foreign loan words." Anthropologist James Stanlaw has shown that the mixed origins and complex changes in these words make them a rather sophisticated syncretic language. Some, like *apato* for apartment, *pan* for bread, and *depato* for department store, are still fairly easy to discern. Others take some solid detective work. For instance *pasukon* is difficult to trace to "personal computer," but not so very different than the American "PC" (which can also mean "politically correct") or CPU. The popular breaded fried food called *tempura* must be traced back to the sixteenth-century Portuguese *temporas* to refer to nonmeat (primarily fish) foods that Roman Catholics could eat during Lent.

Other words boggle the imagination. *Nokon* refers to a baseball pitcher who has "no control" over his pitches. Men who fantasize about teenage girls are said to have *rori-kon*, or a "Lolita complex." *Arubaito* is a part-time job, usually for college students and must be traced back to the nineteenth century when German ōyatoi offered their students "*arbeit*" (work) cleaning their homes. Some *gairaigo* require whole paragraphs to explain. Historian Roy Hanashiro notes that foreigners laugh when they first hear their Japanese friends use these new terms, but have incorporated them into their own speech within days when they find how handy the words become as a linguistic "shorthand." Historian Lane Earns notes dryly that as convenient and cute as these *gairaigo* are, they only add to the complexity of an already impossible language and can place even more distance between generations of Japanese.

BEAUTY IN THE EYE OF THE BEHOLDER

It should at this point be noted that for the most part Japan is enthralled with American ideas of beauty. Not only are foreign models more likely to be hired to endorse products than are Asian stars, but the Japanese spend thousands of dollars to have themselves surgically reconstructed to appear more Western. The most common procedures are "nose jobs" and surgery to remove the Asian eyelid fold to make eyes appear "rounder." Japanese men spend lots of money to have their hair chemically curled. Curiously, Japanese have not followed the American lead in whitening, "capping," or straightening teeth with braces. Slightly crooked teeth and overbite are considered attractive features for young women. But, like in the United States and Europe, youth and slimness, particularly in women, are prized as attributes. Japan, of course, has no corner on this market when one considers the impossible culturally imposed body styles for young women in America. Breast implants, rib removals, nose jobs, liposuction, tummy-tucks, face-lifts, and lip collagen procedures in the United States far out-distance such "elective surgeries" in Japan. Anthropologist Laura Miller has written much about the fetish.

Many observers have commented on how long young women continue to act girlish in Japan. They affect high, squeaky childish voices. Young saleswomen are trained to speak in this manner. Many of Japanese male sex-ual fantasies have to do with school girls. Showgirls, bar hostesses, and pros-titutes often dress in middle schoolgirl uniforms. Thankfully, cases of rape of adolescent girls are extremely rare. Women in their 20s continue to dress, act, and speak as if they were still 15 years old.

MANGA AND ANIME

Another part of popular culture that cannot be seriously considered to be either art or literature in the usual sense but deserves serious consideration is *manga*, the pulp comic. Unlike the usual comic-book genre of the United States, which has been primarily relegated (until very recently that is) to the interests of adolescent boys, *manga* has taken on considerable more influence throughout the society. The garishly drawn illustrations take on somewhat more importance when we consider that over a million booklets (each issue is commonly more than 100 pages) are published daily in Japan. In 1996 there were over forty thousand titles published, and at least 1,000 of them were serials with at least 12 editions each year; about 100 of them being is-sued weekly. Most of the stories are geared to young male readers, but many are intended for young women and adults. One cannot enter a café, tavern, barber or beauty shop, train station, or subway car without stumbling over hundreds of copies lying about. The people who clean the subways report that they recycle (thankfully) upwards of 100,000 copies of discarded *manga* booklets per day!

Unfortunately, many of the *manga* topics border on the pornographic, and virtually all of them contain some kind of violence, particularly against women and schoolgirls. It is disconcerting to see so many young men reading such misogynist trash. It continues to be a favorite complaint of the feminist movement in Japan.

That being said, the illustrations of *manga* can be very artistic. They take on a cinematic quality that has heavily influenced the television and film indus-tries. There are many *manga* artists and illustrators who have been rightfully recognized for the high artistic quality of their work. One cannot say the same of the writers of the *manga* text. A few *manga* writers have employed tradi-tional Japanese folk tales, but most rely on very-low-quality plots and banal story lines. Obviously if one has to turn out eight or nine story lines per week, one does not take the care and time of Marcel Proust.

A related phenomenon is the film genre called *anime*. These animated futur-istic cartoons have spawned a whole industry of children's television cartoon shows, but they have also led to very sophisticated computer-generated feature-length movies. *Mighty Morphin Power Rangers* and *X-Men* are examples of this genre.

PRIVATE POSSESSIONS

Disposable wealth among young women is very high. Most young women work for two or three years before marriage. Because they continue to live at home, their living expenses are really only for sumptuous vacations and stylish clothes and jewelry. A newspaper survey in 1995 discovered that the "average" young secretary or office worker spent over $100 per week on clothes alone. Vacations are taken by these young women in groups where they divide their time between lying in the sun and shopping. The same newspaper survey indicated that an average young woman spends over $4,000 on an annual five-day vacation, over half of which is for souvenirs for all her friends and family.

Young men do not spend anything close to these amounts on themselves. This is partially due to the fact that after college young men all wear the same dark blue or black conservative-cut suits, muted striped ties, and black shoes. In relaxation they all seem to wear identical golf shirts or polyester exercise suits. Most are saving every spare yen in hopes that one day they can afford to buy a house. Land prices in Tokyo are notoriously expensive.

Even in the economic downturn of the mid-1990s, a tiny (less than 500 square feet) two-bedroom "mansion" apartment costs over $450,000! Houses are even more expensive. It is now common to spend over $1,000,000 for a small 750-square-foot house. One-hundred-year mortgages have been recently introduced because it is now nearly impossible to pay for a home in a single lifetime. One hopes that the house will last long enough for one's grandchildren to inherit because they will inherit the mortgage as well. Long-term leases are increasingly popular as well, but most people would prefer to own *mai-homu* ("my home").

In the immediate Postwar era Japanese struggled to eke out a living. Not surprisingly, once people began to make a living, they began to save at a very high rate. By the late1960s, when Ikeda's "Income Doubling Plan" was become a reality, estimates of per capita savings rates were that the average worker was saving up to twenty percent of disposable income. By the 1970s, most Japanese began to spend that money, mostly on private homes. In the 1980s and beyond, people began to splurge a bit on personal possessions. Virtually every home now contained the basic "necessities" of life: refrigerators, televisions, air conditioners, electric rice cookers, bathtubs, and heaters.

One surprising expense is for high-tech toilets. Apart from the standard porcelain models many Japanese homes are outfitted with toilets with heated seats, electronically controlled bidets, music, and aromatic misters. Some models cost over $1,000!

Automobiles are very expensive to buy and to maintain. In Tokyo, one cannot register a car unless one can prove that one has an off-street parking space.

Apartment complexes charge up to $300 per month for a *hanga* ("hanger"), which is a mechanical elevator contraption that stacks up to four cars above each other in the space ordinarily used for one car. Rent for single spaces can go as high as $700. Pollution control restrictions can add $10,000 to the price of a new car, and one must pay for the inspection of emission control devices every year. Most people ride public transportation, but would prefer to own their own car, if only to drive around on weekends.

Much has been made of Japan's dronelike male workers who work six 12-hour days per week, sometimes literally working themselves to death. That vision needs to be qualified somewhat. Men are away from home for long hours; they average a two-hour commute on crowded trains per day. They may work only six or seven hours at their desks but routinely spend another two hours drinking tea, smoking, gossiping, or reading the newspaper. They may spend another two or three hours drinking with coworkers after work. Men commonly spend another four or five hours per week bowling, playing golf, or on a company sports team. As with most activities, they do these things collectively with coworkers.

Japanese men often even vacation together on company-sponsored group tours. It is quite common for coworkers to even honeymoon together! Because they are so involved with coworkers, it is natural that many are introduced to and end up marrying female coworkers or their sisters.

MARRIAGE CUSTOMS

The marriage industry is, after golf, the most lucrative nonproductive enterprise in Japan. It is even more prosperous than patent diet medicines and exercise salons (both of which are enormously profitable). Marriages are a combination of Western and Japanese traditional customs, which anthropologists Walter Edwards and David Plath have made familiar to American readers.

The *Mi-ai* (appropriately "see-meet") are arranged by matchmakers, coworkers, and siblings. Prospective spouses are introduced after a careful investigation of their backgrounds. Detective agencies do a very profitable business tracing ancestry; school (as far back as kindergarten) records; and employment, medical, and credit histories occasionally as far back as the lives of one's grandparents. The prospective couple first independently examines pictures and the dossiers (provided by detectives) of each other, and if they agree to meet, they carry on a carefully monitored and prescribed courtship that can be terminated by either person at any time. After the third date, however, fewer than five percent break off. By that time, the expectations of both families run so high that it would be a major social embarrassment to do anything but the "proper thing" and be wed. Engagements are rarely shorter than a year in order to gird one's loins and to save up for the wedding.

The marriage ceremony itself is a tremendous undertaking. Weddings are carefully staged events that in 2008 cost on the average of $32,000! Special professional wedding "palaces" are booked for a year in advance. Most major hotels have one on their premises and rely on 20 percent of their revenue from weddings alone. The bride and groom actually go through at least two, sometimes three distinct ceremonies, each one requiring a change of costume. They dress in Western-style swallowtail tuxedos and white wedding dresses and go through a quasi-Christian ceremony, often conducted by a Westerner, sometimes in Latin! Quite a few foreigners who are not even clergy can make a substantial fee for playing the role of a priest. Then the couple changes into traditional (usually rented) kimono for a Shinto ritual. Another costume change brings them back into the reception room (where the guests have been dining on expensive food) for a series of toasts and speeches made by virtually everyone whom one has known in one's lifetime.

It is considered prestigious and trendy to have a foreigner as a guest, so one can be quite amazed to be invited to a wedding of someone with whom one shared a dictionary one rainy afternoon in a college library. One may well imagine the depth of sincere emotion of that speech!

The only legally binding part of the whole ritual is the signing of official marriage certificates witnessed by a bureaucrat, the rest is window dressing. But the show is the thing. Wedding couples emerge from trapdoors in the floor in billows of colored dry-ice smoke or descend suspended from the ceiling on silk swings accompanied by a blare of trumpets. Revolving stages, laser light shows, cascading waterfalls, taped music, flying birds, and even fireworks are not uncommon. The recent wedding of a sumo Grand Champion and a rock star included a procession of twenty of his fellow behemoths, all bearing samurai swords and dressed in their colorful ceremonial silk robes. Her friends came dressed as courtiers from Louis XIV's Court at Versailles.

The guests bring gifts of money ($400 per guest is usual) and are in turn given elaborate expensive souvenir gifts by the bride and groom. Only after a grueling three hours is the wedding couple allowed to leave, usually to collapse from nerves and fatigue in their hotel rooms. A young man recently confessed that he and his wife spent the first 18 hours of their honeymoon fast asleep recovering from the wedding.

It is common to coordinate one's wedding and honeymoon with one's coworkers. Entire tours to Guam, Hawaii, Fiji, and Thailand are made up of honeymoon couples. They are conspicuous because brides commonly purchase matching outfits for both of them to wear. It is not uncommon to see tour buses disgorge an entire busload of perfectly matched, color-coordinated couples at tourist sites. Foreigners are sometimes startled to find that they are the only non-Japanese, non-honeymooners in the entire coach section of an airplane bound for Honolulu. One foreigner observed that it was "like being on Noah's Ark with two birds of each color of the spectrum."

NIGHT LIFE

Restaurant, bar, and night life in Japan are unlike anywhere else in the world except perhaps Copenhagen and San Francisco. Newspaper surveys indicate that the average male eats in a restaurant four times per week. Women average slightly less than that because most are home with their children. Most restaurants, even expensive French and Italian ones, display their menus made up in realistic plastic mock-ups in their windows. One may decide which restaurant is suitable by a mere glance to see what is on the menu along with the price. Menus are therefore unnecessary within the restaurant, often the customers shout out their orders as they enter in response to a shouted *"Irrashai!"* (welcome!) greeting by the waiters/cooks.

Bars can be tremendously expensive even if there is no live entertainment. Bar types can be grouped into several general categories. At music or "theme" bars one can listen to a particular genre of recorded music. Jazz clubs are most popular, but there are many classical, blues, rock, and even country western establishments, particularly in Tokyo. Live entertainment bars are very expensive with steep "cover" charges or drink minimums. Jazz is again the most popular genre. Expensive snacks are also sold.

Hostess bars provide female companionship at high prices. These young women are not usually prostitutes, they are professional "listeners," who offer only light conversation and companionship for harried men who feel unappreciated by their wives. There are a growing number of bars that cater to women as well. Young attractive men act as hosts for bored housewives.

Semiprivate clubs are where most of the clientele are regular nightly customers. These usually cater to the employees of one or two neighboring companies. The coworkers sit in groups segregated from workers of other companies. It is not uncommon for employees from different companies to compete against each other in singing contests across the room. Some of these bars cater to graduates of particular colleges. Most of the customers are on expense accounts paid by their employers. Industry managers believe that coworkers "bond" together while drinking and therefore subsidize these after-hours meetings. Hot snacks are popular.

Private clubs where members buy their whiskey by the bottle (commonly over $150 for a fifth of ordinary Suntory Japanese scotch—$250 for imported brands), which is then displayed prominently behind the bar with members' names on brass nameplates hung on chains around the bottle necks.

Karaoke bars are the most peculiar of the lot. The idea of these bars is for customers to take turns warbling their favorite tunes accompanied by taped music (hence the name, which means "empty orchestra") cued by videos displaying scenes appropriate to the music. Patrons can also rent private rooms for small parties. It is common for men to take weeks of private lessons to be prepared to sing in a casual and spontaneous manner. One can buy videotape souvenirs of one's performance.

SPORTS CULTURE

A few words should be said about Japan's popular sports culture. The most popular participatory sport is golf. This is somewhat amazing because the crowded conditions and high land prices make the expanse of a golf course highly irrational. Yet virtually every young male professional plays religiously. Driving ranges are precariously built on the roofs of tall buildings or against the side of many surrounding hills. In Tokyo there are several bars with from 8 to 10 postage stamp–sized practice putting greens.

The green fees of full golf courses are tremendously expensive. The few public courses cost upwards of $150 per round. Private clubs sell memberships for more than $1,000,000. Memberships are sold and traded like stocks and bonds. They very often become the "perks" for executives of large companies. Golf tours are common where golfers pay thousands of dollars to fly to Australia, the Philippines, or even to Scotland or the United States to play endless rounds of golf. Many women play as well.

Golf equipment is very expensive as are all the clothes, hats, shoes, and gloves necessary to look like a serious player. It is common for Japanese businessmen abroad to return with three or four sets of clubs. Foreigners about to visit Japanese friends are often amazed to be asked to bring a set of graphites; to be paid for by the Japanese of course.

A very popular family sport is bowling. There were two or three alleys in prewar Japan, but they were closed by the militarists because such pastimes were deemed to be unpatriotic. Bowlers were urged to take up grenade throwing. During the Occupation, scores of alleys were built to entertain the troops. After the Occupation, many Japanese continued to enjoy the sport as good family entertainment. The sport remains very popular, particularly out in the smaller towns of Japan. Roller skating and ice skating are popular pastimes, too.

Skiing is tremendously popular among the youth. Special trains leave hourly from Tokyo and Ōsaka on Friday afternoons bound for the nearby mountains in the interior and return Sunday evenings. Like golf, the Japanese spend amazing amounts of money to outfit themselves with colorful clothes and the very best in ski equipment. Hiking and mountain climbing have their aficionados as well. It is said that after the Spencer Tracy–Robert Wagner movie *The Mountain* was shown in Japan in the late 1960s, sales of climbing equipment skyrocketed. The same is true after Sylvester Stallone's *Cliffhanger* ran in the 1990s.

BEISBORU OR YAKYU

The most popular spectator sport in Japan is *beisboru* (baseball). The sport was introduced by American sailors in the 1880s and became very popular within a generation. It became so popular that it survived during the war, though many of the terms were changed. *Yakyu* or "fieldball" is still used by sportswriters in the same way that Americans refer to "horsehiders" or "pigskin."

There are more than a dozen professional "major league" teams and a score of "minor leagues" (some in Korea and Taiwan) as well. The major colleges field very competitive teams as well. A number of American professionals have extended their careers by playing ball in Japan for very high salaries. Some, like Cecil Fielder and Julio Franco, returned to the United States after a few years in Japan to become major stars. In the mid-1960s one Japanese, Murakami Masanori, pitched briefly with the San Francisco Giants, but it was not until 1995 that Japanese players began to routinely go to the United States to play in the major leagues. Nomo Hideo caused tremendous interest when he became the National League 1995 Rookie of the Year with the Los Angeles Dodgers. Merchandise bearing his picture became wildly popular (as well as those of his batterymate catcher Mike Piazza). At least three pop songs about him became hits in Japan, and the nation seems to pause to watch live (at 9:00 a.m.) television satellite broadcasts when he pitches. It was not unusual to have the broadcast simply stop when he was lifted for a pinch hitter.

Once Nomo set the precedent (he "retired," allowing him to leave the Japanese baseball system), many top players left Japan to play in the American major leagues. By 2008 some 50 players had made the jump (though only about 20 stayed). Many Japanese sportswriters worried that the outflow would doom the Japanese game. Japan would become little more than another minor league they warned.

The sport differs from the American game. Stealing bases is discouraged because it embarrasses the pitcher. Batters who are knocked down by a pitch wait for the pitcher to tip his hat in apology. Ties count in the standings. Spectators return balls that are hit into the stands. Teams have organized cheering sections much like in American college football. They are raucous and constant in their support, even when their team is ahead or behind by a dozen runs. Dried squid is more popular than hot dogs, and sake is as prevalent as beer at the concession stands.

Effort, earnestness, and practice are prized high above accomplishment. It is not unusual to see the pitcher who has just been replaced run to the bullpen to work earnestly to remedy the flaws in his delivery that caused him to be lifted. Spring training takes on the ambience of military boot camp. Players drill, train, run, and exercise constantly, often to the point that they do not perform well in games because they are simply too tired from practice. Journalist Robert Whiting has written extensively about the differences between Japanese and American baseball. He argues that they are as different as Ping Pong and tennis.

As popular as professional baseball is, high school baseball is even more so. Every summer all of Japan grinds to a halt when the annual high school championships are played in Tokyo. Teams train all year round, and it is common to have parents move their residences to neighborhoods where the great teams play. Again, effort is very important. There are countless legends of players who played despite broken bones or in spite of the fact that a parent or sibling was being buried that day.

There have been numerous cases of players who committed suicide for having committed an error that lost the championship. The television cameras zoom in on tears pouring down the cheeks of the sobbing losing players after the game. Most players bring plastic bags to fill with the "sacred earth" of fabled Koshien Stadium. It is not unknown for middle-aged men to list their membership on a championship team on their business cards twenty years after the game. In short, the Japanese have transformed this "most American of games" into something that is distinctly Japanese.

PACHINKO

Much has been written lately on the topic of Pachinko. This pinball-like game has been popular in Japan since the late nineteenth century (named after the sound that the cascading steel balls make against the metal divider pins), but became the rage in the postwar era. It is a mindless game that requires absolutely no thinking and little skill other than common finger dexterity. Thousands of people sit at the noisy machines like zombies for hours, pausing only to load the machine with money.

The steel balls that make the game work can be traded for cheap gaudy prizes that can be exchanged for money in tiny huts just outside the door. It is well known that the people who run the money exchange counters are in league with the Pachinko parlor owners. Virtually every city block has a garishly decorated, neon-lit parlor.

Police estimate that Pachinko is a multibillion-dollar industry. They may never really know because the parlors are owned by yakuza gangs who pay off police and tax officials to turn their heads at this vice. Much money "laundering" is done through these parlors, and they are also the centers for the small drug trade (mostly in methamphetamines) and for pickpockets.

SEX AND THE SINGLE MAN

Perhaps one final category of popular culture needs to be examined. That is, the sex industry. This includes the usual sterile and degrading pornography that occurs in all parts of the world of course. That is, except to say that pornographic magazines can be purchased virtually anywhere, in convenience stores, train station kiosks, and even in bakeries and ice cream parlors. What is different in Japan are Soap Lands and Love Hotels. Soap Lands are saunas, massage parlors, and public baths that cater to men. The name comes from the young women "bath attendants" who lather their own bodies with soap and then rub them on male bathers. Obviously prostitution is common in such places as well.

These places should not be confused with traditional public bathhouses, which are legitimate family-run establishments that had their beginnings in village public bathhouses because most homes could not afford private baths. (Anthropologist Scott Clark has done a serious academic study of the social importance of public bathing in Japanese history.)

The Love Hotels are fantasy establishments where couples can sneak away for brief sexual encounters. There are lots of extramarital affairs going on in these places, of course, but it is also common for young married (or engaged) couples to meet for privacy. High housing costs force many couples to live with their parents for years after the marriage. Some Love Hotels also cater to homosexual couples.

Typical Love Hotels are garishly decorated in neon on the outside and are fancifully exotic on the inside. Each room is decorated on a distinct theme such as Arabian Nights, King Arthur's Court, spaceships, pirate galleons, and even with Disney-like cartoon characters.

Interestingly, many rooms are fitted with special telephone booths where one may call home to say one is going to be late for dinner. Taped background noises of a busy office, train station, or restaurant can be played to convince people that the caller is otherwise engaged. It is interesting to note that many have "beauty parlor," "Mah-jong parlor," or "PTA Meeting" selections to accommodate women patrons. Customers never actually see or are seen by the hotel attendants. The couples go directly from underground parking garages into their private rooms. Credit card receipts are disguised with charges for "golf lessons," "translation services," or "auto repair."

COMMUTER CULTURE

Without question, the singular salient aspect of modern Japanese society is that its cities are tremendously overcrowded. Indeed, with the exceptions of anomalies such as the city-state of Singapore, Japan is among the most densely populated countries on earth. Keeping in mind that almost 80 percent of its landmass is mountainous forest, the rest of Japan is perhaps the most crowded urban country in the world.

Japan pays a price for its densely concentrated urban population with its urban air pollution, huge garbage and sewer disposal needs, astronomical land prices, high city taxes, and its immense transportation problems. The movement of goods and services are significant problems that add to the cost of living of course. But even more vexing is the attendant problems of humans commuting to and from their homes to their livelihoods. In prewar days virtually everyone worked within a short distance of where they lived. In the postwar period more and more workers began to commute to their jobs at the periphery of the cities.

In 2008 it was reported that the average commuting time for Japanese urban residents is more than two hours per day. The averages for Tokyo and Osaka are approaching three hours. The surprising thing about that figure is that only about 20 minutes of that time involve walking or cycling to and from a bus stop or train station, the rest of the time is riding trains. Virtually every square meter of urban Japan is well served by several interlocking networks of bus, train, and subway lines. Transportation systems, which by the way are clean, safe, reliable, punctual, and relatively inexpensive. But they are also unbelievably crowded.

Every Western visitor is aghast at the crush of humanity on every mode of public transportation. Subway cars that carry 50 people in New York, Paris, London, and Chicago are stuffed with 80 riders in Tokyo. Even accounting for the difference in relative body mass between Westerners and Japanese, this is still simply amazing for most outsiders. Every station is staffed by courteous uniformed workers whose chief duties, other than giving directions, are to help stuff more people into already crowded cars. Most Japanese know instinctively that even if a car is overflowing with riders, one need only turn one's back at the door and then shove backward against the crowd already in the car. Then train "stuffers" discretely shove shoulders, arms, and legs until the automatic doors close and the train whisks off down the line to be replaced by another overcrowded train scarcely five minutes later; and the shoving starts again. Few people complain, indeed few people even notice that a dozen strangers are pressed around them closer than they will ever be with another person except with one's spouse.

Regarding the crush of people on commuter trains, it should be noted that some men like to take advantage of that forced crowding by groping, fondling, or rubbing up against women who are nearly defenseless in such circumstances. After all, these degenerates can claim that it was the jostling of the train or push from other riders that caused them to inadvertently touch women and girls. Some women have taken to carrying long dress-maker pins to stab the offenders, others carry tiny electric devices that deliver a painful shock, much like an electric cattle prod. So many women have complained that many of the rail lines have established Women Only cars during rush hours.

Most citizens are inured to the grind of commuting, having grown up since kindergarten with the need to cram oneself into tiny spaces. People simply adjust. Many commuters can "tune-out" their surroundings enough to read a book or newspaper, many more literally tune-out by virtue of their iPods or cell phones (see the following section "Cell Phone Culture").

COMMUTER CONSUMERISM

What is fascinating to many social scientists is how Japanese culture has evolved (some say devolved or mutated) to accommodate the commuting process. Every subway and train station is surrounded by 7-Eleven, Lawson, and other similar *Kombi* (convenience) stores that cater to the commuter who has either just seconds or sometimes hours to spend between commutes. The *kombi* are stuffed with items that in regular stores would languish on the shelves for weeks, if not months. Quick-repair kits to baste a hem, reattach a button, or secure a zipper are the most obvious items because they contain at best one needle, a meter of thread, and perhaps two buttons and two safety pins for approximately four dollars. One could purchase 10 times the amount of sewing supplies in bulk for the same price that one pays for the tiny kit. Disposable cameras, high-lighter pens, sticky notes, two-pack AAA-sized batteries, single-dose aspirin, antacid, antidiarrhea pills, and hay fever tablets crowd the shelves in these claustrophobic shops. The sheer number of one-use toiletries boggle the mind. Disposable toothbrushes, tiny toothpaste blister-packs, three-pack of dental floss loops, half-ounce vials of hair gel, tiny plastic pillows of underarm deodorant, mini-razors, and ampoules of shaving gel are just a few of what one might call emergency-size personal "convenience" items. Only someone who is truly desperate would purchase these items for the prices charged. But then, does one have the time to find a regular-sized store in the 10 minutes between trains? And even if one does find such a store, what does one then do with a 12-ounce bottle of mouthwash for the rest of the day?

Single-serving snack foods and drinks are like those in every industrialized city in the world of course. But the Japanese have created a whole genre that would astound Westerners. Seaweed-wrapped rice balls, cellophane-wrapped bits of raw fish and sea products. Peeled fruit, cooked vegetables, cups of soup, noodles, and rice abound. Even those stations that are more remote are girded by banks of vending machines that dispense all of the above and more. Individual machines pour out scalding-hot coffee, tea, and soup from one side and dispense cold drinks and ice cream from the other side. And, one may be surprised to be entertained with music or videos from the same machine while obtaining a snack or drink!

Apart from these ubiquitous *kombi* around every transportation nexus, Japan is rife with tiny food stalls around the stations. Japan has for centuries led the world in cheap, tasty, "finger food" shops that cater to Kabuki, Bunraku, and Noh theaters in the so-called Gay Quarters. For the same reason that burger and taco shops populate the areas around bars and taverns all over the world, the Japanese in effect invented "fast food." The truth is, drunks tend to eat junk. Food that one would not even consider for dinner looks very attractive when one's natural culinary tastes are suppressed (or destroyed) by liquor. Salty, spicy, and sweet tidbits have always encouraged people to drink more. Japan's subway and train stations are jammed cheek to jowl with such commuter-friendly fast food shops. Magazine surveys report that the average Japanese adult eats such food five or six times a week. Teenagers frequent such places even more.

Which brings us to the other "conveniences" around transportation hubs: sex. The garish "love hotels" and massage "soap palaces" are very often conveniently located where people tend to congregate. Love trysts are facilitated by convenient transportation. Working men and women often take an hour to "relax" before hurtling home from work. Those who do not have convenient partners available can arrange for such companionship within minutes of every station. Risqué picture cards are plastered over every imaginable flat space around stations, advertising such companionship. In the days before inexpensive cell phones, every public pay phone was plastered with such advertisements; many with toll-free telephone numbers. Often nearby coin machines dispense pornographic magazines. Often these garish machines are cheek-to-jowl with "regular" drink and food machines.

BICYCLE WARS

Millions of Japanese adults ride bicycles from their homes to train stations. Perhaps 90% of the bicycles are identical utilitarian black single rear coaster brake models that employ a simple one-gear chain drive on wide "balloon" tires. Many are neither male (horizontal pole from handlebar to seat) nor female (45-degree diagonal pole from handlebar to pedal assembly) models, but are modified unisex models with a more gradual diagonal slope (from handlebar to midway on the vertical pole that extends from seat to pedals). Most have a simple friction-generator headlight and two or three reflectors on the front (green) and rear (red) wheel fenders. Most have thumb-activated "grind" bells on the handlebars to warn others of approach. Many feature a simple wire-cage "basket" mounted on the handlebars, a few sport "saddlebag" baskets mounted on the rear fender assembly. Some come standard with a simple caliper lock that is meant to immobilize the rear wheel when locked with a key. Others employ a mesh steel cable with a combination lock to fasten the bicycle to an immobile object (light standard, utility pole, bicycle rack, etc.). Very few bicycles are of a different color or employ more gears with derailer sprockets and hand brakes. Even fewer have battery-driven lights, sirens, horns, saddle seats, and other flashy decorations.

In short, most adult commuter bicycles are almost interchangeable; and therein lies the tale. Bicycles are very often parked seemingly haphazardly close to train station entrances. Uniformed municipal "guards" are often employed to watch over the gaggle of parked bicycles, sometimes to painstakingly thread a long steel cable through the frames in order to pull them even closer together so that during the day the assembled bicycles resemble a pressed block of black steel that one might encounter at a junkyard. Beginning at about 3:00 p.m., the "guards," often retired middle-aged men (see section on retirement below), begin to recoil the steel cable in anticipation of the arrival of commuters. Each train disgorges a pack of men and women who rush to retrieve their bicycles for their short ride home.

At first glance, one wonders how commuters can identify their own machine from the pack of identical black bicycles, particularly if they are in the center of the pack. The answer is: they don't! They simply grab one that is convenient, ride it home, and then return it to the pack the next day. No one is accused of "stealing;" they have no intention of keeping it, they are just using it, expecting that the owner will borrow someone else's bike and everyone will have one to ride. Of course that can only happen if everyone does not lock the caliper. Those that do, know that the caliper can be easily disabled, there being only about 10 distinct key types in the country. It is not uncommon for complete strangers to offer their own keys to help someone whose key is not opening the lock!

Foreigners have some difficulty with this because hardly anyone admits that they are not riding their own bicycle. Indeed, commuters who painstakingly lock their bicycles with personal combination lock steel cables are considered selfish "nerds" who gum-up the process because they have great difficulty finding and dislodging their own machine from the center of the crush of bicycles. Often one can spot these steel cables wrapped around the seat pole assembly where of course they serve no purpose. One can imagine that the owners simply gave up using those locking devices because they were too inconvenient. The "guards" will sometimes tie a warning tag to bicycles that are tethered to railings, poles, and the like. The tag warns that those bicycles are blocking public access and may be ticketed and impounded. The implication is that the owners are inconsiderate and are not playing the game.

Children are taught the expectations of the Bicycle Wars at an early age. Of course flashy brightly colored bicycles with many attachments and accoutrements are carefully locked because of course these are "personal" machines. Usually, by the time the child enters high school they have left those bicycles at home and are using the utilitarian black anonymous models that are part of the system. Some Japanese claim that the same bicycles have been circulating train stations for generations. One retiree "guard" pointing at the pile, confided that his old bike was "probably still in there somewhere."

"Communal bicycle" systems exist in many European cities whereby municipalities supply the bikes and the public simply uses them and returns them to convenient drop-off points. When questioned why the Japanese don't simply employ the same system, Japanese dismiss the suggestion with responses such "Oh, that would never work in Japan!" The truth is, it does.

CELL PHONE CULTURE

Telephones were always a unique public convenience in Japan, different from in America or Europe. In the 1970s through the 1990s public coin phones were ubiquitous in all public spaces in an array of color-coded varieties. Pink phones were intended for local calls. Ten-yen coins were the standard for local calls. A "beep" would indicate that one's three minutes were about to expire and one would have to drop in another coin to extend the call. Some phones (usually yellow or light blue ones) would accept 100 yen coins but give no change for unused minutes. Green phones were designated for international calls and were usually the only phones in booths, the rest were kept on counters or were mounted in corners. The green phones featured several different numbers for phone companies that one could choose instead of the standard NTT (Nippon Telephone and Telegraph). Recently, almost all phones accepted plastic prepaid magnetic phone cards that one could buy in *Kombi* shops or in cash-operated dispensers in varying denominations. The standard were 500- and 1000-yen cards that were punched with tiny holes by the phone as the minutes were used. Most of the cards featured cute pictures and souvenir postcard scenes. Young girls seemed to buy them for collecting purposes and could frequently be observed trading with friends like baseball cards are traded in America. Some companies gave them away as incentive or *Orei* (thank-you gifts) to customers. Some individuals bought personalized phone cards to present in lieu of *Meishi* (see the following section "Meishi") business cards.

Since the mid-1990s almost every adult now carries a personal cell phone. Many commercial companies have availed themselves of a new technology in order to tap into the deluge of cell phone users. When several companies began to produce e-mail newsletters ("e-mail magazines,"*meru-maga*) for their employees, a few began to convert these into abbreviated versions for cell phones. The articles were reduced to a few lines that could fit on a standard cell phone screen. Since then, commercial advertisers have seized on the idea and have sponsored these abbreviated messages. That is, commercial ad agencies would set up the company mini-newsletter in return for being allowed to imbed their ads therein. Many major newspapers in Japan have noticed a drop in subscription rates, particularly among the young adult demographic and have invested in their own versions of *meru-maga* and cell phone ads. Subscribers sign up for these free services in return for incentives such as video games.

Younger adults buy cell phone models that include tiny video screens to play games or watch short videos. Teenagers have created their own cell phone culture that is truly amazing. Not only do they play a plethora of buzzing, beeping, honking, and squawking video games but they also watch short music videos on the tiny screens. Teenagers send text messages to each other endlessly, even if they happen to be sitting next to each other.

Each text must then be shared with everyone in the coterie and screams of laughter accompany each message, followed by another exchange, seemingly for hours. Like in America, Japanese teens have invented their own "emoticons" shorthand (like the :) sideways smiley face). But *kanji* and *kana* characters are very much more expressive that abbreviations such as the now banal LOL ("Laughing Out-Loud") or IMS ("I Am Sorry") of American chatrooms and text messages. Most Japanese adults have absolutely no idea of what is being said since they do not know the codes. Teenagers seem to have invented their own language that contains Japanese, English, French, and "TV-ese." Otherwise innocuous *kanji* elicit screams and gales of laughter from teenagers. Adults seem to be constantly perplexed at this activity.

These emoticons (called *emoji*) are a hybrid of the usual American emoticons where asterisks (*_*) indicate the eyes. In *emoji* the eyes are the central character with an underscore (_) serving as the mouth, and the parentheses, form the outline of the face. A significant difference from American emoticons is that in *emoji,* the emotion is connoted with the eyes contrasting the Western emoticons emoting through the mouth. Different emotions can be expressed by changing the character representing the eyes, for example T can be used to express crying or sadness (T_T). What is significant is that T indicate tears using the English word. The Japanese word for tears is *namida*. The emphasis on the eyes is reflected in the common usage of emoticons that use only the eyes (^^). Looks of embarrassment are either represented by (x_x) or (-_-). Characters like hyphens or periods can replace the underscore; the period is often used for a smaller, "cuter" mouth or to represent a nose, (^.^). Alternatively, the mouth/nose can be left out entirely (^^). The parentheses also can often be replaced with brackets {^_^}.

One final aspect of interest is that sometimes homophone *kana* characters are inserted to give even more expression. Sometimes the word *emoji* itself is "spelled" using the *kanji* characters for "picture" (pronounced "e") and "written character (pronounced "ji"), which creates something of a rebus picture. New *emoji* are constantly being invented. Students who have been out of Japan for a semester return to find that they cannot readily "read" *emoji*. Some Brazilian-Japanese have adapted Portuguese words into their *emoji.*

About a third of Japanese sixth graders have cell phones, while 60 percent of ninth graders have them, according to the education ministry. Parents typically pay about 4,000 yen (US$39) a month for cell phone fees per child.

Most mobile phones in Japan are sophisticated gadgets offering high-speed Internet access called 3G, for "third-generation," allowing Japanese to do most everything that can be done on personal computers on cell phones, including messaging, electronic shopping, social networking, Net searches, and video games.

Some youngsters are spending hours at night on e-mail with their friends. One fad is "the 30-minute rule," in which a child who doesn't respond to e-mail within half an hour gets targeted and picked on by other schoolmates.

The cell phone culture has changed teenage behavior on trains and subways. Up to the early 1990s, teenagers slumped in their seats listening on earphones to their usual cacophony of music while absorbed in their *manga* comic books. Now, one seldom sees them reading anything. They are hunched over their cell phones playing games or texting their friends. The two fundamental changes are that previously they usually sat in relative silence and read. Now their music or game noises are deafening, and they rarely read. Their teachers claim that fundamental literacy has plummeted. Many cannot write even simple *Toyo-kanji* (the 3,000 "common-use" characters used in most newspapers). It is similar to the 1970s when teachers complained that students could no longer use a *soroban* hand-held abacus or "do" the standard multiplication tables after the advent of the inexpensive hand-held electronic calculator.

Private landline domestic telephones were always expensive and cumbersome because one had to pay exorbitant deposits and sign long-term rental agreements. Recently it was reported that standard home phones were rapidly disappearing and coin public phones were being pulled out of most restaurants because virtually everyone now has a personal cell phone. The green international phones remain in tourist sites, but now it is possible to rent inexpensive cell phones capable of making international calls. One NTT bureaucrat was recently quoted as saying that more public phones were now being purchased as curios and antiques than as actual telephones.

CLOTHES CULTURE

Japan has been almost a caricature of a clothes-conscious society since the immediate postwar era. Except for the drab sameness of the Peoples' Republic of China during the Mao years (and its analog in North Korea), Japan has been until recently perhaps the epitome of social conformity. Virtually every segment had its own dress code. Employees in manufacturing wore the same work uniform, school children dressed in middie-style uniforms, and corporate employees dressed the same as their peers. In industry, the uniform cover-all or work shirt-trousers combinations made sense for company laundries and the like of course. Even some public schools in America have discovered that standard school uniforms help avoid many school problems such as apparel with inappropriate cartoons or logos, economic-class distinctions, and the proliferation of gang colors.

In Japan, however, there was also a corporate "uniform" of dark blue or black suits with muted-colored neckties and white shirts for men and the equivalent female "uniform" of dark middie-jacket and mid-calf skirt over white blouses with string ties. In mid-Spring, charcoal grey–colored uniforms would begin to appear as soon as middle managers started to switch over. City sidewalks and commuter trains were seas of the dark uniforms. Indeed, many manga and anime mocked the gaggle of "black crows" as they were called.

Recently, however, more casual wear has begun to appear, particularly during the summer. The first blossoms of color began with forays into neckties (dark reds followed by patterns and eventually into bright pastels) then into dress shirts (blue predominantly, but recently some pastels for women). Now one can occasionally see browns and even plaid jackets.

For years, sociologists have claimed that the conformity in clothing was a symptom of Japan's communalist society. So what are we to surmise from the recent changes? Some claim that the shifts in clothes began with employees returning from overseas postings, others suggest that the more casual dress is a measure of how Japan is slowly becoming less formal in business. Still others claim that with more women joining the middle levels of corporations, the color shift is inevitable. Perhaps this is a symptom of all three prevailing trends.

MEISHI

As noted previously, Japan is very much a status-conscious society. In feudal times one's status was determined by one's professional social class and of course by one's gender and age. An elaborate language system called *keigo* ("Honorifics") marked one's status. Samurai talked "down" to townsmen and villagers and the latter in turn used honorific-marked words to speak to their samurai superiors. Men talked "down" to women, children, and animals; sons honored their parents; and masters talked "down" to their servants and apprentices.

In Japan today the status is often determined by one's occupation, gender, age, and by the ascribed status of one's employer or academic alma mater. Virtually everyone seems to know where one stands in relation to others and one can readily adjust their language to others based on these nebulous social markers. A popular genre of newspaper article is to rank companies, universities, occupations, and even favorite sports teams.

Not surprisingly, the Japanese wish to know how one relates to strangers. A simple way is for strangers to exchange name cards (*meishi*). These cards grew out of "calling cards," which announced visitors to their hosts. When one called on one's boss or other superior, one did so by handing the servant one's name card. Curiously, these cards were often used ritually and perfunctorily. One was required to visit one's superiors on New Year's Day and at other ritual occasions. Often lower-ranking employees "called" at the residence of their immediate superior, who of course was not at home; he was calling on his own superiors! A way of "marking" one's obligatory visit was to leave one's name card and go on to the next stop.

In the postwar era, the name card evolved to mark one's relative status when meeting strangers. The card contained one's name of course, and often one's address or telephone number; but also the cards began to list one's employer and one's title. A stranger now can glance at one's *meishi* and know immediately one's social status. One can then adjust one's language according to one's perceived social relation to the stranger. A middle manager of a lower-ranking local company must honor an executive of Toyota of course. A local school superintendant can talk "down" to a mere teacher at another school, but must honor a member of the Ministry of Education, no matter what the latter's position.

Blind studies have been done whereby Japanese are observed when meeting strangers. Very often Japanese will treat the same strangers differently when presented with "lofty" *meishi* than they do when presented with "lowly" *meishi*. Language honorifics and "body language" change perceptively. In one study a group of secondary school administrators met a group of strangers at an academic conference. When presented with meishi that indicated the stranger was roughly equal in status (another school administrator like themselves) they behaved quite informally. When presented with *meishi* indicating prefectural ministers, or national educational executives, their language was much more deferential and their greeting bows were much deeper and more pronounced.

Westerners who live in Japan often miss the subtleties of the *meishi* exchange because Japanese usually treat most foreigners the same, unless the alien is an important government official or an academic officer at a prestigious foreign university. I have observed how differently a colleague is treated at national libraries when he presents a *meishi* indicating that he is a professor at Harvard University versus how he is treated when presents a *meishi* from his real Mid-western state college.

SMOKERS AS LEPERS

Until about a decade ago smoking was a huge problem in Japan. About two-thirds of adult males smoked and about half that number of women did as well. Almost every restaurant, tavern, bathroom, waiting room, and other public spaces were choking with cigarette smoke. Smoking was allowed in virtually every public space and almost all rail lines made special Smoking Cars available. Japan's growing incidence of lung cancer was skyrocketing and many children suffered from breathing problems caused by "second-hand smoke." This caused a great public outcry and public opinion polls indicated that concerns about smoking were quickly becoming a major social issue rank-ing with other issues of pollution and political corruption. In the early 1990s a number of "Green" political parties began to hold public demonstrations and to petition their legislatures to ban smoking in public places. Smokers were accosted and ridiculed by gaggles of activists in restaurants, theaters, train stations, and other public areas. Public opinion carried the day in most small and medium-sized cities. By the turn of the century, even the large cities had begun to catch up and recently smoking bans have cropped up all over the country. Some major cities even ban smoking on public sidewalks.

POPULATION ISSUES

Japan became one of the world's first nations to seriously attack the prob-lems of the postwar population boom. With millions of male soldiers return-ing to their homes after several years abroad, Japan's population naturally increased initially. Demographers suggest that the human "procreation surge" occurs naturally after every catastrophe and war. Japan's population probably doubled in the 30 years after World War II, but then leveled off and actually regressed somewhat in the 1980s. This population plateau probably came as a result of the World Health Organization's "Zero Population" program that was trying to address the threat of famine and disease in the so-called Third World (Africa, Latin America, and Asia).

The death of Mao Zedong in China (1976) removed one of the last hurdles to population control in Asia. In 1979 the Peoples Republic of China instituted the national One Child Campaign to address the boom that had carried China past the dreaded one billion mark in population. At about the same time Japan became one of the first developed nations to report a net loss in population.

What is amazing about this feat was that it was accomplished virtually without the aid of cheap, safe and readily available low-dose estrogen birth control pills. Japan's medical establishment has dragged its feet on certifying these pills as safe despite now more than 30 years of "trial" in America and Europe. Cynics claim that Japanese doctors have been reticent in approving the "pill" because they can make much more money by performing clinical abortions than they can by writing prescriptions for the drug. After all, it took only months to approve the sale of the male impotence drug Viagra.

In the twenty-first century, Japan has begun to experience some attendant problems with Zero Population Growth. In 2008 the government announced that the number of children under the age of 14 had declined for the twenty-seventh straight year. The 17.25 million children represented slightly more that 13 percent of the total population, almost the same fraction of adults over the age of 55. The National Institute of Population and Social Security Research estimated that the number of children will drop below 15 million and their proportion below 12 percent in 2015. Japan already has 13 million citizens aged 75 or over, about one-tenth of its population and the figure is forecast to rise to 22 million in 2025. Two in five Japanese are expected to be aged 65 or over by 2050, double the current percentage. The problem of course is that Japan's retirement system would quickly founder and go bankrupt absent serious and substantive changes. Most Japanese retire at about age 55. Since Japan is among the global leaders for life expectancy (approaching 80 years for women, men only slightly lower), there would not be enough workers to support Japan's burgeoning retired population.

The average age of first marriage has been increasing for years (26.7 for women, 28.5 for men) as the average number of live births per couples (1.64) continues to decline. Moral and material incentives have been offered by Japan's politicians in a predictable male chauvinist way. Young women have been castigated for their selfishness and have been offered cash bonuses to have more than two children.

As mentioned above, most Japanese males retire between the ages of 50 and 55. This seems to be "early" to Americans and Europeans who are more accustomed to standard retirement ages of 60 or 65. All retirement age standards are arbitrary of course; the American 65 standard was established by the creation of the Social Security Administration in the late 1930s when the average life expectancy for males was around 60 years. The 50–55 Japanese custom became common in the immediate Postwar 1950s when large companies used the "early" retirement as a method to weed-out less productive members of the work force. The idea was that in the so-called "lifetime employment system" companies would hire a cohort of young college graduates who were expected to stay with the same company for 30 years. Employees would be "promoted" in lock-step with their cohort, all receiving the same raises as everyone in their cohort as a reward for their loyalty. Finally at age 50 or so, the "high-flyers" would be retained to become middle managers while the rest of their less-productive cohort would be retired. That is, those employees who were not in the company's long-term plans would be forced out.

Company retirement systems were woefully inadequate (less than 20 percent of final annual wages) so workers were constantly urged to "save for retirement" on their own. This created a huge personal savings fund that could be used by those very companies for capital investment at very low interest rates. Obviously, this "55-and-out" system worked very well for these companies. They could shed workers just when their salaries were becoming a financial burden and they could borrow money from those funds at very low rates in the meantime. Also, they were not burdened with company-funded retirement systems as were American and European companies.

Until 2007 much of the retirement savings was concentrated in the government-run postal savings system (Nippon Yusei Kosha or NYH), which contained over $2.1 trillion in savings. NYH paid very low interest rates (usually less that one percent) to savers. In 2007, NYH was privatized with much of the capital flowing to higher-interest plans.

In the late 1980s into the middle 1990s when Japan's financial "bubble" burst, the retirement system became a problem. Economic problems forced a number of Japan's largest and most prestigious companies to shed "surplus" labor to cut costs. This broke the social contract of "lifetime employment." Workers could no long rely on their paternalistic employers so they began to adjust by moving from one company to another that promised higher wages. As labor sorted itself out, so did the retirement accounts. Savings accounts began to seek higher interest rates and cheap capital became rare. Inevitably, high-risk financial schemes began to crop up everywhere and thousands of middle-aged men lost their retirement nest eggs. Now the government was faced with a real social problem; thousands of bankrupt retirees flooded back into the labor market seeking a living wage. It became very common to see these middle-aged men in menial jobs (such as bicycle guards at train stations). Regrettably, the suicide rate (see section below) for retirees skyrocketed during this period.

"Silver Talent Centers" sprang up in most cities where retirees could be matched up with private employers who needed part-time workers. Obviously this did not solve the fundamental problem. Many companies began a scheme whereby their own newly-retired workers were "rehired" as part-time workers at much lower wages.

A related issue is the imminent crisis of care for the aged. In the past it was always assumed that children would care for their aged parents. Most postwar households consisted of at least three, and very often four generations under the same roof. But now with the precipitous decrease in the number of young married adults living with their parents, who takes care of the aged?

The mathematics are simple, if not simplistic. If one assumes that Japanese procreate at less than the minimum two per couple, within a few generations they will create an "inverted pyramid" demographic. That is, one grandchild for each four grandparents; each set of grandparents produced only one child, and those two offspring produced only one child. It would be an onerous burden indeed for that one child to support four grandparents (if they survived into their 70s) and two parents who retired at 55.

Traditionally, the eldest son inherits both the family home and the duty to take care of his parents in their old age. Many young women balk at the idea of caring for a grandparent-in-law. A current joke among young women when asked "what do you want your prospective husband to be?" is the response: "Healthy, wealthy, and an orphan."

The shame of relegating an infirm and aged relative is not as great as it once was. Recently there have been an increased number of nursing homes established to take care of the aged. Not surprisingly, the system could not hire enough caretakers and nurses to tend to the growing numbers of retirees. Fewer young women were going into the nursing profession so Japan began to solve the problem in the same way it had dealt with a shrinking industrial work force: namely hire foreigners. By the 1990s more and more of the employees of those nursing facilities have been Filipino nurses brought to Japan. In 2007 the government signed an agreement with Indonesia to bring over one thousand of their nurses and care givers to Japan, promising to provide a wage higher than they could earn in Indonesia. According to this plan, the Indonesians will be given a half-year of language lessons at hospitals and nursing homes in Japan, appropriate places for such training, as much of the vocabulary used is specialized.

By 2003 the government reported that more than 20 percent of retirees were living below the poverty line. Reforms were tried to provide public assistance, but the paternalistic government urged the children of these retirees to "try to settle the minds" of their parents. Suggestions were made whereby adult children were instructed on how to build additions to their own homes where their retired parents could live. Young mothers were reminded that their own parents made excellent babysitters.

Not surprisingly, public opinion turned against these pandering bureaucrats. A number of reform candidates, including many women, were elected on reform platforms that promised to revamp the government National Pension System as well as to regulate the Employees Pension Scheme for private companies. Very slow progress has been made.

One positive result of Japan's new focus on retirees was the foundation of *rojin daigaku* ("elder universities") where retirees are subsidized to attend cultural classes. Some of the retirees themselves taught those classes (for pay of course) and others received a small stipend as long as they attended. The classes gave the elder students something worthwhile to do with their free time as well as provided employment and stipends. Most large cities have set up "Golden Age" centers in their municipal facilities. These government-subsidized centers facilitate common-interest clubs for the elderly and include cultural arts, traditional music, dance, and amateur theatrical productions and the like.

In 2008 the government announced a new program for dealing with some of these retirement issues including gradually revamping the national retirement system. Private companies were to be given material incentives to continue to employ those who had reached age 55. Variations on European and American Individual Retirement Accounts with company tax-free contributions were to be instituted to supplement traditional retirement accounts. Time will tell if they will be successful. If the past is prologue in Japan, the society will adjust and prosper. Virtually every crisis has been surmounted by the persistent Japanese.

SUICIDE IN CULTURE

Suicide in Japan has for centuries been an accepted solution to some social problems. Much has been made of the ritualized *hara kiri* (or seppuku) suicide of the samurai class during the seven centuries (1192–1867 c.e.) of feudalism. Slicing open ones' abdomen (which is what *hara kiri* means: "cut stomach") with a razor-sharp short-sword (reserved for taking the heads of enemies as war trophies and for killing oneself) was an accepted method for ending one's life. *Hara kiri* was fairly rare, though common enough to become a trope in Japanese literature. It was preferable to other more painful methods of death of course (witness the "death of a thousand cuts" torture famous in Japanese movies), but what made it become popular among samurai is that it connoted sincerity and expiation. A samurai might atone for grievous misdeeds, disloyalty, or cowardice by committing *hara kiri*.

In the modern era, however, *hara kiri* nearly died out with the samurai class after the 1870s. Other forms of suicide have continued into the Heisei Era. Thousands of military men committed suicide during World War II when it was far preferable to ignominious surrender in defeat. Since then it has been much rarer of course, but not so much that it surprises society at large. Financial failures are forgiven businessmen if they take their own lives. It is accepted as an act of atonement. In the 1970s and early 1980s there was a rash of suicides by students who had failed college entrance exams. Middle-aged men in the late 1980s and 1990s took their lives when the financial "bubble" burst. Double suicides by thwarted lovers were so common that they became a literary convention in the feudal era. They continue to crop up from time to time.

Suicide rates are quite high in Japan (but lower than many northern European societies-Finland and Sweden for example). Psychologists and sociologists are at a loss to explain why this is so. Some suggest that neither Buddhism nor Shinto condemn suicide, and society at large continues to believe that it is a rational escape from some otherwise insoluble social problems. Unrequited love, bankruptcy, crushing social shame, incurable diseases, and mental depression are the most conventional reasons

Japanese aged 60 and over were the fastest growing age group among suicide cases, jumping by 987 in 2007 to 12,107 deaths, an increase of 8.9 percent from 2006. The age group made up 36.6 percent of all suicides in Japan in 2007. The second-largest age group in the suicide study were Japanese in their 50s, accounting for 21.3 percent of the total, though the number dropped 2.8 percent in 2007 to 7,046 cases.

Curiously, "suicide pacts" by non-lovers and even strangers became rife in the 1990s and continues today. Internet websites for such pacts blossom from time to time. Complete strangers agree to meet to help each other commit suicide in popular places (the edge of forests, along rivers, near waterfalls, and even remote train crossings).

In 2008 a new wrinkle cropped up. Some 34 people committed suicide in central Tokyo by generating deadly hydrogen sulfide gas during the first six months of that year. Some twenty suicides were by mixing detergents and generating hydrogen sulfide in Tokyo in April alone, followed by six in May. Nineteen of those who committed suicide with the deadly gas were aged in their 20s, seven were in their 30s, while there were two each in the age brackets of teens, 40s and 50s. Eighty percent of those who committed suicide with the lethal gas were men; 13 were unemployed and six were students. Few of them knew each other and the Tokyo authorities were at a loss to explain why. Critics blamed a local television news show that demonstrated the method of combining laundry detergents used by one couple to kill themselves.

A SAFE COUNTRY

In June 2008 a young madman announced to his friends that he was about to kill people at random. He then drove his car into a crowd in Akihabara, a district of Tokyo otherwise known for its dozens of electronic stores. He then jumped from the vehicle and began to stab and slash people at random, ultimately wounding dozens and killing seven strangers before he was subdued. For weeks the media was rife with reports on the incident. Many newspaper and television reporters decried the incident as only the latest manifestation of rising crime, particularly among Japanese youth. They reminded the public about how a man wielding a knife killed at least eight pupils in a rampage at their school in western Japan only seven years before in June 2001.

Obviously both of these crimes were horrible acts of violence, but we should be reminded that Japan's crime rate remains low by international standards, with 1.1 homicides per 100,000 people in 2005 compared with 3.5 in France, 3.2 in the United Kingdom and 5.6 in the United States. Japan, a country of 127 million people, had just 1,391 homicides in 2005, compared with 16,692 in the United States. Gun violence is quite rare in Japan, in part because of Japan's very stringent gun control laws. Yet feminists in Japan have noted a rising tide of domestic violence, particularly against women. Sexual violence is on the increase as well. Critics point at Japan's rising rates of pornography, homelessness, poverty, and drug abuse as issues of concern. But when taken together, despite some increase in violence, Japan remains one of the safest societies in the world.

For the present, Japan can justly pride itself on the relative safety of its neighborhoods. Elementary school children ride buses and trains to and from school with little danger of violence. Women and children can walk city streets even in late evenings without fear. Inebriated men with pockets stuffed with cash on paydays are rarely accosted or robbed. Petty theft is relatively rare and personal items lost on subways and trains are routinely turned in to Lost and Found offices. Rural police report that citizens routinely turn in lost coins and paper currency. Foreigners in Japan from all over the world are astounded at the level of peace and safety even in its huge cities.

Various opinions are offered by criminologists and sociologists for why Japan is safer than other developed industrial nations. Some suggest that latent ideas of Confucian familialism might be the answer since South Korea, Singapore, and Taiwan have similar low rates of social violence. Others adduce the safety to Japan's school system that keeps a very tight rein on youth violence. Certainly the pacifist teachings of Buddhism have something to do with it too. Shinto's ideas about the inter-connectedness of all life contribute to Japan's ideas of nonviolence as well. Perhaps if the formula could be isolated conclusively, then it might be duplicated elsewhere.

Some of the more radical neo-nationalists (the *Nihonjin-ron* advocates alluded to in the introduction to this chapter) have pointed to Japan's preference to nonviolence to try to prove that Japan could not have possibly committed the alleged war crimes during World War II. The argument is that the Communist Internationale invented the atrocities for public relations reasons. Of course the argument is specious. All one has to do is to point to the very real atrocities documented at Bataan, the Philippines, Indonesia, Korea, Taiwan, and virtually everywhere the Japanese Imperial military held sway.

Those atrocities make the nonviolence in modern Japan all the more problematic. How could the same society nurture both extremes? One has only to note that the same society that gave the world Bach and Beethoven also bred

Hitler and Himmler. And, to be more parochial, the same country that bred the Ku Klux Klan also nurtured Quakers and the Salvation Army.

A FINAL WORD

Japan has had turbulent times in the past two decades. Its economy suffered in the 1990s from what has been called the "bursting of the bubble;" its government has been rocked by constant scandal and controversy. Japan's East Asian neighbors have criticized and held dangerous public demonstrations against it and its political system seemed to writhe and shudder as its political parties shifted, dissolved, and reassembled in different coalitions. Yet Japan manages to keep a relative even keel. Governments rise and fall without social chaos and huge economic companies crumble without national collapse.

Japan has managed to weather the storms. When foreign "shocks" buffeted the nation, the Japanese persevered. When distant wars threatened Japan's energy supply, Japan adjusted and prospered in the new global realities. Before the Arab Oil Embargoes of the 1970s, Japan was a producer of durable goods and heavy industry. Japan understood that to continue would threaten economic collapse of those energy-dependant industries. So it went "high-tech" and began to produce electronic goods instead. When faced with rising American protective tariffs, Japan shifted and began to export its automobile manufacturing to the United States to avoid those import tariffs.

The truth is that Japan is a mature and stable society able to withstand shocks that would cripple many nations. As cynical as most Japanese are about their political parties, they continue to rely on a ponderous yet capable bureaucracy to see them through turbulence. The Japanese continue to go about their lives without much concern for the future. They educate their children, they save their money, they pay their taxes, they obey the laws.

If its political system is flawed in that women and other political minorities continue to suffer from inequities, then the Japanese will need to address those problems. In most other aspects of society the Japanese benefit from a safe and stable country.

Regrettably, the dark side of every culture festers just beneath the surface of civility. Fascism in Germany, Spain, and Italy reared its ugly head in the 1930s. Communism in Russia and Eastern Europe suppressed human rights for a half century and continues to do so in China, North Korea, and Cuba. The cultures of the Middle East, South and Southeast Asia, Africa, and Eastern Europe currently writhe in racial and religious genocide. America teetered at the very brink of revolution in the 1930s, suffered from vicious McCarthyism in the 1950s, and was rocked by racial riots in the 1960s and anti–Vietnam War violence in the 1970s. In the 1960s it appeared that Japanese leftist student radicals might gather public support. When North Korean missiles flew over northern Japan in the twenty-first century, it appeared that conservative neo-nationalist elements might gain some political clout. Fortunately, Japan's vast middle class seemed to shy away from either extreme. Japan has managed to keep both the radical left wing and the irrational right wing at bay. One hopes that one descent into the Valley of Darkness for Japan was enough.

Appendix A: Notable People in the History of Japan

Akihito (Heisei)—Emperor (1933–); son and successor to Emperor Showa (Hirohito) after 1989.

Amaterasu Omi-Kami (mythical)—The Sun Goddess and ancestor of all Japanese; the chief kami in the Shinto pantheon.

Ashikaga Takauji (1305–1358)—Founder of the bakufu that bears his name; championed, then imprisoned the Emperor Go-Daigo.

Etō Shimpei (1834–1874)—Meiji Restoration activist from Saga han; led a brief samurai rebellion against the government in 1874, then arrested and executed.

Fukuzawa Yūkichi (1835–1901)—Japan's greatest popularizer of foreign ideas in the early Meiji era; traveled extensively to the West; founder of newspapers and Keio University.

Go-Daigo (1288–1339)—Emperor 1318–1339 when attempted imperial restoration brought down the Kamakura Bakufu; escaped from Ashikaga Takauji's confinement and formed a rival southern court at Yoshino.

Gotō Shimpei (1857–1929)—Colonial administrator and reformer in Manchuria and Taiwan; credited with rebuilding Tokyo after the 1923 Great Kantō Earthquake.

Gotō Shōjiro (1838–1897)—Tosa activist in Meiji Restoration; involved with Itagaki in Jiyū tōpolitics; served with Mutsu as a conduit for genrō bribes to Jiyūtō.

Hara Takashi (1856–1921)—Protégé of Mutsu and Itō, rose to become Japan's first commoner premier after the 1918 Rice Riots; leader of Seiyūkai party.

Townsend Harris (1804–1878)—Became America's first Minister to Japan in 1856; negotiated the first of the Unequal Treaties in 1857.

Himiko (Second Century)—Emperor-shaman of Japan who first received sanction from the Chinese Emperor. Her name means "Sun Princess."

Hiratsuka Raichō (1886–1971)—Feminist founder of *Seitō* (Bluestockings) magazine; founder of New Women's Association in 1919 to work for women's rights; elected to Japan's first postwar Diet but purged because of her progovernment wartime actions.

Hirohito. *See* Shōwa.

Hōjō Masako (1157–1225)—Called the "nun shōgun" because as the widow of Minamoto Yoritomo, after his death in 1199, ruled behind the scenes.

Hōjō Tokimune (1251–1284)—Leader of the Japanese forces that helped drive away the attempted Mongol invasions in 1274 and 1281.

Hoshi Tōru (1850–1901)—Protégé of Mutsu and Itō, served in the Diet as Speaker, Ambassador to America 1896–1898; called Japan's "Boss Tweed" for his corrupt political financial practices; assassinated while serving as president of Tokyo City Council.

Ii Naosuke (1815–1860)—Tokugawa loyalist who forced the signing of the American treaty in 1858; assassinated by Mito loyalists for his actions against their daimyō Tokugawa Nariaki.

Inoue Kaoru (1835–1915)—Longtime ally of Itō and close friend of Mutsu; a Chōshū genrō who served as foreign minister and other cabinet positions in early Meiji; closely tied to the Mitsui Zaibatsu.

Inukai Tsuyoshi (1855–1932)—Longtime Diet member, president of Seiyūkai and premier in 1931 until his assassination over his criticism of the Mukden Incident; Japan's last prewar party Premier.

Itagaki Taisuke (1837–1919)—A Tosa leader of the People's Rights and Freedom Movement; founder of Jiyūtō.

Itō Hirobumi (1841–1909)—Chōshū genrō, called the "Father of the Meiji Constitution," often premier and president of the Privy Council; founder of Seiyūkai; assassinated by Korean patriot.

Itō Noe (1895–1923)—Editor of Seitō; feminist and socialist leader; murdered with her socialist lover by police during the Kantō Earthquake.

Iwakura Tomomi (1825–1883)—Courtier hero of Meiji Restoration; led the Iwakura Mission to the west, 1871–1873; nearly assassinated for his action in avoiding the Korean Expedition in 1873.

Iyo (Third Century)—Successor at age 13 to Emperor Himiko. She was also an emperor-shaman.

Izanagi ("He-Who-Invites")—The creative male deity in the Japanese creation story. The father of Amaterasu, the Sun Goddess.

Izanami ("She-Who-Invites")—The creative female deity in the Japanese creation story. The mother of Amaterasu, the Sun Goddess.

Katayama Sen (1860–1933)—Christian Socialist and leader of anti-Russo-Japanese War peace movement; lived in Moscow working for the Comintern from 1921 until his death.

Katsura Tarō (1848–1913)—Chōshū army protégé of Yamagata; alternated as premier with Saionji during the 1910s; recognized as a genrō in later life.

Kido Takayoshi (1833–1877)—Choshu samurai who helped to engineer the Meiji Restoration. One of the early Meiji modernizers until he resigned from government in 1873.

Kishi Nobusuke (1896–1987)—Industrial administrator in wartime Manchukuo; listed as Class A war criminal, released in 1948, rose in Jiyūtō to become premier in 1957; resigned after the Security Treaty Incident in 1960; remained a kingmaker in the Diet until his death; brother of Satō Eisaku.

Kita Ikki (1883–1937)—Right-wing nationalist philosopher; implicated in the February 26, 1936, attempted military coup in Tokyo, executed.

Konoe Fumimaro (1891–1945)—Descendant of the Fujiwara courtier family; premier during the early part of the Pacific War; committed suicide rather than be tried as war criminal.

Kotoku Shūsui (1871–1911)—Socialist philosopher executed for his alleged participation in the Great Treason Incident, an attempt to assassinate the Meiji Emperor.

Kuroda Kiyotaka (1840–1900)—Satsuma genrō, served in various cabinet ministries, briefly premier, and then president of Privy Council until his death.

Matsukata Masayoshi (1835–1924)—A genrō from Satsuma han; served as premier; famous for the 1881 Matsukata Deflation.

Matsuoka Yōsuke (1880–1946)—Worked his way through school at Oregon University; later director of South Manchurian Railroad, a delegate to League of Nations, walked out over the Lytton Report; Foreign Minister at the beginning of World War II; indicted as a Class A war criminal but died before judgment was reached.

Meiji (1852–1912)—Emperor from 1867 until his death; gives his name to the modernization era; given name was Mutsuhito.

Minamoto Yoritomo (1147–1199)—Defeated the forces of the Taira and became the first shōgun and founder of the Kamakura Bakufu.

Minamoto Yoshitsune (1159–1189)—Younger brother and chief general for Yoritomo; when he became more popular than Yoritomo, was hounded until he committed suicide.

Minobe Tatsukichi (1873–1948)—Authority on constitutional law at Tokyo Imperial University; was hounded from public life and nearly assassinated for his views that the emperor was an organ of the government, not the totality of the state.

Murasaki Shikibu (Eleventh century)—Court lady author of Tale of Genji.

Mutsu Munemitsu (1844–1897)—Born in a Tokugawa shimpan han, became a rōnin with Sakamoto Ryōma; convicted of treason in 1878, rose to become foreign minister in 1892; engineered revision of the Unequal Treaties, the Sino-Japanese War, and the Treaty of Shimonoseki.

Nichiren (1222–1282)—Founder of Buddhist sect that bears his name.

Ninigi—The first human and first emperor in the Japanese creation story. Son of Amaterasu, the Sun Goddess.

Nogi Maresuke (1849–1912)—Commanding general at the Siege of Mukden (1905); committed ritual suicide with his wife upon the death of Emperor Meiji.

Oda Nobunaga (1534–1582)—First of Japan's three great unifiers; incorporated use of Portuguese arquebuses to warfare; called the "Destroyer" for his harsh use of terror; committed suicide rather than be taken prisoner by rebels.

Ōkubo Toshimichi (1830–1878)—A Satsuma hero of the Meiji Restoration, became the de facto leader of the government after 1873; assassinated in retaliation for his actions in the Satsuma Rebellion and the death of countryman Saigō Takamori.

Ōkuma Shigenobu (1838–1922)—Longtime Meiji leader ousted from government in 1881, but subsequently served as premier; lost his leg in an assassination attempt in 1889; the founder of Kaishintō party as well as Waseda University.

Ōshio Heihachirō (1792–1837)—Bakufu Ōsaka city administrator who led a failed rebellion as a demonstration against the bakufu's mishandling of the Tempo Famines.

Ōyama Iwao (1842–1916)—A Satsuma genrō, cousin of Saigō; longtime minister in various cabinets; a commanding general in Sino-Japanese and Russo-Japanese wars.

Harry Parkes (Sir) (1828–1885)—British diplomat first to China, and then to Japan during the Meiji Restoration until 1883.

Matthew C. Perry (1794–1858)—American commodore who "opened" Japan in 1853, forcing the Treaty of Kanagawa in 1854.

Saigō Takamori (1827–1877)—The Satsuma hero of the Meiji Restoration; left government over the Korea Affair in 1873 and committed suicide at the head of the failed samurai (Satsuma) rebellion in 1877.

Saigō Tsugumichi (1843–1902)—Half-brother to Takamori, he was a Satsuma genrō; led the ill-fated Taiwan Expedition in 1874.

Saionji Kinmochi (1849–1940)—A late addition to the genrō; only member not from Satsuma or Chōshū; alternated as premier with Katsura in the 1910s; adviser to Shōwa (Hirohito) Emperor.

Sakamoto Ryōma (1835–1867)—A Tosa rōnin who brought the Chōshū and Satsuma factions together in the Meiji Restoration; traded in guns for the loyalists; assassinated just before the restoration.

Satō Eisaku (1901–1975)—Longtime premier, brother of Kishi Nobusuke; Japan's first Nobel Peace Prize winner.

Ernest Satow (Sir) (1843–1929)—Translator and assistant to British Minister Harry Parkes during the early Meiji Era; British envoy to Japan, 1895–1900; wrote the influential book A Diplomat in Japan, 1921.

Shinran (1173–1262)—Founder of the Jōdo "Pureland" Buddhist sect.

Shōtoku Taishi (574–622)—As imperial regent for his aunt, is credited with introducing Confucianism into government; is considered the first Japanese boddisatva (saint); introduced the Seventeen-Article Constitution.

Shōwa (1901–1989)—Emperor from 1926 until his death, regent for his father from 1921–1926; given name was Hirohito; renounced his "divinity" in 1946.

Taira Kiyomori (1118–1181)—As leader of the Taira faction, ruled Japan behind the scenes for a decade; defeated by Minamoto Yoritomo.

Taishō (1879–1926)—Emperor from 1912 until his death; physically and mentally infirm during most of his reign; given name was Yoshihito.

Tanaka Giichi (1863–1929)—A Chōshū army man, became premier but resigned when Shōwa Emperor chided him on his handling of the killing of the Manchurian warlord Zhang Zuolin.

Tanaka Kakuei (1918–1993)—Premier in 1972 when Japan normalized relations with the People's Republic of China; long rumored to be involved in political financial corruption, convicted in the Lockheed Scandal; resigned as premier but continued to influence politics as LDP "Shadow Shōgun."

Tanuma Okitsugu (1719–1788)—Political and economic reformer within Tokugawa Bakufu in late eighteenth century.

Tōjō Hideki (1884–1948)—Military and political leader in World War II; convicted and hanged by the Tokyo War Crimes Tribunal.

Tokugawa Ieyasu (1542–1616)—Founder of the bakufu that bears his name; last of the three great unifiers with Nobunaga and Hideyoshi.

Tokugawa Yoshinobu (1837–1913)—The last Tokugawa shōgun; resigned in 1867, restoring power to Emperor Meiji.

Toyotomi Hideyori (1593–1614)—Only son of Hideyoshi; died at Ōsaka Castle with his mother after a brief attempted rebellion.

Toyotomi Hideyoshi (1536–1598)—Vassal and general of Nobunaga; succeeded in unifying Japan for a decade until his death; named himself regent for the emperor.

Yamagata Aritomo (1838–1922)—Leader of the Chōshū faction of genrō; called the "Father of Japan's Army"; often Premier and Home Minister; controlled the government after the death of Itō in 1909.

Yamakawa Kikue (1890–1980)—Leader in the Proletarian Socialist and feminist political movement; became the head of Japan's first Labor Ministry's Women's and Minors Bureau in 1947.

Yoshida Shigeru (1878–1967)—Delegate to Treaty of Versailles; briefly imprisoned for attempts at peace in 1945; premier for much of the American Occupation; credited with the "reverse course" of the Occupation.

Appendix B: The Sat-Chō Oligarchy (Genrō)

The genrō were the "second generation" of Meiji-era modernizers who inherited the mantle of leadership after 1877. The original seven were all from the feudal domains of Satsuma and Chōshū and therefore the oligarchy that they formed was called "Sat-Chō" from the first syllable of the names. With the exception of Ōyama, they all served as Premier at one time or another. They all also rotated through the other cabinet ministries during the early period of modernization (1881–1900). The "Later Genrō" were protégés of the original seven.

Inoue Kaoru (1835–1915), Chōshū

Itō Hirobumi (1841–1909), Chōshū

Kuroda Kiyotaka (1840–1900), Satsuma

Matsukata Masayoshi (1835–1924), Satsuma

Ōyama Iwao (1842–1916), Satsuma

Saigō Tsugumichi (1843–1902), Satsuma

Yamagata Aritomo (1838–1922), Chōshū

Katsura Tarō (1848–1913), Chōshū

Saionji Kinmochi (1849–1940), Courtier

Appendix C: Premiers

PREWAR PREMIERS

Itō Hirobumi, 1885–1888

Kuroda Kiyotaka, 1888–1889

Yamagata Aritomo, 1889–1891

Matsukata Masayoshi, 1891–1892

Itō Hirobumi, 1892–1896

Matsukata Masayoshi, 1896–1898

Itō Hirobumi, 1898

Ōkuma Shigenobu, 1898

Yamagata Aritomo, 1898–1900

Itō Hirobumi, 1900–1901

Katsura Tarō, 1901–1906

Saionji Kinmochi, 1906–1908

Katsura Tarō, 1908–1911

Saionji Kinmochi, 1911–1912

Katsura Tarō, 1912–1913

Yamamoto Gonnohyōe, 1913–1914

Ōkuma Shigenobu, 1914–1916

Terauchi Masatake, 1916–1918

Hara Takashi, 1918–1921

Takahashi Korekiyo, 1921–1922

Katō Tomosaburō, 1922–1923

Yamamoto Gonnohyōe, 1923–1924

Kiyoura Keigo, 1924

Katō Takaaki, 1924–1926

Wakatsuki Reijirō, 1926–1927

Tanaka Giichi, 1927–1929

Hamaguchi Osachi, 1929–1931

Wakatsuki Reijirō, 1931

Inukai Tsuyoshi, 1931–1932

Saitō Makoto, 1932–1934

Okada Keisuke, 1934–1936

Hirota Kōki, 1936–1937

Hayashi Senjūrō, 1937

Konoe Fumimaro, 1937–1939

Hiranuma Kiichirō, 1939

Abe Nobuyuki, 1939–1940

Yonai Mitsumasa, 1940

Konoe Fumimaro, 1940–1941

Tōjō Hideki, 1941–1944

Koiso Kuniaki, 1944–1945

Suzuki Kantarō, 1945

POSTWAR PREMIERS

Higashikuni Naruhiko, 1945

Shidehara Kijūrō, 1945–1946

Yoshida Shigeru, 1946–1947

Katayama Tetsu, 1947–1948

Ashida Hitoshi, 1948

Yoshida Shigeru, 1948–1954

Hatoyama Ichirō, 1954–1956

Ishibashi Tanzan, 1956–1957

Kishi Nobusuke, 1957–1960

Ikeda Hayato, 1960–1964

Satō Eisaku, 1964–1972

Tanaka Kakuei, 1972–1974

Miki Takeo, 1974–1976

Fukuda Takeo, 1976–1978

Ōhira Masayoshi, 1978–1980

Suzuki Zenkō, 1980–1982

Nakasone Yasuhirō, 1982–1987

Takeshita Noboru, 1987–1989

Uno Sosuke, 1989

Kaifu Toshiki, 1989–1991

Miyazawa Kiichi, 1991–1992

Hosokawa Morihiro, 1992–1994

Hata Tsutomu, 1994

Murayama Tomiichi, 1994–1996

Hashimoto Ryutaro, 1996–1998

Obuchi Keizo, 1998–2000

Mori Yoshiro, 2000–2001

Koizumi Junichiro, 2001–2006

Abe Shinzo, 2006–2007

Fukuda Yasuo, 2007–

Asō Taro (2008)

Glossary of Selected Terms

AINU: Indigenous people of northern Japan, distinct from Japanese race.

AMIDA BUTSU: A manifestation of the Buddha.

ANIME: Computer-generated futuristic cartoons.

ARQUEBUS: Medieval European gun.

ASHIGARU: "Footmen"; feudal foot soldier, pikeman, archer.

AUM SHINRIKYO: A quasi-Buddhist cult that used poison gas attack in Tokyo subways in 1995.

BAKUFU: "Tent government"; name applied loosely to feudal governments between 1192 and 1868; headed by a shōgun.

BAKUMATSU: "End of the Bakufu"; indicates the last three or four decades of the Tokugawa era.

BEISUBORU: The game of baseball, also called Yakyu.

BODDISATVA: A Buddhist saint who becomes an intermediary in salvation.

BONSAI: Miniature tree sculpturing; Zen art of plant husbandry.

BUNMEI KAIKA: "Civilization and Enlightenment"; phrase or slogan used during early Meiji era to indicate modernization.

BUNRAKU: Puppet theater evolved from Jōruri.

BURAKUMIN: Social underclass descended from eta. *See also* ETA.

BUSHI: "Warrior"; term used interchangeably with samurai.

BUSHIDŌ: "The Way of the Warrior"; ethos of the warrior.

CHA-NO-YU: Zen art of tea ceremony.

CHŌ: 2.45 acres of rice paddy land.

CHŌNIN: "City Folk"; all non-samurai (merchants, artisans, and the like) residents of feudal cities.

DAIMYŌ: "Great Name"; designation for feudal warlord.

DESHIMA: Artificial island in Nagasaki harbor where Dutch were isolated from 1640s to 1860s.

EDO: Former name of Tokyo; capital of Tokugawa Bakufu.

EMOJI: "Emoticons," text message symbols (e.g., the :) "smiley face").

ETA: Outcast people probably descended from captive slaves, made to do tasks that are morally corruptible (butchers, undertakers, and the like); from about the fourteenth century.

FUDAI: "House men"; designation of Tokugawa's most trusted daimyō allies.

FUJIWARA: Name of cadet imperial house that came to control the emperors. *See also* KUROMAKU.

FUKOKU KYŌHEI: "Rich Country—Strong Military"; slogan used by Meiji modernizers.

FUMI-E: "Treading Pictures"; ritual, from 1630s to 1870s, to prove that one was not Christian; people required to step on pictures or icons of Christ or the Virgin Mary.

FURUSATO: "The Old Place"; one's native home.

GAGAKU: Ancient imperial court dance genre; Chinese-type music and dance performed by masked dancers.

GAIRAI-GO: Syncretic words that originated from foreign language, now part of Japanese language.

GEISHA: "Artiste"; musicians and entertainers, usually women, particularly in the Tokugawa era.

GEKOKUJO: "Inferior ruling superior"; phrase used to indicate control of figurehead leaders by subordinates.

GENRŌ: "Senior Statesmen"; used to indicate the nine most trusted Meiji advisors from 1890–1940.

GIRI: Confucian social obligation and duty to be honored above ninjo *See also* NINJŌ.

GOKENIN: "Honorable Housemen"; title given to closest feudal vassals, particularly during the Kamakura era.

HAIHAN CHIKEN: "Abolition of Domains—Establishment of Prefectures"; slogan to indicate the end of feudalism and the establishment of the modern Meiji state in 1871.

HAIKU: Seventeen-syllable poem alternating five, seven, and then five syllable lines as meter scheme.

HAN: Feudal domain controlled by daimyō.

HANIWA: Clay figurines found in imperial tombs, third to seventh centuries.

HARA KIRI: "Belly slitting"; ritual suicide usually by feudal samurai.

HATAMOTO: "Bannermen"; close house vassals of the Tokugawa.

IKEBANA: Zen art of flower arrangement.

IJIME: Bullying in school.

IKKO: "Single-purpose"; Pureland Buddhist sect organized on military hierarchy in Central Japan during fifteenth century.

JIYŪ MINKEN UNDŌ: "People's Rights and Freedom Movement"; 1870s liberal rights movement led by Itagaki and others.

JIYŪTŌ: "Liberal Party"; founded by Itagaki Taisuke and others in 1881; also the name of the postwar party founded by Hatayama Ichirō in 1945; merged with Democratic Party to form the Liberal-Democratic Party (LDP) in 1955,

JŌDO: "Pureland" sect of Buddhism founded by Hōnen in the twelfth century. Invocation of the name of Boddisatva Amida would take one to the Pureland, and there to be saved.

JŌDO SHINSHŪ: Buddhist Pureland sect founded by Shinran in the twelfth century; adherents formed military brotherhood called Ikko.

JŌRURI: Early feudal mime theater and dance; evolved into puppet shows; forerunner of Bunraku.

KABUKI: Theater form incorporating drama, dance, and music.

KAISHINTŌ: Constitutional Party founded by Ōkuma Shigenobu in 1882.

KAMI: "Spirits" or gods of Shinto.

KAMIKAZE: "Wind of the Gods"; used to designate the typhoons that drove away Mongol invaders in the twelfth century; also used to designate suicide bomber pilots during World War II.

KANA: The name given to the two phonetic syllabaries used together with Kanji characters to write Japanese.

KANJI: Sino-Japanese ideographic characters used in writing.

KANTŌ: The plains region around Tokyo.

KARAOKE: Literally "open orchestra." Entertainment form where amateurs sing to recorded music in special bars.

KARMA: "Dependent causality"; the sum total of human actions in life that effect the next life in Buddhist thought.

KEIGO: "Honorific language." Polite speech patterns to indicate social deference.

KIMONO: Loose, sleeved robe worn by both sexes, wrapped around the body and tied with sash around the hips.

KOAN: Zen nonsense riddle to shock the mind out of reasoning in order to achieve enlightenment; advocated by priest Eisai.

KŌDŌ-HA: "Imperial Way"; faction of the army in early 1930s.

KŌGAKU: "Ancient School" of thought in Tokugawa period that harkened back to early Confucian texts at the expense of Neo-Confucianism.

KOJIKI: "Record of Ancient Matters"; eighth-century imperial history recounting nearly mythological past.

KOKU: A 4.98-bushel measurement instituted by Hideyoshi.

KOKUGAKU: "National Learning" school of nativists in late Tokugawa period.

KOMBI: Convenience stores (7-Eleven, Lawson).

KOMEITO: "Clean Government Party" founded in 1964; closely allied with the Buddhist Soka Gakkai movement until mid 1990s.

KUROMAKU: "Black curtain" government; behind-the-scenes government employing regents; practiced first by the Fujiwara over imperial house in Heian era.

MAHAYANA: "Greater Vehicle"; Buddhist school of thought that teaches tolerance.

MAI-HOMU: A neologism that transliterates "my home;" refers to personal property (not just houses).

MANGA: Comic books.

MAPPŌ: Buddhist idea of degeneration; led to rise of Pureland Buddhism in twelfth century.

MEISHI: Name cards exchanged when people meet.

MERU-MAGA: Literally "mail magazine;" company electronic newsletters.

NEMBUTSU: Chant or invocation of Amida's name in Pureland Buddhism.

NIHONGI: "Chronicles of Japan"; eighth-century imperial history, written in Chinese.

NIHONJIN-RON: Philosophy that everything Japanese is unique, and superior to all things foreign.

NINJŌ: Human emotion to be suppressed in favor of giri in Neo-Confucianism. *See also* GIRI.

NIRVANA: "Blowing out" of human passion; salvation from reincarnation in Buddhism.

NOH: Pantomine theater, heavily influenced by Buddhism; evolved from sarugaku, patronized by bakufu.

ONNA DAIGAKU: "Greater Learning for Women"; Confucian tract written by Kaibara Ekken to demonstrate ideal female behavior.

ŌYATOI: "Honorable employee"; foreign experts hired by Meiji government to teach Japanese cadre the applied arts and sciences of the West.

OYOMEI: Japanese pronunciation of Wang Yang-ming, the intuitive philosophy in Confucianism.

RANGAKU: "Dutch Studies"; designation given to all Western studies in late Tokugawa period.

RENGA: "Linked verse" 31-syllable poem. One poet writes 17-syllable haiku, second poet responds with two seven-syllable lines.

ROJIN DAIGAKU: "University for Elders." Cultural classes held in municipal centers; for elderly.

ROMAJI: Roman alphabet used to write Japanese phonetically.

RŌNIN: "Wave men"; masterless samurai.

SAKOKU: "Closed Country"; edict forbidding travel abroad and limiting visits by foreigners during the Tokugawa era.

SAMURAI: "He who serves." Generally used to mean class of warriors.

SANKIN KOTAI: "Alternate Attendance" system of hostages and political control used by Tokugawa Bakufu whereby all daimyō alternated their residence between Edo and their han.

SANYAKU: Top three ranks in Sumo.

SARUGAKU: "Monkey Music" that evolved into Kabuki, Noh, and other theater forms.

SAT-CHŌ: Nickname of the Satsuma and Chōshū-dominated oligarchy during Meiji era.

SEITŌ: "Bluestockings" feminist journal; also the name of the feminist movement in early twentieth century; founded by Hiratsuka Raichō and later edited by Itō Noe.

SEIYŪKAI: Political party founded by Itō Hirobumi and later controlled by Hara Takashi.

SENGOKU: "Warring States"; term loosely applied to the period of civil war, 1467–1570.

SHAMISEN: Three-stringed banjolike musical instrument.

SHIMPAN: Daimyō related to the Tokugawa.

SHINGAKU: "Heart Learning"; chōnin school of Neo-Confucianism during Tokugawa era; emphasized the "way of the merchant" by Ishida Baigan.

SHINGON: Buddhist sect founded in the eighth century.

SHINTO: The native animist religion of Japan.

SHISHI: "Men of Spirit"; zealots who assassinated philosophical rivals in Bakumatsu in the 1930s.

SHŌEN: Prefeudal independent manors; tax-free estates.

SHŌGUN: "Generalissimo"; title used for military "deputy" who ruled for emperors; leader of bakufu.

SOKA GAKKAI: "Value-Creating Society"; a Nichiren Buddhist reform movement that emerged in early postwar period; strongest among urban low middle class; controlled Komeito "Clean Government Party" until mid 1990s.

SONNŌ-JŌI: "Revere Emperor—Expel Barbarians"; slogan used by anti-bakufu forces at the end of the Tokugawa era.

SOROBAN: Abacus.

SUMI-E: "Ink-wash" style of Zen-influenced painting; Chinese in origin but popularized by Sesshu.

SUTRA: Buddhist scripture.

TAIHŌ: "Great Law"; institution of Confucian laws in 702.

TANKA: Thirty-one syllable medieval poem.

TENDAI: Buddhist sect founded in the eighth century; controlled Mt. Hiei above Kyoto.

TERAKOYA: "Parish schools" run by chōnin and peasants who hired Confucian teachers for their children in the late Tokugawa era; housed in Buddhist temples.

TOKUSEI: "Act of Grace"; moratorium canceling of debts; employed by daimyō and shōgun to give economic relief to their vassals.

TŌSEI-HA: "Control Way Faction"; faction within the Japanese Army in the 1930s that advocated Total War.

TOZAMA: "Outsiders"; least-trusted daimyō of the Tokugawa.

UBASOKU: Shamanist lay Buddhist preachers.

UJI: Kinship group; clanlike regional governments.

UKIYO-E: "Pictures of the Floating World"; woodblock prints of late Tokugawa era.

WAKO: "Japanese Pirates"; name given by Chinese to all pirates in the fourteenth through sixteenth centuries.

YAKUZA: Criminal underworld urban vice cartels; primarily in large cities; loosely allied with many right-wing splinter parties.

YAKYU: "Field ball," the war time Japanese name for baseball; still used along with the more common beisuboru.

YAMABUSHI: "Mountain priest" shamanists who practiced secret Buddhist rituals in the mountains.

YAMATO: "Name" of the Japanese people, especially the imperial house.

YAMATO-E: "Japanese Pictures" to differentiate from Chinese-style painting after the ninth century.

YASUKUNI: Controversial Shinto shrine in Tokyo dedicated to souls of war dead.

YOKOZUNA: Grand Champion, the top rank in Sumo.

ZA: Guildlike merchant and artisan associations.

ZAIBATSU: "Financial Cliques"; large commercial and industrial combines after early Meiji.

ZAINICHI: Resident aliens in Japan.

ZAZEN: Quiet Zen Buddhist meditation advocated by priest Dōgen.

ZEN: Anti-intellectual Buddhist schools.

Bibliographic Essay

The greatest change in the past decade in regards to research has been the maturation of the Internet. In the 1990s research on the Net wasn't worth the effort one put into the keyboard strokes; now with some care, the Internet can be a valuable resource. I always caution students, however, that virtually anyone with a little computer expertise can post to the Internet. Many martial arts aficionados, *manga* and *anime* fans, as well as anyone who saw *The Karate Kid* on television, can and do write some outrageously misinformed articles. The rule of thumb is to check bona fides; that is, check who wrote it and check their expertise.

Generally speaking, most of the material found at university-sponsored sites can be trusted because the material has been checked by professionals. A good place to start is the Stanford University site (http://jguide.stanford.edu/site/history_267.html). Another is Academic Info (http://www.academic info.net/japanhist.html). Also, one can generally trust a site maintained by Robert Y. Eng called the Annotated Directory of Internet Resources (http://newton.uor.edu/Departments&Programs/AsianStudiesDept/japan-history.html).One source commonly used by undergraduate students is Wikipedia which advertises itself as the "Free Encyclopedia" (http://www.wikipedia.org/). Generally speaking, this can be a reliable source except that virtually anyone can post to its Web site. I have sometimes corrected inaccuracies (as have many academic specialists), but who has the time and/or inclination to act as their editor? Occasionally I have encountered some fairly silly statements there. That is to say, it is not always trustworthy. One has to use great caution when using the various sites that claim to provide "study guides" for students on various subjects. One such is Spark Notes. Generally they provide accurate, if sometimes imprecise, information. The site is good for timelines. One should generally steer clear of sites that contain catchy terms in the URL such as "samurai," "ninja," and "geisha."

Still the most readable and accessible general histories are a trilogy by Mikiso Hane: *Premodern Japan: A Historical Survey, Modern Japan: A Historical Survey, and Eastern Phoenix: Japan* since 1945, all published by Westview Press (Boulder, Colo.: 1991, 1986, and 1996, respectively). I say this in spite of the fact that I have undertaken the task of revising them since the author, a good friend, died a few years ago. Edwin Reischauer's *Japan: The Story of a Nation* (New York: McGraw-Hill, 1990) is quite good. George B. Sansom has also written a three-volume history, but his best work is still *Japan, A Short Cultural History* (New York: Appleton, 1943). Readers should be warned that Sansom's prose is dense and flowery—it is also wonderful.

Readers who are interested in literature could start with Donald Keene's *Japanese Literature: An Introduction for Western Readers* (New York: Grove, 1955). He has authored several other books on the subject as well. A classic study is Ivan Morris's *The World of the Shining Prince: Court Life in Ancient Japan* (New York: Knopf, 1964). One would do well to read some early Japanese literature. Helen McCullough has done a series of translations of the warrior tales. Edward Seidensticker's two-volume translation of Murasaki Shikibu's *Tale of Genji* (New York: Knopf, 1978) is a classic, as is Karen Brazell's *Confessions of Lady Nijō* (Stanford University, 1973). Coverage of modern literature is nearly impossible, but one should look at the translated works of Abe Kōbo, Ariyoshi Sawako, Dazai Ōsamu, Endō Shusaku, Kawabata Yasunari, Mishima Yukio, Murakami Haruki, Natsume Sōseki, Ōe Kenzaburō, Tanazaki Junichirō, and Yoshimoto Banana (really!) for a good representation.

The most accessible book on religion is H. Byron Earhart's *Japanese Religion: Unity and Diversity* (Rutherford, N.J.: Farleigh Dickinson, 1974). His bibliography is excellent.

Surprisingly, after four decades, the best book on art is still Hugo Munsterberg, *The Arts of Japan: An Illustrated History* (Tokyo: Tuttle, 1957), but one would have to look elsewhere for a current bibliography on the subject.

A good place to start reading about education is Ronald P. Dore's *Education in Tokugawa Japan* (Berkeley: University of California, 1965) and Herbert Passin's *Society and Education in Japan* (New York: Columbia University, 1965). One should also look at Thomas Rohlen's *Japan's High Schools* (Berkeley: University of California, 1983) and Benjamin C. Duke's *Education and Leadership for the Twenty-First Century: Japan, America and Britain* (New York: Praeger, 1991).

For the status of women, Sharon Siever's now-classic work is *Flowers in Salt: The Beginning of Feminine Consciousness in Modern Japan* (Stanford University, 1983). Also, Gail L. Bernstein's various works, Takie S. Lebra's *Japanese Women: Constraint and Fulfillment* (Honolulu: University of Hawaii, 1984), as well as the recent scholarship by Sally Hastings and Helen Hopper are all important.

For other topics, one may consult the bibliographies of Mikiso Hane's books as well as the *Bibliography of Asian Studies* published annually by the Association for Asian Studies.

Index

About the Author

LOUIS G. PEREZ is professor of Asian history at Illinois State University. He is also the author of *Daily Life in Early Modern Japan* (Greenwood, 2001), *Japan Comes of Age: Mutsu Munemitsu and the Revision of the Unequal Treaties* (1999), and several other books.

Other Titles in the Greenwood Histories of the Modern Nations
Frank W. Thackeray and John E. Findling, Series Editors

The History of Afghanistan
Meredith L. Runion

The History of Argentina
Daniel K. Lewis

The History of Australia
Frank G. Clarke

The History of the Baltic States
Kevin O'Connor

The History of Brazil
Robert M. Levine

The History of Canada
Scott W. See

The History of Central America
Thomas Pearcy

The History of Chile
John L. Rector

The History of China
David C. Wright

The History of Congo
Didier Gondola

The History of Cuba
Clifford L. Staten

The History of Egypt
Glenn E. Perry

The History of El Salvador
Christopher M. White

The History of Ethiopia
Saheed Adejumobi

The History of Finland
Jason Lavery

The History of France
W. Scott Haine

The History of Germany
Eleanor L. Turk

The History of Ghana
Roger S. Gocking

The History of Great Britain
Anne Baltz Rodrick

The History of Haiti
Steeve Coupeau

The History of Holland
Mark T. Hooker

The History of India
John McLeod

The History of Indonesia
Steven Drakeley

The History of Iran
Elton L. Daniel

The History of Iraq
Courtney Hunt

The History of Ireland
Daniel Webster Hollis III

The History of Israel
Arnold Blumberg

The History of Italy
Charles L. Killinger

The History of Japan, Second Edition
Louis G. Perez

The History of Korea
Djun Kil Kim